Elizabethan Popular Theatre

Theatre Production Studies

General Editor
John Russell Brown
School of English and American Studies,
University of Sussex

£15.95

Elizabethan Popular Theatre

Plays in Performance

Michael Hattaway

Routledge & Kegan Paul
London, Boston, Melbourne and Henley

First published in 1982
by Routledge & Kegan Paul Ltd
39 Store Street, London WC1E 7DD,
9 Park Street, Boston, Mass. 02108, USA,
296 Beaconsfield Parade, Middle Park,
Melbourne, 3206, Australia, and
Broadway House, Newtown Road,
Henley-on-Thames, Oxon RG9 1EN

Set in Plantin, 10 on 12pt, by
Rowland Phototypesetting Ltd, Bury St Edmunds, Suffolk
and printed in Great Britain by
St Edmundsbury Press, Bury St Edmunds, Suffolk
Plates printed by
Headley Brothers Ltd, Ashford, Kent

Library of Congress Cataloging in Publication Data

Hattaway, Michael.

Elizabethan popular theatre.
(Theatre production studies)
Bibliography: p.
Includes index.
1. Theater – England – History – 16th century.
2. English drama – Early modern and Elizabethan,
1500–1600 – History and criticism. I. Title.
II. Series.
PN2589.H33   792'.0942   82-5429
ISBN 0-7100-9052-8

Contents

Preface and acknowledgments · ix

Introduction · 1

PART ONE The idea of Elizabethan theatre

1 **Playhouses and stages** · 9

    Seven playhouses · 11
    A drawing of the Swan · 15
    Halls and fairgrounds · 16
    The stage, the tiring-house, and the canopy · 23
    The furnishing of the stage · 34
    The auditorium · 40

2 **Performances** · 42

    City and Court · 42
    Audiences · 44
    Preparation and rehearsal · 50
    Scene building · 56
    Music and dancing · 61
    Dumb shows, set pieces, and jigs · 63

3 **Players and playing** · 70

    Playhouse economics · 70
    Acting styles · 72
    Plays and games · 79
    Boy players · 83
    Make-up and costumes · 85
    Clowns and tragedians · 88
    Shakespeare, Marlowe – and Brecht · 92
    Speaking the speech · 97

PART TWO Plays

4 *The Spanish Tragedy:* **architectonic design** · 101

5 *Mucedorus:* **the exploitation of convention** · 129

6 *Edward II:* **dramatic documentary** · 141

7 *Doctor Faustus:* **ritual shows** · 160

8 *Titus Andronicus:* **strange images of death** · 186

Abbreviations · 209

Notes · 211

Select bibliography · 227

Index · 229

Illustrations

(*between pages 86 and 87*)

1 Detail from 'The View of the Cittye of London from the North
   towards the South', an engraving found in the manuscript journal of
   Abram Booth (*c.* 1599), now MS.1198 Hist. 147. Library of the
   University of Utrecht
2 Detail from 'Civitas Londini', an engraved panorama of London by
   John Norden (1600). Royal Library, Stockholm
3 Details from J. C. Visscher, 'Londinum Florentissima Britanniae
   Urbs' (Amsterdam, 1616). British Museum
4 Detail from Wenceslaus Hollar, 'Long View of London' (*c.* 1642).
   British Museum
5 A sketch of the Swan (1596) by Arnoldus Buchelius after a drawing by
   De Witt. Library of the University of Utrecht, MS.842 f.132ʳ
6 Detail from Pieter Brueghel the Younger's 'Village Fair' (Brueghel's
   dates are 1564–1637). Auckland City Art Gallery
7 Fludd's *Theatrum Orbis*, from his *Ars Memoriae* (1623). Folger
   Shakespeare Library
8 Plans by Inigo Jones (for the conversion of the Cockpit in Drury Lane
   in 1616?). Worcester College, Oxford
9 Edward Alleyn as Tamburlaine, from Richard Knolles's *A Generall
   Historie of the Turkes* (1603), p. 236. British Library
10 Drawing of Titus Andronicus, attributed to Henry Peacham (*c.* 1595).
   Library of the Marquess of Bath, Longleat House, Wiltshire (Portland
   Papers, I, f.159ᵛ)
11 John Scottowe, Portrait of Richard Tarlton (1588?). British Library,
   Harleian MS.3885, f.19
12 Title-page to the 1615 edition of *The Spanish Tragedy*. British Library
13 Pieter Brueghel the Elder, 'Mascarade d'Ourson et de Valentin'.
   Bibliothèque royale, Brussels (Van Bastelaer 215, Lebeer 60)
14 Title-page to the 1624 edition of *Doctor Faustus*. British Library

Preface and acknowledgments

The dates I have ascribed to the plays I mention come, unless stated otherwise, from Schoenbaum's revision of A. Harbage, *Annals of English Drama*. I have been my own editor and modernised all quotations from dramatic and literary texts, having derived them from the standard editions of the works concerned.

Professor John Russell Brown, the general editor of the series, provided admirable encouragement and criticism as the writing progressed. At Kent R. A. Foakes, Kate McLuskie and Peter Davison read parts of the manuscript and weeded out numerous errors and infelicities as well as suggesting additional references. The typists of Eliot College deciphered my preternaturally untidy typescripts. To them and to librarians at Kent, the Universities of Massachusetts at Amherst and Texas at Austin (where Professor Lynda Boose offered me generous hospitality while I was in the last throes of revision), Harvard, Yale and the British Library I am exceedingly grateful.

I am grateful for permission to reproduce the following: Plates 1 and 5, University Library, Utrecht; Plate 2, the Royal Library, Stockholm; Plates 3 and 4, the Trustees of the British Museum; Plate 6, the Auckland City Art Gallery; Plate 7, the Folger Shakespeare Library; Plate 8, the Provost and Fellows of Worcester College, Oxford; Plates 9, 11, 12 and 14, the British Library; Plate 10, the Marquess of Bath; Plate 13, Bibliothèque royale Albert 1er, Brussels (Cabinet des Estampes). Copyright is retained by the owners of the originals.

Introduction

This study of the popular drama of the late Elizabethan age begins with an account of the stages, performance conditions, and acting of the period and then turns to the analysis of five well-known plays of the 1590s. Two were written by Marlowe, a university-educated man, one (*Mucedorus*) by an anonymous disciple of the university wits, one by Kyd who, after leaving Merchant Taylors' School, may have become a scrivener like his father, and the last by Shakespeare – *Titus Andronicus*, a play that displays its author's impressive knowledge of the classics, of Seneca, Ovid, and even Euripides. A reader might be surprised to be reminded at the outset of a discussion of popular theatre of the academic origins of these works. However, an informing proposition of this book is that the value and popularity of this drama owe something to its traffic between the academic and the demotic, the idealized forms of the court show and the energies of carnival, between official subsidized private performance and licensed commercial public performance, between a literary and an oral culture. To the Elizabethans, in fact, 'public' and 'popular' were virtually synonymous: Sir Thomas Elyot noted that 'public' was derived from *populus*, 'in which word is contained all the inhabitants of a realm or city, of what estate or condition so ever they be'.[1] Conversely in our context 'private' described not the way that some playhouses were owned but the restricted nature of their audiences. The popularity of these plays, in other words, is a function of their appeal to the whole spectrum of Elizabethan society, and this study will show that the aristocratic withdrawal from popular culture[2] (dramatized, say, in Beaumont's *The Knight of the Burning Pestle* written for an elitist audience about 1608) had not really begun before the turn of the century. Plays and players, 'the abstract and brief chronicles of the time', were, like sermons (their rivals as entertainment), important components of a mass culture.

'Drama for the people' therefore is one definition of popular drama. Another might be 'drama of the people'. Study of theatrical conditions reveals not only that plays were occasions for community revelry but that texts were enlivened in performance by elements of aristocratic game and folk ritual. Moreover, although it is a dangerous generalization, I would argue that the ethos of these plays is sceptical and anti-authoritarian (although not anti-aristocratic) or, less attractively, chauvinistic and anti-Catholic.

Writers on Elizabethan drama have, until recently, tended to go to literary and printed sources, to philosophic and theological tracts, and too often have turned Marlowe, Shakespeare, and their fellows into Tudor propagandists, apologists for establishment order or 'the Elizabethan world picture'. Certainly we find order restored at the end of many of these plays, but they also expose what Elizabethans associated with 'the politician', corruption wrought by acquisitiveness, and the machinations for power in the courts and cities where the dramas are set. Playwrights like Marlowe used the art of the theatre to depict the theatricality of politics; ceremonies are frequently disrupted to signify the vanity of power sustained by theatrical form. Heroes in these plays tend to be outsiders – lovers, warriors, knaves, or saints – and the sheer energy demanded for the performance of these roles must have raised the consciousness of contemporary audiences against all that is destructive of individuality. 'Energy is Eternal Delight' said the voice of the devil through Blake, and delight may be the prime theatrical response here, a response that subverts the reactions predicted by literary theorists, the fear kindled by tragedy and the moralism of satiric comedy.

These plays celebrate the expansiveness of life and use all the resources of the playhouse in that celebration, both technical and verbal. *Queen Anna's New World of Words* was the title of an early Jacobean Italian and English dictionary, a title that commemorates the verbal discoveries of the Renaissance, discoveries which were not in the 1590s at least destroying the homogeneity of English culture. Renaissance concepts of decorum were not restrictive – to the shock of later neo-classicists – and enabled dramatists to explore the grandest and lowest domains of experience. The linguistic profusion of writers like Nashe, Marlowe, and Shakespeare bears witness to another kind of delight as these writers coined words to meet that challenge or delved into folk wisdom, the unmethodical aphoristic world of proverbs. (In modern popular culture we mark an analogous pleasure in neologisms – witness the parades of technical vocabulary in science fiction.) It was only in the Stuart period that decorum became more of a function of class structures and social forms. Men became measured by their linguistic style, and dramatists were constrained by the enticements of gentility (represented in a rhetorical context by 'propriety') and its neo-classical chaperon, verisimilitude. In the playhouses of the English Renaissance it was still possible to explore modes of reality other than the social and the rational. Truth was measured by the internal coherence of the artefact rather than by congruence with life: dramatists resisted the restrictiveness of the universal when reduced to the socially normative, and they revelled in the truth of strangeness, whether that be the archaic, the unexpected, the improbable, or the impossible. Any age which ennobles 'high culture' relegates these themes to subliterary genres – in our age to science fiction, children's literature, or derivatives of the gothic.

Popular drama therefore is, paradoxically perhaps, sophisticated drama. We have already noted that elements of high Renaissance culture were imported into public playhouses: the aristocratic rituals of the Accession Day tilts could appear in plays like *James IV* that also contained folk games. We must also remember that drama partakes of both literary and oral traditions, and that what might appear difficult on the page, inaccessible to an illiterate audience,[3] readily gives up its meaning in the playhouse. The stately or witty styles of the Court were true caviar to the general. Conversely texts like that of *Mucedorus* which might seem lame stuff on the page come to life when their motif patterns, dramatic rhythms, and formulaic plots work upon the group consciousness of a playhouse audience so that action turns to theme, spectacle to emblem, and speech to discourse. Elizabethan audiences were able to enjoy this blend of conventionalism and naturalism as easily as, say, audiences at horror films today: the 'problem of belief' afflicted only academics like Sidney. The fact that for the most part these plays were written in verse, a mode that allows dramatists to move freely between the extremes of naturalism and conventionalism, also made sophisticated demands on their players. They could neither simply stand and elocute as if taking part in a dramatic oratorio, nor could they perform the ordinary unmagnified actions of workaday life. As T. S. Eliot wrote:[4]

> they must somehow disclose (not necessarily be aware of) a deeper reality than that of the plane of our conscious living; and what they disclose must be, not the psychologist's intellectualization of this reality, but the reality itself.

They must have been aware in other words of the form of the action as well as the turns of the plot, their moral and social roles as well as their individual personalities; and their physical and speech acts must have shaped out what the Renaissance called 'figures' and Brecht defined as 'Gests'[5] – a term I shall use frequently in this work. They must have come to poises that captured not just the emotions of the moment but which revealed the conditions of life, the social and moral perspectives on the presented experience – what Eliot called 'the reality itself'.

I think, moreover, that the dramaturgy of this period makes the 'sophisticated' dramaturgy of plays written for learned coteries represented, say, by the court of Louis XIV or the European liberal intelligentsia of the age of Ibsen seem naïve or at least restrictive. For Elizabethan stages provided space for the most dazzling of dramatic sequences that ranged from the creation of partial illusion by mimicry to the exhibition of performance skills, from representation to presentation, and dramatists delighted in switching from one mode to another. Theatricality, exploitation of the archaic as a way of exploring the psyche, the use of 'metadrama' to examine the relationship between individual character and social role, the disruption of spectacle, literary parody, social and sexual travesty, linguistic absurdity, mime, improvisation, musical drama, drama of mechanical spectacle, agit-prop, the theatre of cruelty, and the 'poor' theatre – all were known to Elizabethan audiences. The varying of these dramatic modes meant that theatrical experience was based on awareness; apprehension necessarily involved both the emotions and the intellect, so that players and audiences worked together in the tasks and delights of imaginative recreation.

Neither is it true to say that popular theatre of this period was poor or primitive theatre. Generations past condescended to the supposed simplicities of Elizabethan playhouses or exalted in a puritanical way the virtues of a bare stage (as opposed to the real advantages of an empty space). The very popularity of the plays they offered made Elizabethan entrepreneurs and players comparatively wealthy and they invested some of their profits in playhouses that were renowned for their lavishness, and often moved their productions between Court and playhouse. Lavishness and visual display delighted both courtier and groundling.

The complexity of my subject makes the method of this book eclectic. What little evidence there is for performance techniques and conventions has to be garnered from many sources – playscripts themselves, related literature, playhouse records, legal documents, travellers' tales, psychological treatises. Each category of evidence is highly mediated and poses formidable problems of interpretation. I have started each of the first three chapters with a simple account of the economic factors relevant to my topics: like politics, theatre is the art of the possible. Much of what follows has to be speculative and readers may well find themselves irritated by the necessary qualifications and conditionals in my prose. I have resisted the temptation to divide up the longish chapters of Part One in the belief that accounts of theatrical experience must attempt the description of wholes: there is no virtue, for example, in discussing acting styles without discussing costumes. So too I have attempted in Part Two to give a commentary on the unfolding action of each of the plays. Each chapter there is, however, prefixed by general considerations – some readers may want to skip the commentaries and return only when they are working on a particular play.

Chronology has been another problem. Because evidence is scanty I have necessarily had to trespass on the periods if not the dramatic material of other writers in this series. The playhouses after all survived beyond the turn of the century which marks the close of my period, and the only extant play from the Swan, the sketch of which must remain one of our prime sources, dates from 1611. The Red Bull plays, written at about the same period, provide material illustrative of specifically non-patrician drama which is difficult to resist. Engravings of later playhouses reveal structures similar in function to those of the 1590s and are accordingly suggestive. Adherence to chronology in fact can distort the writing of drama history. It makes us assume, for example, that a first performance is more important than a revival, or that a performance that nourishes the flowers of an author's fancy is necessarily better than the jerks of invention in an adaptation. By analogy we might remember that just as first performances might not have been the most interesting, so the performances in the London playhouses were not the only performances of these plays. They were performed also at Court and, importantly, outside the metropolis, even to audiences on the continent who did not understand English. Elizabethan popular theatre, then, was a truly national theatre.

Finally I would note that a theatre historian or dramatic critic can only make suggestions, help to pose informed or challenging questions. Answers are to be found only in the theatre, in relation to particular productions. Answers are determined by accidents of playhouse construction or casting, and each performance is conditioned by the response of its audience. As the American folklorist Phillips Barry put it, in the realm of oral popular culture 'there are texts but no *text*; tunes but no *tune*'.[6] I have therefore not hesitated sometimes to include suggestive accounts of modern revivals, to work regressively in my attempts to recreate the forms and pressures of these splendid Renaissance occasions which have left so few racks behind.

Part One

The idea of
Elizabethan theatre

I · Playhouses and stages

The construction of James Burbage's playhouse, called simply the Theatre, in Shoreditch in 1576, the first building since Roman times built in England expressly for the presentation of plays, does not, contrary to much received opinion, establish a Renaissance for English drama. Rather it defines a high point in the economic fortunes of one established company, a moment when it had the confidence to raise enough capital to erect a permanent cockpit-like structure for spectators around its stage. On this stage and on those of the playhouses that were built during the next fifty years or so were presented plays that had burgeoned from native theatrical stock that was then reaching maturity after two or three centuries of hardy growth. Unlike modern companies of actors, troupes of Elizabethan players depended neither on particular buildings equipped with technical devices to create illusion or spectacular effects nor on an audience prepared to reserve places in advance for a season that might run through the course of a year. Their plays were constructed on non-illusory principles, their performances often formed part of seasonal festivities, religious, civil, or domestic, and, as had been the case throughout the Middle Ages, they assumed that taking their plays to audiences was as much a part of their job as attracting audiences to them. Throughout the reigns of Elizabeth, James, and Charles players were prepared to present their plays in rooms of state frequented by the nobility, in halls at the universities or the London Inns of Court, in guildhalls or the great chambers of private houses, in inn-yards or inn-rooms. When the pestilence caused the playhouses to be closed and drove them out of London, they performed in 'town halls, or moot-halls, or other convenient places' (the stock formula from a licence issued to Queen Anne's players in 1604),[1] on scaffolds at fairgrounds, in natural, artificial,[2] or, conceivably, ancient amphitheatres – or simply anywhere that an audience might congregate. Between November 1589 and February 1592, for example, Strange's Men are known to have played at the Cross Keys, at Court, and at Henslowe's playhouse the Rose.[3] All that they needed was some space: the Latin word for a stage that occurs sometimes in medieval stage directions is *platea*, which means simply a 'place' or area. Around that, below it, on three sides, two sides, or one side, the audience disposed themselves with various kinds of provision made for their comfort or convenience.

This book examines the playhouses, stages, dramaturgy, acting, and plays of the last couple of decades of the sixteenth century, the age of Kyd, Marlowe, and the early Shakespeare. It is a study of popular drama and in this context as we have seen 'popular' means 'written for whoever chose to frequent plays': it does not designate the lower orders of society. For this was the age of 'public' playhouse monopoly. Although plays had been performed in the 1570s and early 1580s by children of the royal chapels in the former monastery of the Blackfriars, a place used intermittently for aristocratic revels since the reign of Henry VIII, these performances were essentially private and occasional. They ended in 1584 although the Paul's boys performed occasionally at Court during the remainder of the decade. With regard to regular commercial performances, the distinction between public and private playhouses, between large mixed and small coterie audiences, did not emerge until about the turn of the century when the Blackfriars was refurbished, first for another generation of child players, Hamlet's 'little eyases', then for the King's Men who virtually bought them out in 1608. The companies of the 1580s and 1590s – and I do not intend to chart the immensely complicated permutations and combinations they underwent – performed to whoever could pay a penny, the minimum necessary to enter their playhouses. There was no regulation by price or by the exclusion of certain social groups.

Performances therefore did not depend upon the facilities offered by particular playhouses and, moreover, the companies with which we have to deal moved frequently between playhouse and Court. The Corporation of London complained in 1574 that the common players: 'present before her majesty such plays as have been before commonly played in open stages before all the basest assemblies in London and Middlesex.'[4] Two important corollaries follow from this, themes that will run through the argument of this book. The first is that I believe that the difference between staging at private and public performances, in halls and playhouses, has been over-stressed. Many historians have argued (following Chambers) that performances in the public playhouses of this period were mounted on simple stages sparsely furnished in contrast with the lavish spectacles offered at Court. Admittedly there is far more evidence for the construction of 'mansions' and scenic devices for Court performances, but it may well be that the equivalent playhouse evidence has simply been lost. Henslowe's inventory of the Admiral's Men's properties used at the Rose does include a number of large and presumably elaborate items: it is likely too that it was as expensive to transport these up the river to Whitehall or Hampton Court or down to Greenwich as it was to make new ones when the company was summoned before the Queen. Second, it is likely that audiences could be attracted by being offered the same productions as had been seen by the Monarch and nobility. Third, many modern accounts of performances at this time have been vitiated by the deep-rooted prejudice against spectacle held even today by their authors. Aristotle's deprecation of spectacle has penetrated deep into the European critical consciousness – spectacle, moreover, is difficult for critics to reconstruct and describe. Yet it provides one of the basic theatrical experiences. I firmly believe that the visual texture of these plays equals their verbal elements in importance.

The second corollary involves the relationships between plays and audiences. If, as I have argued, the same plays were performed before noble and common audiences and if the audiences at particular performances were more heterogeneous than used to be thought (see Ch. 2), it follows that it is not possible to postulate a simple connection between the social composition of its audience and the sophistication of a dramatic text. Certainly there must have been groundlings who loved nothing more than inexplicable dumb shows and noise, wits from Court who set down the intricate verbal conceits of the plays in their 'tables'. Equally certainly there must have been nobles whose taste ran only to jigs or tales of bawdry, illiterate but intelligent commoners whose sole access to literature lay in the playhouses. No playwright of the period can therefore have written for the instruction or delight of a particular class.

Seven playhouses

Between 1576 and 1600 seven playhouses were built on the outskirts of the City. The first, as we have noted, was called simply the Theatre and was situated north of the river in Shoreditch at the corner of Curtain Road and New Inn Yard about a mile north of Bishopsgate at the east end of the city. It was surrounded by open ground, the scene of several recorded frays (Plate 1).[5] It was built by James Burbage, a joiner as well as a player and the father of Richard Burbage, one of the greatest actors in Shakespeare's company. Most of what we know about the Theatre unfortunately is limited to the records of squabbles between the Burbages and leaseholders: other documents reveal at least that it was round, had three galleries for spectators, and was used by most of the important troupes of the time. The clown Tarlton played there, *Doctor Faustus* and the plays Shakespeare wrote before 1597 were performed there. At the end of 1598 the Theatre was pulled down and its timbers carted across the river to Bankside to be used for the construction of the Globe during the next year.

Adjacent to the Theatre stood Henry Lanman's Curtain, built within months of the Theatre and used until 1627. Like the Theatre it was used by a large number of companies. Another famous clown and singer, Robert Armin, played there and it was probably used by Shakespeare's company, the Lord Chamberlain's Men, between the demolition of the Theatre and the erection of the Globe. As with the Theatre, the Curtain was used for 'activities' – for fencing and later prize-fighting. The epilogue of a Curtain play, *The Travels of the Three English Brothers* (1607) speaks of its 'round circumference' (it may in fact have been polygonal) and it was there that the Swiss traveller Thomas Platter saw 'tents' used on the stage during the performance of an unknown play in 1599.[6] Of the next playhouse at Newington Butts, a village a mile south of London Bridge, mentioned from 1580 to 1594, we know very little. It may have been owned by Philip Henslowe, the greatest Elizabethan impresario, for it was at Newington that the Admiral's and Lord Chamberlain's Men mounted a combined season after the plague of 1592–4 and before they went their separate ways to the Rose and the Theatre respectively.[7]

Henslowe's main playhouse, the Rose, built south of the river about 1587, was the first of the Bankside playhouses and one of the most prestigious of its age. It was situated within the Liberty of the Clink – like all the other playhouses outside the jurisdiction of the City. There the companies associated with Henslowe, Strange's Men, Sussex's Men, the Queen's Men, and, notably, the Admiral's Men, performed. The Admiral's Men transferred to the Fortune in 1600 and about 1605 the Rose was pulled down. There, however, *Titus Andronicus* was played together with most of Marlowe's works and plays by Kyd, Chapman, Dekker, Drayton, Greene, and Lodge.

To the west, immediately opposite Blackfriars, stood the Swan, built about 1595 by a goldsmith called Francis Langley who leased the playhouse to the Earl of Pembroke's men. A performance there in 1597 of *The Isle of Dogs* (lost), claimed by the City to be seditious and slanderous, prompted the order by the Privy Council to close and pull down all public playhouses. The order was never put into operation but the Swan never recovered its status although it continued in existence, used for entertainments like prize-fights and an extemporal versifying contest involving Robert Wilson (1598) until about 1637. The prime piece of visual evidence for Elizabethan playhouses, the copy of a drawing by Johannes de Witt who visited London probably in 1596, is of the Swan – I shall examine this shortly. Like the Rose it was more lavish than the playhouses built north of the river. Unfortunately the suggestiveness of de Witt's evidence is unmatched by details drawn from playtexts: only one extant play, Middleton's *A Chaste Maid in Cheapside* (1611–13), is known to have been performed there. Views and maps of the period confirm the de Witt drawing and indicate that like its predecessors the Swan was round or polygonal (Plates 2–4). It was to the

Swan that a trickster and poetaster called Richard Vennar attracted a crowd of spectators to a fictitious entertainment called *England's Joy*. The plot promised such spectacles as Queen Elizabeth 'taken up into heaven, when presently appears a throne of blessed souls, and beneath under the stage, set forth with strange fireworks, diverse black and damned souls, wonderfully described in their several torments.' As the admission prices were 'two shillings or eighteen pence at least' – they usually ranged from one penny upwards – Vennar must have been expecting a highly privileged auditory. In the event he eloped with the takings, whereupon the audience, 'when they saw themselves deluded, revenged themselves upon the hangings, curtains, chairs, stools, walls, and whatsoever came in their way, very outrageously, and made great spoil.'[8]

It was to the Globe, which was built in 1599 and which stood until it was destroyed by fire in 1613, that the Lord Chamberlain's Men (later the King's Men) moved from the Curtain. There the plays of Shakespeare's maturity were performed. It stood to the east of the Rose, and was the nearest of the playhouses to London Bridge. Unfortunately again the richness of the dramatic fare offered there is unmatched by a richness of detail concerning the playhouse itself. It was round and its stage with canopy above was the model for the last of the Elizabethan public play-houses, the Fortune, built in 1600 by Henslowe and Edward Alleyn, to the north of the city just outside Cripplegate. Perhaps Henslowe and his men moved there from the Rose because they were being eclipsed on Bankside by the success of plays at the near-by Globe. The Fortune was occupied by the Admiral's Men, who became first Prince Henry's Men and then the Lord Palsgrave's Men, until it too was destroyed by fire in 1621. This playhouse was the main rival to the Globe, offering to a possibly more plebeian audience revivals of the Elizabethan dramatists as well as new works by authors such as Heywood, Middleton, Rowley, and Field. As at the Red Bull built near by in Clerkenwall about 1606, the diet seems to have been of heroic and spectacular plays, laced with offerings of sentimental comedy.

These then were the playhouses. Without minimizing the differences, evidence suggests that their external structure and internal layout were broadly similar. The Globe, after all, was built with the same timbers as the Theatre, and the Fortune contract specified that although the auditorium was to be square the stage was to be modelled on that of the Globe. Both the Globe and the Fortune were built by the same builder, Peter Street. The measurements in the contract for the last of Henslowe's playhouses, the Hope (1614), match those of the Fortune, and we know that the stage there was modelled on that of the Swan (although it was to have no stage columns so that the stage could be easily removed when the playhouse was to be used for bear-baiting).

Our examination of the varied places in which players were required to perform makes it apparent that in fact we should concentrate our examination of Elizabethan popular theatre on stages rather than playhouses. We shall then be able to set in perspective a lot of the vast amount of research and description that has taken place during the last couple of generations. As first-hand accounts of English Renaissance playhouses are very scanty, attempts at reconstruction have inevitably drawn upon theory as much as upon evidence. Because Elizabethan players performed in buildings and structures other than playhouses, scholars have very properly examined the similarities between these buildings and the playing places but, very naturally, their descriptions have often turned unwittingly into explanations which, moreover, often rest on implicit cultural assumptions. If, for example, we are concerned with performances in fairground booth theatres, it is easy to describe the drama so performed as an element of a folk or unsophisticated culture. If we consider performances in inn-yards, it is easy to postulate a tiring-house equipped with windows, doors, and rooms, and therefore appropriate to domestic bourgeois realism. If we notice that in performances in banquet-halls or great chambers the audience may well have sat or stood on four sides of the playing space, it is easy to associate the drama with the vogue for theatre in the round of the 1950s and 1960s, a vogue which attracted to itself writers and actors whose views about dramaturgy or social structures were quite un-Elizabethan. If we compare Elizabethan theatre buildings with those of the seventeenth century or later where perspective devices were employed to create illusion and where knowledge of neo-classical theory encouraged dramatists to set their plays in particular times in particular places, we are likely to look only for structures in early playhouses that might evolve into the proscenium arches and flat painted scenery with which an age of naturalism was more familiar. Undoubtedly the players did adapt themselves to the physical features of their playing places, and these features must have made impressions on contemporary audiences and been included in the total meaning of the play. What is distorting, however, is to assume that the history of the theatre proceeds by rules of growth. Theatre history is indeed a strangely unsatisfactory intellectual discipline because the effect of particular productions depends so much upon the way a company can adapt itself to the particular place in which it has to play and upon the accidents of particular performances. Induction from such a range of contingent phenomena is impossible and deductive accounts of the 'nature and origins' of a theatre or group of theatres are correspondingly invalid. It is impossible therefore to produce one monolithic theory about the nature of the Elizabethan public playhouses. All we can do is discuss the effects of different sorts of playing spaces and different sorts of dramatic occasion.

A drawing of the Swan

It is convenient to examine here the primary piece of visual evidence for the Elizabethan public playhouses, Arend van Buchell's copy of de Witt's sketch of the interior of the Swan, made in 1596 but discovered only in 1880 (Plate 5). I shall relate this to the primary piece of written evidence, the contract for the building of the Fortune playhouse of 1600. The sketch notoriously raises a lot of problems and presents us with evidence of only one of the fifteen playhouses that flourished in London from the last decades of the sixteenth century until the Civil War. Even if the sketch can be questioned as to detail, however, the accompanying notes and the labels attached to parts of the structure enable us to clarify some terms.

The centre of the drawing and the centre of the playhouse is the large flat stage. It is raised above the level of the yard which is labelled *planities sive arena*, 'a level surface or the place of combat in an amphitheatre'. (*Arena* is derived from the Latin word for sand and it is possible that the yard was so strewn rather than being paved with brick.) De Witt was concerned to draw similarities between the Elizabethan playhouses and ancient theatres. Accordingly he labelled the stage *proscaenium*, 'the area in front of the scenic wall' – the Latin word *scaena* derives from the Greek word *skene*, a tent. It is worth noting that the English word 'stage' means originally a standing-place, then a raised floor, platform, or scaffold, then specifically 'the platform in a theatre upon which spectacles, plays, etc. are exhibited' (*OED*). It does not in the sixteenth century refer as the modern word does to the whole complex of acting area, wings, flies, cyclorama, etc. (Incidentally in the sixteenth century 'platform' means a ground plan: a 'raised platform' is therefore almost a contradiction in terms.) Behind the stage stands the elaborate structure that de Witt labels *mimorum aedes*, 'the actors' house' or tiring-house. Two large entrances fitted with functional doors or gates give out on to the stage and above them in a gallery (called sometimes the 'tarras' – terrace – or referred to simply as 'aloft'), of which the turned columns can just be made out, there seem to be sitting, on the occasion of de Witt's visit at least, a row of spectators (or possibly musicians). There are several references in Elizabethan documents to the habit of sitting 'over the stage', sometimes in 'the Lords' room'[9] – the Swan gallery is divided into rooms and boxes. Two massive and decorated colums support a (tiled?) canopy above the stage, called a 'shadow or cover' in the contract for the Fortune,[10] and above that we see the 'hut' which is conspicuous in all the engraved maps of London and which housed the winches used for flying larger properties. From it flies the Swan's flag and from it a trumpeter emerges to proclaim the beginning of the performance. As players are already performing, it seems likely that de Witt was recording not a specific moment in a performance but the function of the various parts of the playhouse.

What is also interesting about the sketch (despite its crudeness) is that it is apparent that the stage and the tiring-house seem to stand independently of the encircling structure (a point to be developed later). This amphitheatre is galleried in three tiers which accords with the witness of other visitors. (The label *porticus* means simply a gallery and de Witt indicates that the galleries contain seating, *sedilia*.) No divisions are shown, but in most playhouses the amphitheatre galleries also were divided into rooms or boxes. Spectators ascended from the yard to the first gallery by the entrance marked *ingressus*: presumably the entrance from outside to the playhouse yard was opposite the tiring-house. De Witt labels part of the first gallery *orchestra*, which therefore has not its original Greek meaning of the round dancing-place of the chorus but its Latin sense, 'the senators' or noblemen's places in a theatre between the stage and the common seats'.[11] This part of the gallery may accordingly have been one of the 'Lords' rooms'. The sketch shows no trapdoor on the stage, no curtains or arras on the tiring-house, and it is difficult to tell whether the shaded areas below the stage represent massive supports or gaps between hangings (no corners appear).

That is the visual evidence. We must now attempt to correlate that with evidence gathered from theatrical history and dramatic texts in order to work towards a reconstruction of public playhouse performance. That is best done by considering the dramaturgy of plays that were performed on stages elsewhere so that we might then attempt a synthesis of our knowledge of dramatic convention with that of theatrical resources.

Halls and fairgrounds

There are two categories of performances by professionals away from playhouses: performances indoors for the privileged, and outdoor perform-ances at places of popular resort or recreation such as fairgrounds or bear-baitings. The first task is to establish whether the plays performed at Court were in fact similar to those performed in the popular playhouses at the same time. The evidence is scanty as most of the texts have been lost, but references to Court performances such as *The Knight in the Burning Rock* (1579), played by Warwick's Men, or *Felix and Philiomena* (1585), played by the Queen's Men, suggest that a large number of the productions there were of romances or romantic treatments of historical or classical legends. When we turn to the lost plays from the popular playhouses, titles that derive largely from Henslowe's accounts for the Rose and elsewhere in the 1590s, we find a preponderance of romance or romanticized history confirming our hypothesis that the plays offered there were broadly similar in kind.[12] (In Marston's *Histriomastix* (1599) Sir Oliver Owlet's men choose to play before a nobleman rather than at the town-house (Act II) simply because he will pay them more than the mayor.) For an extant example of a romance which we know to have been performed both at Court and in the playhouse we can look to *Mucedorus* (see Ch. 5). A second confirmation comes from comparing properties and costumes listed in the expense accounts for the Office of the Revels at Court with the inventories of Henslowe's Admiral's Men while they were playing at the Rose and elsewhere. Tombs, chariots, mossy banks, trees, 'houses' made of lath and canvas, weapons, crowns, horsehair accoutrements for wild men are found in both sets of documents.[13] Productions of this kind are indeed neither aristocratic nor plebeian in appeal; rather they are designed for the whole community, being entertainments in which legends or folk-tales were translated into a timeless aristocratic milieu. Not only did these works violate classical unities of time and place but they paid no account to theories of decorum: clowns like Tarlton from the inns and public playhouses mingled with kings from history and fiction in presentations as popular with the Queen as with the playhouse groundlings. Entertainments of this kind preclude in turn any dramatic verisimilitude based on illusion. We get a glimpse of such dramatic occasions in V.i. of *A Midsummer Night's Dream* where players and musicians, professional and amateur, are competing to appear before Duke Theseus.

What then was the style of a performance in a great chamber? The first thing to note is that the nature of the building did not provide for a physical division between players and audience. Records reveal that performances took place either in the centre of the hall with the audience arranged around, or sometimes on the raised area on which the high table stood with entrances provided by the doors to kitchens or private rooms behind.[14] If the latter arrangements were used, it was common for provision to be made for the master or monarch to view the play from a special seat or 'state' which would itself serve as one of the focal points for the staging and form part of the spectacle. (In Peele's *Arraignment of Paris* (1581), for example, the play's conflict is resolved when Queen Elizabeth is complimented by being judged the fairest goddess present.) No attempt was made in hall performances to deploy the action so that the sightlines of the hall itself converged on the players, and although lighting was used, it was not the practice to illuminate the players and not the spectators: indeed members of the audience would have been as aware of each other's presence as of the play. We can see how the playing area was not confined to the 'stage' alone by looking at the description of the fourth dumb show from *Gorboduc* performed at the Inner Temple and again at Whitehall in 1562. Although the example is early and the play might have been performed by gentlemen of the Temple rather than professionals, there is no reason to suggest that the conventions were different in professional Court performances later in the century:

First the music of the hautboys began to play, during which there came forth
from under the stage, as though out of hell, three furies, Alecto, Megaera,
and Tisiophone, clad in black garments sprinkled with blood and flames,
their bodies girt with snakes, their heads spread with serpents instead of hair,
the one bearing in her hand a snake, the other a whip, and the third a burning
firebrand . . . after that the furies . . . had passed about the stage thrice, they
departed, and the music ceased.

Just as at *England's Joy*, infernal beings were to come out from under the
stage to the space modern theatregoers would assume to possess for
themselves. Moreover the physical inhibitions that exist in proscenium arch
theatres on direct address to the audience or soliloquy did not exist, any
more than they do now in circuses or music halls.

There was then no categoric division between the space of the audience
and the space of the players; neither was the stage 'localized' in the manner
suggested, even today, by many editors of Renaissance texts. Scenes like the
dungeon scenes in *Edward II* or scenes that begin as at the opening of *Doctor*
Faustus with the discovery of a 'study' (see below) may be said to be set in a
specific place only in the sense that an appropriate space and axis for
performance was created – there was *no illusion of place*. Even Ben Jonson
who, more than any other dramatist, took care to establish the fictive
bounds of his actions, setting specific parts of London, say, very particularly in the minds of his spectators by a density of verbal reference, assumed
that his spectators would share actively in the making of the scene and not be
just passive spectators of a ready made object. So Musco (Brainworm in the
English version) comes forward at the beginning of Act II of *Every Man in*
his Humour (1598) and reveals his strategies in direct address to the
audience, thus revealing that Jonson was making no attempt to sustain
illusion. When players were performing on stages without tiring-houses,
say on a stage in the middle of a hall, it is probable that sometimes they
would have been visible before they 'came on'. Coming on to the stage in
such a theatre does not establish a place but merely begins an action. In *The*
Famous Victories of Henry V (1586) we several times come upon the
instruction for a character to enter *'roaming'*. Presumably the player came
out and moved about the stage, possibly exchanging quips with the
audience, until he was stopped not in a particular 'place' but simply for an
encounter with another character.

Like the playing spaces, the plays themselves did not postulate a division
between the world of the play and the world of the audience. Although the
sixteenth century saw drama change from an occasional and amateur
activity to an enterprise where professionals performed regularly throughout the year, Elizabethan drama never lost completely its associations with
seasonal revelry, those games and rituals that were part of the great
festivities of the year – Christmas, Shrovetide, Maytime. The same com-

panies that were playing in the public playhouses were called to Court at Christmas or contributed to the staging of the great civic pageants like the Midsummer Shows. Occasional and festive plays were then brought to the public stage – *A Midsummer Night's Dream* and *Twelfth Night* are examples. Plays in halls, in fact, subsumed two kinds of dramatic performance: those by professional actors and revels staged by those whose skills were not simply mimetic. Elizabethan players were the descendants of those individual artists of the Middle Ages, minstrels, musicians, fools, tumblers, and jugglers who made a living moving from house to house, fair to fair. From the point of view of the government and civic authorities they fell into the same category as 'masterless men'. For their own protection, some of these travellers became attached to particular households, others took the name and livery of particular aristocrats, even though they continued to live as roving players. The kind of dramatic fare they originally provided was based more on performance than narrative, on the exhibition of skills rather than the imitation of action, and was akin to the kind of drama we now associate with circuses or the ballet.

By the middle of the sixteenth century, however, a specific kind of play had evolved that might be performed by players of this kind. This was the interlude, a short piece that could be simply the dramatization of a folk-tale, of a bawdy anecdote, or a brief moral debate like that provided in *Fulgens and Lucrece* (1497), where a lady of birth has to choose between suitors whose nobility derives from birth and conduct respectively. The matter of the play is amplified by two comic servants, parts that require professional comic skills. In their first interchange which opens the play the author deliberately welds the action and audience together:

A: I trow your own self be one
   Of them that shall play.
B: Nay, I am none.
   I trow thou speakest in derision
   To liken me thereto.
A: Nay, I mock not, wot ye well,
   For I thought verily by your apparel
   That ye had been a player.
B: Nay, never a dell.
A: Then I cry you mercy,
   I was to blame, lo, therfore I say.
   There is so much nice array
   Amongst these gallants nowaday
   That a man shall not lightly
   Know a player from another man. (ll. 44–56)

Interludes, imitations of the Italian *intermezzi*, were performed between the courses of banquets: they were like cabaret acts or a modern 'dinner theatre'.

Another tradition was that in which the performers were non-professional, drawn from or becoming part of the audience. This was the tradition of tournament, of mummings, disguisings, and masques, the forms of which might sometimes be shaped by their story or 'action'. As Glynne Wickham has shown, it was fairly common for shows of arms or 'barriers' to include a moral narrative: knights would compete to rescue a maiden from a monster. Or the ritual plays of the mummers' tradition, plays about St George or Robin Hood, would be performed by amateur actors as part of an evening's festivities. Finally the disguising, the visitation of a house by a group of young men in masks to pay court to a group of young women, might include a symbolic pageant followed by dancing in the hall by all that were present. Masqued balls are the modern descendants.

As a second example of a hall entertainment we might take the interlude *Mankind*. This is the earliest interlude which we know to have been performed by an English troupe, probably about 1466 somewhere near Cambridge. It used to be thought that the play was performed in an inn-yard or fairground; I agree with Richard Southern[15] that the references to doors on to the playing place, the mention of a yard outside (l. 556), the orders to the spectators to stand back as the players made their entrance, as well as the line 'I pray God give you good night!' suggest that the text derives from an after-dinner revel in a great hall.

This speculation is confirmed by the nature of the play. Like the morality plays, its characters bear allegorical names and it deals with matters of religion, but the plot is of the loosest (even the arrangement of the leaves in the sole manuscript from which modern editions derive is in doubt), and the play is little more than a sequence of comic turns for the players involved. The actors do not really 'enter' to advance the progression of the narrative, but step into the playing space to present their impersonative and performing skills. Parts were undoubtedly doubled, and the play is a sequence of set pieces: there is a dance and a bawdy song when the audience is invited to sing along, a spectacular entrance for the devil Titivillus which is proclaimed by his calls from behind the hall screen as he hurriedly dons his costume, and which takes place only after the other players have halted the action to go around the audience and gather money. This sequence must have been like the entrance of the Green Knight, amusing and horrific, described in *Sir Gawayn*. *Mankind* begins and ends with a solemn proclamation by Mercy, but the action calls for turns of zestful knockabout as the devil prevents Mankind from tilling the ground by placing a board under his spade, or as the vices urge Mankind to end his misery by leaping off a gallows brought into the hall. Some of the effects, like the appearance of Titivillus, depend on an entrance being made through a door, but the nature of the play suggests that members of the troupe may have remained in the hall throughout the performance and have 'put on' their roles or indeed their costumes in sight of the audience as is done in a game of charades. Many scenes in Elizabethan drama centre on the donning of costumes appropriate to a character's role: *Tamburlaine* (1587) I.ii. provides the classic example. In *Mankind*, as in the plays of the public playhouses (*Doctor Faustus* although possessing a stronger narrative structure belongs in the same tradition), there is no attempt at verisimilitude and no attempt to persuade the audience that they are privileged spectators of a particular event that might have happened thus in the past. The play demands mere space and not place, roles and not characters, and action is defined not against a specific physical background but simply when actors address or gesture to one another.

When we come to consider outdoor performances which generally took place on the scaffold stages of fairgrounds we are fortunate in that these often appear in European if not English paintings and engravings of the time (Plate 6). From the examples that appear in the Flemish paintings, for example – and there is no reason to suppose that theatres of this kind were different in England – we can see that the stage consisted simply of a board platform supported by trestles or barrels at about head height, and that behind this was a simple rectangular tent which served as a tiring-house and, perhaps if its curtains were painted, as an emblematic summary of the play. Generally the 'action' (using the word now in its Elizabethan sense of the gestures of the player) depicted in these paintings seems to be of a vaudeville type, and it is reasonable to suppose that the plays were based on familiar roisterous tales, the dialogue mannered and studded with catch phrases. The 'motion' (puppet play) of *Hero and Leander* in Jonson's *Bartholomew Fair* (1614) shows how Marlowe's 'learned and poetical' book (V.iii.104) was reduced to knockabout bawdy and comedians' cross-talk routines. Presumably the audience paid about as much attention to the 'story' as they do to a modern Punch and Judy show – there was no question of 'a willing suspension of disbelief' – and exchanged quips with the players, a convention that survived into the Elizabethan playhouses.

Inevitably no scripts from performances of this kind have survived – if indeed scripts ever existed. The players most probably improvised and, moreover, adapted their routines to cope with interjections from boisterous members of their audience or to hold the attention of spectators distracted by other spectacles in the fair until one of the company could go around the crowd to gather what trifling sums he could. Performances in such settings must have made the collection of money a chancy business: one obvious solution was to put the booth theatre within an enclosure so that admission could be charged as the audience approached the stage. There are several European engravings extant which show precisely this arrangement: a booth theatre standing within a galleried Fencing School. In the case of the engraving of the Nuremberg Fechthaus of about 1690 reproduced by Wickham,[16] the players are tumblers and are competing with a fiddler, a tight-rope walker, and a performing ape. This same building was also used for bear-baiting, and it seems that such stages were built within inns and in the bear- and bull-baiting circles that stood on London's Bankside. What is more interesting is that this conception of stage and auditorium as separate structures survives in the contract for the Fortune theatre where the builder was instructed to build his stage 'within the frame' of the auditorium, and the Hope contract of 1613 stipulated that the stage was to be built of trestles that it might easily be taken down. The implications are that the frame or auditorium was considered as a construction for accommodating the maximum number of spectators and only incidentally as a structure which might serve the stage by providing a picture frame for the action or machinery for handling large properties. The basic elements of the Elizabethan public playhouse therefore are the elements of the booth theatre, a tiring-house and a stage, the two structures in fact that Peter Quince designates in the rehearsal for Pyramus and Thisbe.

We can now see that indeed the building of the Theatre in 1576 is an event in economic history rather than in the history of dramatic form, a moment that Wickham describes as 'a watershed between what may reasonably be called "a public service theatre" and what thereafter may with equal fairness be described as "a commercial theatre"'.[17] It occurred when Burbage had accumulated enough capital (probably as much as from his mining interests as from his theatrical ventures) to build a wooden O around the kind of portable stage he and his fellow players had been using for centuries. Travellers report that the London playhouses could accommodate 3,000 spectators and we know that the method of collecting admission charges preserved the idea of keeping the stage concealed from those who had not paid. Admission was through an outer door where spectators paid a penny to a 'gatherer' to be given entrance to the yard. If they required 'standing' (seats, in fact) in the galleries, they paid another penny to move there from the yard, and they could pay further sums to move into 'the Lords' room' or, late in the period, for a stool on the stage itself. As we shall see, the atmosphere within certain playhouses must have reminded spectators of fairgrounds with orange-sellers and fosset-women, boys bringing around beer, sellers of plays and ballads, and prostitutes soliciting for custom.[18] (The availability of rooms just off the galleries around inn-yards was one of the reasons why the city fathers abhorred the stage.) It is also interesting that, although some of the playhouses had stone foundations (probably necessary for those built on the Bankside marshes), Elizabethan methods of construction – the timbers of the frame were slotted and pegged together – made these buildings portable constructions. For the Theatre was pulled down in 1598 and rebuilt 'in another form' as the Globe in 1599. That fact is not in itself of great significance, but we might mentally contrast the sense of improvisation, of having to establish on unworthy scaffolds the setting and mood of a play by no more than word, gesture, and properties, with the sense of permanence and ritual that is suggested by the great stone amphitheatres of the ancient world, and with the expectations of elaborate spectacle or exact illusion that modern expensive and technologically equipped theatres arouse.

The stage, the tiring-house, and the canopy

What then were the constituent elements of an Elizabethan playhouse? First, of course, the stage. All the evidence points to its having been rectangular and large. We can deduce the size of one stage from the Fortune contract. The playhouse itself was to be square and to have sides 80 feet long enclosing a yard 55 feet across. The stage – meaning simply the raised platform – was to 'contain in length forty and three foot of lawful assize and in breadth to extend to the middle of the yard of the said house'.[19] Hosley has calculated that accommodating the tiring-house façade to the two 10-inch overhangs of the galleries in the frame would have reduced the depth of the stage to 25 feet 10 inches.[20] It presumably stood at head height or somewhat lower, may have been bounded by a low balustrade, and the contract calls for it 'to be paled in below with good, strong and sufficient new oaken boards'. (The Swan drawing suggests that there curtains were used to conceal the cellarage beneath.) The dimensions indicate that on either side of the stage there was a kind of passage some 6 feet wide between the stage and the lower gallery of the frame. These passages may have served as entrances for the spectators, but there is no reason to doubt that when the yard was full they provided extra standing space with the result that the stage would be surrounded on at least three sides. It is important to stress this fact as some of the descriptions that have been applied to the Elizabethan stages, 'thrust' or 'apron' stages, suggest that the stage was ancillary to some other part of the structure. So too those reconstructions which have postulated a stage tapering towards the front have simply demonstrated how the attention of their designers is really on the tiring-house. No, that platform was the centre, the focus of attention for the audience. Not until 1605 when Inigo Jones constructed at Court a proscenium stage with a painted landscape behind it for Jonson's *Masque of Blackness* were the audience given the impression that they were looking through into another world. The stage was, for the Elizabethans, not a remote other place but a space on which men of their own time and of their own community might play, prate, strut, laugh, and fret before their fellows.

To this description we can add two details. Like the floors of halls or great chambers the stage may have been strewn with rushes – although it is difficult to think why this was done in outdoor playhouses. Evidence for this comes from Ch. VI of Dekker's *The Gull's Hornbook* (1609), 'How a Gallant should Behave himself in a Playhouse'. One paragraph is worth quoting in its entirety as it economically describes (when due allowance is made for satiric exaggeration) the practices and atmosphere of a performance as the gallant advances to take his stool on the stage:[21]

> Whether therefore the gatherers of the public or private playhouse stand
> to receive the afternoon's rent, let our gallant (having paid it) presently
> advance himself up to the throne of the stage. I mean not into the Lords'
> room (which is now but the stage's suburbs [a quarter of London
> notorious for its brothels]). No, those boxes, by the iniquity of custom,
> conspiracy of waiting-women and gentlemen-ushers that there sweat
> together, and the covetousness of sharers [playhouse proprietors], are
> contemptibly thrust into the rear, and much new satin is there damned
> by being smothered to death in darkness. But on the very rushes where
> the comedy is to dance, yea and under the state of Cambises himself
> must our feathered estridge, like a piece of ordnance, be planted,
> valiantly (because impudently) beating down the mews and hisses of the
> opposed rascality.

(The passage, incidentally, implies no distinction between staging practices at public and private playhouses.) Second, in those playhouses where the trestles beneath the stage were concealed by drapes rather than palings, it seems that the drapes were changed according to the nature of the play being performed. In the anonymous *A Warning for Fair Women* (c. 1590) we find History remarking to Comedy in the Induction:

> The stage is hung with black; and I perceive
> The auditors prepared for tragedy. (82–3)

In I.v. of *Britannia's Pastorals* (1613) William Browne spoke of:

> What time the world, clad in a mourning-robe,
> A stage made for a woful tragedy. (163–4)

The implications are that other colours were used for other plays (blue for comedy?), but there is no contemporary evidence for this.[22]

The appearance and nature of the tiring-house façade has given rise to more controversy than has surrounded any other part of the Elizabethan playhouse. The primary historical document, the Swan drawing, shows a flat unadorned façade with two massive sets of rustic-looking double doors. This accords with a stage direction in that one Swan play, Middleton's *A Chaste Maid in Cheapside*, which specifies an entrance '*at one door . . . at the other door*' (V.iv.). Hosley[23] thinks that there were three entrances at

Shakespeare's playhouse, the Globe, and therefore at the Fortune which was modelled on the Globe. Other playhouses may have had up to five entrances in façades that, in the case of playhouses that were round or polygonal, were concave or, like the influential Teatro Olimpico at Vicenza designed by Palladio in 1579–80, stood between two side walls. The arguments derive from two bodies of evidence: stage directions and analogies between Renaissance illustrations of classical theatres and Elizabethan playhouses. Passages in *Fortunatus* (1599) and *1 Henry VI* (1591), two Rose plays, suggest at least four entrances [24] and it is possible that the design of some façades was influenced by European engravings in editions of Terence which show characters emerging from arcades or 'houses' with up to five openings. Alternatively there could have been three entrances on stage, corresponding to the palace door and doors for strangers that Vitruvius describes in the scenic walls of Roman theatres, and two more entrances, also used by the audience, leading to the passageways at the sides of the stage. These corresponded to Vitruvius' entrances from the forum and the country in the *versurae* or angles of the wall. [25] If such layouts did exist, it is possible that the common processional stage direction for players to '*pass over the stage*' meant that they entered the yard through such an entrance, mounted on to the stage to march across it (possibly prolonging the spectacle by marching about it), and then descended to the yard again to leave by the passage opposite. The yard might have been used for other kinds of action: Hodges suggests that in *Pericles* a practical boat was brought into the yard and 'moored alongside the stage, which was the ship' and that occasionally entrances may have been made on horseback into the yard[26] as in *Woodstock* (1592), III.ii, possibly acted at the Theatre, or as in Scene i of the anonymous *Famous Victories of Henry V*.

One suggestion for the appearance of the tiring-house façade is provided by an engraving found in Robert Fludd's *Ars Memoria* (1623, Plate 7). It is not necessary to rehearse here the arguments over whether this in any way represents a real or simply a mnemonic theatre or whether, if real, it is a depiction of a London public or private playhouse. [27] Suffice it to point out that the engraving shows two kinds of entrance, two round arches without practical doors, and a larger rectangular opening furnished with practical gates. This document has led some theatre historians to suggest that some playhouses observed a distinction between doors and gates, and that this central entrance was used when characters found their way barred, as for example in siege scenes or in farce which is so dependent on whether doors are open or shut. [28] The rigours of English winters make it unlikely, in fact, that any entrance to the tiring-house was left without a practical door. The implications are that players must have come through a door on to the stage when the dialogue indicates clearly that they are 'outside' or even when they are on the point of going 'inside'. (Many plays contain the stage direction

'*Enter and knock*', which suggests an entrance through one door and a cross to knock at another.) Often a scene played 'outside' a house is immediately followed by a scene 'inside' the house as happens in Act V of *The Alchemist*. No change of scenery took place, so the audience must have been able to accept that an entrance could represent a door 'seen' from either outside or inside. All this reminds us again that an entrance by a character in an Elizabethan play did not help to establish a sense of place but merely marked the beginning of a dramatic sequence.

As for the style of the tiring-house façade, the Swan drawing suggests that it was almost completely undecorated, but de Witt's notes that accompany the sketch speak of the magnificence of the London playhouses, and he compares them with the forms of Roman theatres, notes that the Swan was 'built of a mass of flint stones', and that the playhouse was 'supported by wooden columns painted in such excellent imitation of marble that it is able to deceive even the most cunning'.[29] These may be the columns that belong to the 'frame' but it is more likely that they are the columns that support the canopy over the stage and which are drawn in comparative detail in the sketch. Other travellers to London also speak of the ornateness of the playhouses and these are frequently described as 'sumptuous' or 'gorgeous' in Puritan attacks on the stage. Admittedly the Puritan evidence is open to doubt, but it would be surprising if the European travellers, familiar with court and religious spectacles, would have exaggerated. While I accept that there is no conclusive proof that the interiors of the playhouse were ornate, I find too many reconstructions which seek to stress their plainness unconvincing. They were after all public buildings, and yet the models and plans of say J. C. Adams, Kernodle, and Rhodes seem to have taken their styles from Elizabethan domestic architecture, or rather a folksy version of it, all thatch, black beams with white plaster, and latticed windows. Other drawings suggest otherwise: the sketches of Inigo Jones for the tiring-house façades of an unknown private theatre before 1616 (Plate 8) and the Cockpit at Court of 1629–30, for example, although a generation later than the Elizabethan public playhouses, preserve the basic disposition of their parts,[30] and are clearly Renaissance buildings in a harmonious style. Whether any of the public playhouses of the sixteenth century displayed this degree of classical influence – the elaborate painted columns with Corinthian capitals of the Swan suggest that one playhouse did – is debatable. But we may imagine the façade to have been similar in form and decoration to the carved screens in Elizabethan halls. These were often based on a simple classical plan and ornamented with the elaborate bas-relief carving that is so common also on the tombs of the period. Such seems to have been the style of the Fortune: the contract stipulates that 'the principal and main posts of the said frame and stage forward shall be square and wrought palasterwise, with carved proportions [figures] called satyrs to be placed and set on the top of every of the same posts'.[31] The phrase 'stage forward' refers to the palings that concealed the supports of the stage. It is highly probable that the ornamentation of the tiring-house would have matched that of the frame and stage paling.

The Swan drawing suggests an undecorated façade, but we know that in many playhouses the tiring-house was hung with arras (tapestry) or curtains which were often painted with symbolic motifs. Whether or not they were changed to provide figures that were appropriate to the subject of particular plays is difficult to tell.[32] It is also difficult to know whether these hangings more usually concealed the doors and thereby served as what were referred to as 'traverses'[33] – Volpone is called upon to peep *from behind a traverse* at V.iii.9 – or whether they hung between them. Vignettes from the title-pages of two late texts, *Messalina* (1640) and *Roxana* (1632), show that the hangings extended right across the façade, although one of these stages is much smaller than stages in the public playhouses. It is important to remember, however, that these hangings did not fulfil the function of a proscenium curtain that can be completely drawn aside to reveal, say, an extensive interior. Rather they were parted to allow for entrances, thus obviating much awkward opening and closing of heavy doors like those shown in the de Witt drawing, or they could be drawn sufficiently to expose the door.

This brings us to the difficult problem of 'discovery' scenes.[34] Earlier theatre historians who tended to assume a single line of evolutionary development and who focused their attention on the tiring-house façade tended to assume that there was, behind the tiring-house hangings, a largish 'inner stage' that was used for interior scenes and which was the precursor of the proscenium stage – a box with its fourth wall removed – with which they were familiar.[35] A stage direction that is frequently cited by them is found in a Rose play of 1587–8, Greene's *Alphonsus, King of Aragon*, which calls for a brazen head to be set in the *middle of the place behind the Stage* (IV.i.). It is necessary to point out first that the Elizabethans never used the phrase 'inner stage', nor, as is frequently supposed, did they use the word 'study' as a general name for such a place although there are references to 'studies' in some plays when the action is set in a small room.[36] In fact, many of the scenes which early editors placed on the 'inner stage' contain explicit stage directions or indications in the dialogue which show that the players walked on and off the stage rather than being discovered by drawing a curtain.

Again the Fludd engravings are suggestive in two points: the façade does have an architectural unity, even though its coarse rustic style is unusual and hardly functional or elegant. It is obviously merely a façade – there is no suggestion of *rooms* behind. There are, however, as we have seen, three entrances, the middle one of which is much wider than the other two and is fitted with double doors so hinged that they can be swung back to 'discover' a *space* within.[37] Both the Swan entrances have double doors and could have been used in this manner. Another illustration (admittedly late) supports this hypothesis that entrances were probably used for discoveries. This is the sketch by Inigo Jones, probably for the remodelling of the Cockpit in Drury Lane as a theatre (Plate 8).[38] Again we find three entrances, the middle one large, although there is a great contrast in styles with Fludd's memory theatre, this façade being in the chaste baroque style characteristic of Jones. No doors are discernible and it was obviously not intended to conceal the whole façade with hangings, for the wall is furnished with decorative niches and swags. There is no reason to doubt, however, that the middle entrance, fitted with a curtain, could have been used in the way I have suggested. A final piece of evidence is provided by the screen in the hall of the Middle Temple in London where *Twelfth Night* was performed in 1602. There the entrances are about 5 feet wide, sufficient to discover a group of four or five players. They may well have been used in the scene in that play (not technically a discovery) where the letter is planted on Malvolio.

One further possibility is that the middle entrance stood forward to form a portico, hung with curtains. That structure might have been what was designated as a tent (see below), or could have been used as a bower in *The Spanish Tragedy*, and the platform above would have suited perfectly the demands of the monument sequence in *Antony and Cleopatra*. Unfortunately there is no evidence for such a device beyond suggestions in dramatic text.

Evidence from the plays supports the hypothesis that the space so discovered need not have been large, and that what was revealed was generally in the nature of a tableau to be shown to other characters on the stage and containing little action. A good example is provided by a moment in III.ii. of *2 Henry VI* (1591). There, having heard the news that his uncle Humphrey, Duke of Gloucester, has been murdered, the King commands Warwick to 'Enter his chamber, view his breathless corpse, And comment then upon his sudden death' (131–2). A prompter's note, *'Bed put forth'*, is recorded in the Folio text twelve lines later, and this is followed after two lines by the stage direction *'Warwick draws the curtains, and shows Duke Humphrey in his bed.'* I would suggest that a curtained entrance (rather than a separate tent or booth) was used for this tableau; this is supported by the stage direction for another bedroom tableau that occurs only some 300 lines later. Here the stage direction to the opening of III.iii. in the bad Quarto, a reported text and therefore likely to describe what was done in performance, reads:[39]

> *Enter King and Salisbury, and then the curtains be drawn, and the Cardinal is discovered in his bed raving and staring as if he were mad.*

In *Catiline* (1611), acted by the King's Men at the Globe, the Senecan Prologue rises from the stage trap and after fifteen lines draws a curtain to reveal Catiline in his study. This is probably what had happened at the Rose in *Doctor Faustus*, where the last line of the Chorus, 'And this the man that in his study sits' is followed by the stage direction, *'Enter Faustus in his study.'* In *Friar Bacon and Friar Bungay* (1592?), another Rose play, Friar Bacon reveals his apprentice and the Brazen Head according to the following stage direction:

> *Enter Friar Bacon, drawing the curtains with a white stick, a book in his hand, and a lamp lighted by him; and the Brazen Head, and Miles with weapons by him.* (Scene xi)

The evidence therefore seems to indicate, that (in public and private playhouses alike) curtains and doors were used not simply for places of concealment (Polonius is behind the arras when he meets his end and Falstaff falls asleep there while Hal is dealing with the officers who have come in his pursuit) but as frames for these tableau-like scenes. There is no evidence that they were used to establish the *illusion* of interiors; they could be used only for a small number of players – although some eight players are discovered as a Court of Sessions in scene ii of *Sir Thomas More* (1596) – and they were used sparingly: Hosley computed that twenty-one of the thirty extant Globe plays required no discoveries, and seven of the remaining nine only one each.[40]

Above the entrances there certainly ran a gallery, usually designated in stage directions simply as *'aloft'*. It may have overhung the entrances below so that the arras could be hung from a rail on its forward edge.[41] It was fronted with a balustrade and this may have marked its division into rooms or boxes. The openings could be used as windows when the action demanded them.[42] It is unlikely that the openings were in fact glazed although it is conceivable there were, in some playhouses, glazed functional windows where the tiring-house joined the auditorium. The most graphic description of the use of the gallery for stage action in the public playhouses comes from Jasper Mayne's verse encomium of Ben Jonson:[43]

> Thy scene was free from monsters, no hard plot
> Called down a god t'untie th'unlikely knot.
> The stage was still a stage, two entrances
> Were not two parts o'th'world, disjoined by seas.
> Thine were land-tragedies, no prince was found
> To swim a whole scene out, then o'the stage drowned;
> Pitched fields, as Red Bull wars, still felt thy doom,
> Thou laid'st no sieges to the music-room.

It is obvious from the poem that, in a playhouse like the Red Bull that presented a fairly consistent repertory of blood and thunder plays, the gallery was used for city or castle walls and that one of its 'rooms' or boxes was also used to house musicians. *A Chaste Maid in Cheapside* has a stage direction that includes the following: *'while all the company seem to weep and mourn there is a sad song in the music-room'* (IV.iv.).[44] Other stage directions call simply for *'music within'*.[45]

Besides being used for action, the gallery or at least parts of it were used to house spectators. The Swan drawing indicates that it was so used at least when de Witt was visiting the playhouse and Henslowe records 'pd. for sellynge the Rome ouer the tyerhowsse . . . xs'.[46] Two of the extant playhouse illustrations, although they date from a later period, are again suggestive. The Fludd memory theatre and the Jones plan have galleries that are divided so that they could be used for action and to house spectators simultaneously. The Fludd theatre has a central oriel window which conceivably was a room for spectators and which is flanked with battlements of obvious utility, while the Jones drawing clearly shows seating on either side of a central opening that could have been used for at least tableau scenes. The references to a 'penthouse' in Henslowe's diary may signify a structure like the Fludd oriel at the Rose and it is also possible that the gallery was flanked by boxes which faced inwards towards each other so that spectators or actors sitting there could view discovery scenes in the centre of the tiring-house.[47] Although 'rather more than half of the plays associated with the Globe between 1599 and 1609 require some use of an area above or aloft to supplement the action on the stage proper',[48] most of these scenes were brief, restricted in their action (being based on speech rather than movement), were of a tableau-like nature requiring only a small number of players, and could therefore have been accommodated in a box extending only about a third of the way across the gallery. At the end of *The Jew of Malta*, a Rose play, only Barabas need be visible aloft as he vaunts his plans. In V.i. of *2 Tamburlaine* the Governor of Babylon appears flanked by two kneeling citizens *'upon the walls'*. Theridamus and Techelles appear on the stage below with soldiers and give orders for an assault to be made on them. There is a stage direction, *'Alarm, and they scale the walls'*, but the audience is diverted from what must have been a skirmish in a very cramped part of the gallery by a spectacular entrance beneath of Tamburlaine in his chariot drawn by kings. While he boasts of his victory the unfortunate Governor is bustled into the tiring-house and down the stairs to be brought in again on the stage below. From there he is again conveyed into the tiring-house where he is next discovered, hanging in chains to be shot at by Tamburlaine's henchmen.

Above the gallery and over the stage stood a canopy, supported by the columns so prominent in the Swan drawing and elaborately painted, as I have already noted.[49] The contract of 1614 for the Hope playhouse, however, specified that the canopy was to be supported 'without any posts or supporters',[50] and Hodges has argued that the canopy of the second Globe was likewise without column supports.[51] (These seem to have been the exceptions to a general rule.) Two points about the columns must be made:

there is no doubt that they must have obstructed the view of the stage for some members of the audience – but so must the gallants sitting on stools on the stage. Presumably some movement was possible in the yard if it was not too crowded and the standers must have simply changed their positions if that were necessary. Second, at the Swan at least the columns seem to have been too massive to be easily climbed, which suggests that directions for players to climb trees as in Act IV of *Old Fortunatus* (1599), for example, would have been executed by the provision of sturdy property trees: three trees of various kinds appear in Henslowe's list. The columns may have proved useful in overhearing scenes as when Gaveston stands aside to watch the first confrontation between Edward II and his barons. Like the columns, the canopy seems to have been decorated: references in several plays make it reasonable to assume that its underside (or the 'heavens' as it was often designated) was painted with the signs of the zodiac or with some heavenly allegory set amid clouds and stars. Heywood may have been describing the Rose when he describes 'the covering of the stage, which we call the heavens' in a theatre supposedly built by Julius Caesar: 'In that little compass were comprehended the perfect model of the firmament, the whole frame of the heavens, with all grounds of astronomical conjecture'.[52] The function of the canopy must have been to give some shelter, but only to the players – it did not protect the yard. Webster gives us a glimpse of what conditions in the public playhouses must have been like in winter when he laments in the epistle to *The White Devil* acted at the Red Bull in 1612 that his play 'was acted in so dull a time of winter, presented in so open and black a theatre, that it wanted . . . a full and understanding auditory'. The canopy also supported the hut from which a trumpet was sounded three times at the beginning of performances and which housed not only the winches that were used for 'flying' heavenly thrones and other properties but also certain machinery used for sound effects. The opening stage direction of a Rose play, Greene's *Alphonsus King of Aragon* reads, '*After you have sounded thrice, let Venus be let down from the top of the stage.*' A famous passage from the Prologue to Jonson's *Everyman in his Humour* (1601 version) satirizes such practices:

> He rather prays you will be pleased to see
> One such today as other plays should be;
> Where neither chorus wafts you o'er the seas,
> Nor creaking throne comes down the boys to please;
> Nor nimble squib is seen to make afeared
> The gentlewomen; nor rolled bullet heard
> To say it thunders; nor tempestuous drum
> Rumbles to tell you when the storm doth come.

It was probably from the hut that the cannon was fired during battle sequences as in III.i. of *Edward III* (*c*.1590) or the sea battle in IV.i. of *2*

Henry VI. (Once it discharged the wadding that set fire to the roof and then the whole of the first Globe playhouse during a performance of *Henry VIII* in 1613.) In the more lavish playhouses it may have also contained at least one large bell, possibly equipped with a rope that could be pulled from the stage, to serve as an 'alarum' and, in the absence of clocks, to mark the passage of time. Its sounding was heard to great effect at the close of *Doctor Faustus*.[53] In 1598 the Admiral's Men owned 'ij stepells, & j chyme of belles, & j beacon':[54] probably clock bells, hand bells for musical effects, and an alarm bell respectively. The smaller bells were probably housed in the tiring-house – *A Warning for Fair Women* has the stage direction '*Here some strange solemn music like bells is heard within*' (l. 800). In IV.v. of *Edward III* the text demands '*A clamour of ravens*' then '*Another noise*'. Presumably suitable instruments were kept within.

There has been some debate about the degree to which such properties were 'flown' from the huts during performances. Beckerman concluded that 'about the machinery in the heavens the Globe plays offer no evidence whatsoever',[55] but he was able to analyse only 29 of the 150 plays performed at that playhouse from 1599 to 1609 and it is possible that the plays that have not survived were of a more spectacular sort, not deemed to be of sufficient literary value to merit publication. The engravings of the exteriors of the London playhouses indicate that the huts were quite large, and certainly in late sixteenth-century Italy machines had been developed for lowering thrones and side platforms, and for thrusting up stairs. (Records of late medieval English civic pageantry frequently record the use of winches in elaborate devices for 'discoveries' and for the miraculous appearance of trees.) Henslowe actually stored a throne in the hut of the Rose.[56] The only extant English plays, however, that call for very large numbers of flying entrances and exits are Heywood's mythological spectaculars depicting the Golden, Silver, Brazen, and Iron Ages performed at the Red Bull (1610 –12). Spectacular heavenly phenomena, on the other hand, were fairly frequent, for example the three suns that appear in the heavens in *3 Henry VI*, II.i.25, according to the reported text (Q), and in the dumb show that divides the two parts of an Admiral's play *Captain Thomas Stukeley* (1596):

> so both armies meeting, embrace when with a sudden thunder-clap the sky is
> one fire and the blazing star appears which they prognosticating to be
> fortunate departed very joyful.

It is difficult to know whether elaborate fireworks were used here or whether a cloth like the Admiral's 'the cloth of the sun and moon' would have been drawn across under the canopy.[57] In *A Looking Glass for London and England* (1590), an elaborate emblem was obviously flown: '*A hand from out a cloud threatens with a burning sword*' (IV.iii.) A reasonable conjecture would be therefore that flying apparatus did exist in at least some playhouses, but that it was probably used sparingly – on the ground that anything spectacular overdone soon became tiresome even to an unsophisticated audience.

Gods, then, sometimes descended from the heavens; devils and ghosts certainly appeared through trapdoors in the stage that led to the space beneath, commonly called the 'cellarage'. A Red Bull play, Dekker's *If It Be Not Good, the Devil Is In It* (1611), has stage directions indicating that not only did devils enter from the trap but that some sort of lift existed for rising and sinking effects, and a late Red Bull play, *The Two Noble Ladies* (1622), has a stage direction '*the Devils sink roaring; a flame of fire riseth after them.*' This lift would enable the trap to be used as a grave or pit, fairly certainly for Ophelia's grave, perhaps for the dungeon or sewer in which the King is humiliated in *Edward II*, V.v. The trap may have been quite big: dialogue in *The Silver Age* (1611) indicates that it had to accommodate Pluto's 'iron chariot' shod with brass and drawn by devils.[58] Rhodes notes[59] the stage direction in the prompt-book of Massinger's *Believe as You List* (1631), which reads '*Gascoign and Hubert below, ready to open the trap-door for Mr. Taylor*' (l. 1825) and implies that the Rose trap might have been hinged to the stage at its up-stage end so that the down-stage end could be lowered into the cellarage to provide a ramp.[60]

The fact that the stage stood between a canopy referred to as the heavens and a cellarage associated with devils has encouraged some commentators to think of the playhouse as a model of the world and that the plays performed there were mediated by this physical representation of the theological framework of the universe. A poem by Thomas Heywood prefixed to his *Apology for Actors* (1612) uses this conceit in its argument:

> If then the world a theatre present,
> As by the roundness it appears most fit,
> Built with star-galleries of high ascent,
> In which Jehove doth as spectator sit,
> And chief determiner to applaud the best,
> And their endeavours crown with more than merit;
> But by their evil actions dooms the rest
> To end disgraced, whilst others praise inherit;
> He that denies then theatres should be,
> He may as well deny a world to me.

The poem alludes to the Platonic concept of the perfection of the circle and reminds the reader that characters in plays, like the players, *les enfants du paradis*, are at the mercy of the taste as well as the moral sense of the audience. Yet it is impossible to recover the way contemporaries really conceived of this aspect of the playhouses, and there are several points that should discourage us from being too dogmatic about this iconology. First, as we have seen, plays were often transferred to playing places that did not provide a representation of a three-layered universe. Second, although the *topos* of the *theatrum mundi* is common enough, the actual use of the gallery and cellarage was limited. Third, there is no evidence that the decoration of the tiring-house itself was based on Christian iconography: the canopy may have been painted with heavenly signs, the cellarage have been the habitation of ghosts and devils, but the appearance of the façade and of the pillars would have been no more representative of 'middle-earth' than a screen in a great chamber or the front of a palace.

The furnishing of the stage

It is wrong, as we should now expect, to look for evidence in Elizabethan plays of 'scenery'. The *Oxford English Dictionary* does not record the word in its modern theatrical sense until 1774, and when Dryden used the word in 1695 he was using it in the sense of the Italian *scenario* or, as Dr Johnson defines it, 'The disposition and consecution of the scenes of a play.' Neither is it correct on the other hand to think of Elizabethan dramatists writing for an unadorned and unworthy scaffold, and expecting all that is visual in their plays to be conjured up in their audience's minds by verbal imagery alone. When dramatists do make such an appeal they are not implicitly lamenting the lack of theatrical resources to create scenic illusion but usually seeking to establish economically the time and place of the action. So Bedford at the opening of *1 Henry VI*, II.ii.:

> The day begins to break, and night is fled,
> Which pitchy mantle over-veiled the earth.
> Here sound retreat and cease our hot pursuit.

The stage becomes Orleans at dawn. In fact the lavishness of Elizabethan decoration, and the evidence for ornateness in the style of the playhouses, make it inconceivable that the plays were performed without some visual richness. We can begin by examining the use of properties, and indeed properties, things used by players, give us a useful concept to set against the concept of scenery, physical devices used to give an impression of a specific location, a notion which is un-Elizabethan. A lot of the visual devices were portable: crowns, swords, scutcheons, and targets are often to be found in stage directions. Sometimes these were tokens or metonyms of the person who bore them, sometimes they had the function that such things have in pageantry: in the first scene of Greene and Lodge's *A Looking Glass for London and England*, 'a globe seated on a ship' – signifying dominion over land and sea – is brought on, and in Scene i of Heywood's *The Golden Age* (1610) occurs the following:

> *Enter Saturn with wedges of gold and silver, models of ships, and buildings, bows and arrows, etc., his Lords with him.*

There is a similar procession in I.i. of Dekker's *Old Fortunatus*. The

curtle-axe (cutlass) that Tamburlaine picks up in the second scene of
Marlowe's play and which he presumably carried throughout much of the
play's action is a token emblematic of his power. History plays and tragedies
made great use of such heraldic embellishments. At other times properties
served as a kind of dramatic shorthand to establish what had just gone
before. So the opening of *Woodstock*:

> *Enter hastily at several doors: Duke of Lancaster, Duke of York, the Earls of
> Arundel and Surrey, with napkins on their arms and knives in their hands,
> and Sir Thomas Cheney, with others bearing torches, and some with cloaks
> and rapiers.*

It will be revealed that an attempt has been made to poison all these men at a
banquet: the properties they are carrying immediately establish that it is
night and also establish the chaos of an interrupted ceremony. In contrast
the next entrance presents an emblem of order. Woodstock, uncle of the
profligate Richard II, has been described by York:

> Plain Thomas, for by th'rood so all men call him
> For his plain dealing and his simple clothing.
> Let others jet in silk and gold, says he,
> A coat of English frieze best pleaseth me. (I.i. 101–4)

His appearance in a procession suggesting order restored suits his nature:

> *Enter Thomas of Woodstock in frieze, the mace afore him; the Lord Mayor
> and Exton, and others with lights afore them.*

The opening of the anonymous *Look About You* (1599) reads:

> *Enter Robin Hood . . . with riding wands in their hands, as if they had been
> new-lighted.*

The symbolic importance that could be attached to properties is well
illustrated in I.iv. of *3 Henry VI* where Margaret savagely mocks the
captured York by putting a paper crown upon his head.[61]

The importance of properties in one explanation for the frequent occur-
rence of processions in Elizabethan plays. Tamburlaine's first entrance is
made thus:

> *[Enter] Tamburlaine leading Zenocrate, Techelles, Usumcasane, [Agydas,
> Magnetes,] other Lords, and soldiers loaden with treasure.*

Later in the play his adversaries appear:

> *[Enter] Soldan, [Alcidamus King of] Arabia, Capolin, with streaming
> colours, and soldiers. (1 Tamburlaine, IV.iii.)*

Without lighting or painted scenery these processions were the easiest way
of creating a spectacle[62] and could easily serve an allegorical function in the
way that processional narratives had served in Court masques and, incidentally, in the poems of Langland and Spenser. (See, for example, the
processions of seasons and months in the seventh [mutabitie] canto of *The
Fairie Queen*.) They were also often necessary to clear the stage of bodies at
the end of a tragedy.

Larger non-portable properties were also important. Again they were metonymic rather than representational. Henslowe's inventory lists 'i frame for the heading in Black Jone' (a lost anonymous play of about 1597) and 'i cauderm for the Jewe' [of Malta].[63] The deployment of the latter can be fairly certainly deduced from the text of Marlowe's play. Barabas has planned to invite Selim-Calymath the Turk to his gallery, where a trap has been prepared through which he is to fall into a cauldron beneath. In the event Barabas is himself betrayed by his new Christian allies. They cut the cable and he falls into the cauldron, a traditional instrument of torment for the greedy in visions of hell.[64] The stage directions read after Calymath has said:

> see I pray,
> How busy Barabas is there above
> To entertain us in his gallery . . .
>> *A charge, the cable cut.*
>> *A cauldron discovered.* (V.v.54–65)

Presumably the leading player dropped to the floor of the gallery behind its parapet and went quickly down the tiring-house stairs to climb into the cauldron. His disappearance would be masked by the 'charge' sounded on trumpets and he would be discovered as a door was opened or a curtain pulled back. The stage directions supplied by the nineteenth-century editor Dyce obviously posit an un-Elizabethan naturalistic set:

> *A charge sounded within: Ferneze cuts the cord; the floor of the gallery gives way, and Barabas falls into cauldron placed in a pit.*

The example reminds us that the Elizabethans did of course employ a species of realism in the sense that they enacted what more polite or squeamish ages might have suppressed: bladders of pig's blood might be pierced in stage fights, the corpse of Henry VI followed on to the stage by the Lady Anne in I.ii. of *Richard III* may well have contained a device to ooze blood – as it did in Terry Hands's 1970 Stratford production on her lines:

> O gentlemen, see, see! Dead Henry's wounds
> Open their congealed mouths and bleed afresh! (55–6)

It was not the kind of realism, however, that would encourage a spectator to mistake stage action for reality.

Large properties were not only discovered but frequently brought out on to the stage. A common stage direction is for them to be 'thrust out': larger objects like thrones (generally referred to as 'states'), 'banquets' (tables with plaster moulds of marchpane [marzipan], fruit, and fishes), council tables, tombs (*James IV*, Induction), or beds would be pushed out through the doors on wheels, conceivably on rails, a device that the Royal Shakespeare Company used efficiently in its productions in the 1960s, or even on a small rolling platform like the Greek *exostra* or *eccyclema*.[65] The stage direction in *3 Henry VI* for York and Lords to '*go up*' (I.i.32) to the throne suggests that this may have been set on a platform, but whether or not this was movable we cannot tell. If a platform was used, it may have served for the 'molehills' on which York is humiliated and Henry sits to view the Battle of Towton later in the play (II.v.) – thus providing an emblem of the vanity of worldly power. *A Chaste Maid in Cheapside* has the stage direction '*A bed thrust out upon the stage, Allwit's wife in it*' (III.ii.) – the phrase '*upon the stage*' makes it certain that the bed was not simply set out in an 'inner stage' as nineteenth-century editors used to think. In Heywood's *The Golden Age* the seduction of Danae begins with the following stage direction:

> *Enter the four old Beldams, drawing out Danae's bed: she in it. They place four tapers at the four corners.*

Jupiter enters '*crowned with his imperial robes*', lies upon the bed and thereby wakes her up. After an exchange of dialogue, '*Jupiter puts out the lights and makes unready*'; Danae protests, '*The bed is drawn in, and enter the Clown new waked.*' He has a prose address of about fifteen lines to the audience and exits, whereupon the action is relocated within the bedchamber by the simple re-entrance of '*Jupiter and Danae in her nightgown*':[66]

Alternatively, large properties could be thrust up through the stage trap. A stage direction in II.i. of *A Looking Glass for London and England* reads, '*The Magi with their rods beat the ground, and from under the same rises a brave arbour.*' That was a Rose play: at the Globe a symbolic tree was thrust up in *A Warning for Fair Women* (l. 1266). Possibly the rock, the three tombs, and the two mossy banks that are listed in an Admiral's Men's inventory[67] could have appeared in this way.

I have argued as though properties, those carried on by players, and the larger non-portable devices, generally appeared on the stage only when the action required them. There is another possibility, much debated and which if accepted affects considerably our notions of the dramaturgy of certain Elizabethan plays. This is that sometimes three-dimensional devices or 'mansions' were erected on the stage before the performance and were used as the action demanded, the players moving from one to the other. Changes in location in such plays, in other words, were indicated not by transforming the emblematic structure of the stage but by simply using another part of it. In an admittedly corrupt text, Greene's *George-a-Greene* (1590), we find the following dialogue:

SHOEMAKER: Come, sir, will you go to the town end now, sir?

JENKIN: Ay, sir, come –

Now we are at the town's end, what say you now? (IV.iii.)

This certainly suggests that they move from where the shoemaker had been discovered to a specifically different part of the stage. A key piece of contemporary evidence comes in a passage from the 1590 account of a play at the Curtain seen by the Swiss traveller Thomas Platter:[68]

[The players] represented various nations, with whom on each occasion an Englishman fought for a maiden, and overcame them all except the German, who won the maiden in fights. He then sat down with him, and gave him and his servant strong drink, so that they both got drunk, and the servant threw his shoe at his master's head and they both fell asleep. Meanwhile the Englishman went into the tents [*in die Zelten*], robbed the German of his gains, and thus outwitted the German also.

Now the 'tents' could well have been simply curtains hung across the opening of the discovery spaces, but passages in several plays suggest independent structures. 'Tents' may have been built against the tiring-house wall: Henslowe listed 'j wooden canepie',[69] which may have been the frame for a stage tent or *scena* – defined by Florio as 'a skaffold, a pavillion, or forepart of a theatre where players make them ready, being trimmed with hangings, out of which they enter upon the stage' (*Dictionary*, 1598). It is apparent from a Rose play, Peele's *Edward I* (1591), that at least two tents or pavilions (l. 1932) were used for the King and the Queen respectively, and that the Queen's tent was large enough to contain six players and a bed (l. 1453). In other plays, particularly history plays containing battles, tents were erected during the course of the action, in view of the spectators, and probably further downstage. In *Richard III*, V.iii. opens with the King's command: 'Here pitch our tent, even here in Bosworth field', and six lines later he commands: 'Up with my tent.' Later in the scene a tent must be erected for his adversary Richmond, and changes of place are thenceforward indicated by players entering the appropriate tents.[70]

All of these were or may have been erected during the course of the action. Accounts from the Revels Office, however, indicate that three-dimensional devices or 'houses' were frequently constructed for indoor Court performances and that these were so large and elaborate that it is highly unlikely that they were brought on stage only when needed. Payments are recorded in 1563–5 for 'canvas to cover divers towns and houses and other devices and clouds', in 1572–3 for 'spars to make frames for the players' houses', in 1579–80 for 'fir poles to make rails for the battlements and to make the prison for my Lord of Warwick's Men.'[71] Now E. K. Chambers argued that while such mansions were used at Court there is no evidence of their having been employed on the public stages, that, in other words, synchronous staging was a feature of Court performances, successive staging of public ones. Yet it has seemed highly unlikely to later historians that such a distinction existed. G. F. Reynolds's analysis of the Red Bull plays gave him enough evidence 'to disprove Chambers' assertion that simultaneous settings were not admitted to the public theater stages'[72] and his arguments have been confirmed by several others.[73] It is not possible to review their arguments here but it seems unlikely that the playing companies would have reserved different dramatic principles for their various playing places. The fact that payments are found for the construction of such mansions in the Revels Accounts indicates that the mansions were probably too large to be easily transported from the playhouses and not simply that they were used only at Court. Letters between the Privy Council and the Lord Mayor often mention that public performances were necessary 'exercises' or preparations for those at Court.

Henslowe's 'sittie of Rome' listed among his properties[74] may therefore have been a 'house' rather than a painted cloth, possibly even the device used in III.ii. of *2 Tamburlaine* – it had presumably been used for the coronation of Callapine in the previous scene:

> *[Enter] Tamburlaine with Usumcasane, and his three sons; four bearing the hearse of Zenocrate; and the drums sounding a doleful march; the town burning.*

(The burning of the town was probably done with lighted *aqua vitae*.[75]) The hearse was 'a temple-shaped structure of wood . . . decorated with banners, heraldic devices, and lighted candles' (*OED*, 2c). On to this the sons affix an emblematic pillar, a streamer, and a table of her virtues, before Tamburlaine places Zenocrate's picture upon it. Likewise Henslowe's 'Belendon stable'[76] was probably a 'house' – a lost history play on the reign of Henry I 'with the life and Death of Belyn Dun' is recorded in the Stationers' Register for 1595.[77] Sidney was possibly thinking of a mansion in a public playhouse when in about 1580 he wrote: 'what child is there that, coming to a play and seeing Thebes written in great letters upon an old door, doth believe that it is Thebes.'[78] One famous public playhouse play, Jonson's *Bartholomew Fair*, first acted at the Hope on 31 October 1614, was played at Court the next day. A warrant survives for the payment for 'canvas for the booths and other necessaries for a play called *Bartholomew Fair*.'[79] It is inconceivable that the production would have been radically changed in twenty-four hours. Unfortunately the wording of the warrant does not allow us to be quite certain that these booths stood ready visible before the characters departed to the fair.

In the absence of definitive evidence we have to be open-minded. Elizabethan paintings and engravings employ 'simultaneous time' in that figures appear several times in the same picture at different stages of their lives (as in the biography portrait of Sir Henry Unton): why, therefore, should not Elizabethan audiences have accepted the convention of 'simultaneous place' when the nature of the play demanded it? Would not audiences at public playhouses have been attracted by productions that employed the lavishness of the shows at Court from which they were excluded? And yet the de Witt drawing shows no sign of houses, and many of the references to tents or studies could be accommodated by the use of discovery spaces. As usual we should rest sceptical: mansions may well have been used in some playhouses with larger stages like the Swan and the Rose and in some productions. They were not essential and were almost certainly absent from performances in the provinces. Elizabethan drama was derived from so many sources that it is not surprising to find these devices that were both 'Renaissance' in that they resembled those used in mythological entertainments, and 'medieval' in that they functioned like the simultaneous scenic decors of the mystery plays used on stages by authors such as Jonson whose theoretical inclinations directed them to drama based on neo-classical unity of place.

The auditorium

Of the auditorium or 'frame' there is comparatively little to say. Shakespeare refers to it as a 'wooden O' or a 'cockpit': the latter designation reminding us that the playhouses resembled gaming-houses, that the stage and tiring-house stood independently of the auditorium and could, at the Hope at least, be cleared away for bear-baiting or cockfights. The 'strong iron pikes' mentioned in the Fortune contract[80] which stood around the lowest gallery surrounding the yard were probably a survival from the gaming-houses as well as serving to separate the groundlings from the Lords' rooms. Shakespeare's testimony to the roundness of the playhouses is confirmed by the engraved maps that show the Bankside playhouses and which indicate that they were round or possibly polygonal (Plates 2–4). Some (Plate 1) indicate that they were built with external staircases. The Fortune, constructed in Golding Lane, a more built-up area, was, like the Red Bull after it, square, possibly to take maximum advantage of a smaller building plot (it may have had semi-circular galleries within).

The playhouses were generally of timber and plaster construction (although de Witt notes that the Swan was 'built of a mass of flint stones'[81]) generally three storeys high (the engravings may have exaggerated their height), and roofed with thatch or tile. Their signs hung before them and, during performances, flags with the same motif flew from the huts. The disposition of the stage in the centre of the auditorium (it must be remembered that in the early playhouses at least the tiring-house stood inside the frame and did not form part of it) meant that the majority of spectators were much closer to the players than they are in proscenium arched theatres. Those in the galleries, which were constructed with what the Fortune contract describes as a 'jutty forwards',[82] or projection, were almost overhanging the stage, those in the yard pressing up close to the action. This intimacy made the playhouses very flexible dramatic instruments: it was easy to focus down the audience's attention from a lavish spectacle filling the whole of the stage to a soliloquy spoken by a single player direct to his auditors. A move up-stage or down-stage must have had far greater significance than in a theatre where vertical moves are flattened by the distance between spectators and players. Above all, although the playhouses were open to the skies, players and spectators must have felt themselves, as in a modern circus, to be in the same space, the same 'room', with the consequence that a great variety of playing styles was possible: audiences are far more aware of differences of style if they feel that what they are watching is taking place 'somewhere else'. In such playhouses players could switch from personating to performing, playwrights could alternate scenes with large and small numbers of players without giving the sense that the stage was empty during sparsely populated scenes, audiences could accept the changes from what was instructive to what was entertaining, from sentence to solace. The lack of physical division between audience and players reflected the absence of a categoric distinction between life and art: within the world of the playhouse performer and spectator alike were at play, collaborating in a community act of imaginative and social recreation.

2 · Performances

City and Court

Although, as we have seen, foreign tourists numbered the playhouses among the glories of London, the City authorities engaged in almost constant skirmishes through the last decades of the sixteenth century to have them suppressed and plucked down. The players lost the final battle in 1642 when the playhouses were finally closed, but this was merely the final coup in a war that for decades had cast official disrepute on the very men who were building the most enduring cultural monuments of the age. The reasons for this conflict are complex, involve both questions of religious doctrine and considerations of law and order, and reflect wider tussles between rival centres of power in the Church, the City, and the Court.[1]

Because their profession demanded that they wander from town to town in search of audiences, the first troupes of players had appeared to local and civic authorities to fall into the same category as vagrants whose anomalous status had demanded regularisation during feudal times. In the sixteenth century the Tudors found it convenient to consolidate this legislation against such unstable elements of the population with the result that numerous statutes were passed against rogues, vagrants, and 'masterless men', or, as the Lord Mayor of 1580 called them, 'a very superfluous sort of men'.[2] These statutes compelled players to seek protection from the law by taking nominal service with an aristocratic protector – the reason that most of the sixteenth-century acting troupes bear the names of their noble patrons. This legal fiction generally afforded players protection against summary punishments of whipping, branding, and imprisonment, but just as they were achieving some economic security at the time that the first playhouses were being constructed, they were subjected to further threats to their livelihood from the strengthening power of the City. For this feudal relationship between aristocrats and players was a conspicuous anachronism in the new economic structures of London. Players both offended the religious sensibilities and threatened the commercial order of the City

42

fathers. Although sixteenth-century reformers had used drama for polemical purposes – Bale's historical morality *King John* (1538), for example, is a piece of forceful protestant propaganda – the public playhouses soon proved their ability to distract the citizenry from afternoon church-going, and the habits of players and audiences increasingly offended the more fundamentalist members of the reform movement. Players appeared to be sinners because they would perform on the sabbath and during Lent, making profit out of recreation, because, contrary to biblical injunction, they donned women's attire, because their dialogue might be obscene and scurrilous and their gestures lewd, and because the enthusiasm they generated seemed to be a species of idolatry. (Zeal-of-the-Land Busy enters in V.v. of *Bartholomew Fair* to pluck down the 'heathenish idols' of the Fair, Leatherhead's puppets.[3]) The sumptuousness of the playhouses and of the players' costumes offended too against puritan advocacy of simplicity and plainness. Arguments like these as well as traditional humanist topics that date from ancient diatribes against the decadence of Roman theatrical entertainments appeared in several pamphlets of the 1570s and 1580s and were wheeled out when the collapse of scaffolding and the deaths of spectators provided occasions for preachers to point to Providential punishment on the frequenters of bear-baitings, cockfights, and plays.

This was one kind of attack: others came from the City fathers because they felt that the playhouses were sinks of idleness, that they drew 'apprentices and other servants from their ordinary works'.[4] Considerations of holiness and profit combine in the petition of the corporation to the Privy Council in about 1582 to ban all performances in the suburbs – performances in the City had already been suppressed:[5]

> For as much as the playing of interludes, and the resort to the same are very dangerous for the infection of the plague, whereby infinite burdens and losses to the City may increase; and are very hurtful in corruption of youth with incontinence and lewdness, and also great wasting both of the time and thrift of many poor people and great provoking of the wrath of God, the ground of all plagues; great withdrawing of the people from public prayer and from the service of God; and daily cried out against by the grave and earnest admonitions of the preachers of the word of God; Therefore be it ordered that all such interludes in public places, and the resort to the same shall wholly be prohibited as ungodly, and humble suit be made to the Lords that like prohibition be in places near unto the City.

Other petitions were provoked by specific and inevitable disturbances caused by the crowds that attended the playhouses. As we have seen, plays had been frequently performed in inns, including certain inns within the City itself. Experience of these occasions, the hindrances to traffic caused by the crowds attending and the accompanying frays and incitements to petty crime and vice, made the corporation determined to have no permanent and regular playhouses within the City limits. Accordingly we find that except for the short-lived first Blackfriars, no playhouse was built within the City of London in the sixteenth century. Finally the fear of the plague, alluded to in the petition quoted above, gave the City further cause for concern. Performances were allowed only when the weekly bill of plague victims fell below fifty for three weeks and then thirty a week, with the result that Henslowe's diary and other sources reveal that the playhouses were frequently closed for months on end and the players compelled to seek their living in the provinces.

If they were under attack from the City, the players had protectors at Court. Their patrons, as we have seen, were aristocrats, and playing had long been at the centre of Court revels, particularly the long feast of Christmas. Men who served on the very body, therefore, that was receiving petitions from the City for the suppression of playing, were also engaged in choosing the entertainments to please the monarch from among the competing troupes. It is not surprising that no action was actually taken when the City prevailed upon the Privy Council to write on 28 July 1597 to the Justices of Middlesex and Surrey ordering them to 'pluck down quite the stages, galleries and rooms that are made for people to stand in, and so to deface the same as they may not be employed again to such use'.[6] If the Privy Council, however, chose to exercise only desultory control over the playhouses, it chose to increase its control over the plays that were presented in them. Proclamations as early as 1559 had required the licensing of plays, and in 1581 the Master of the Revels who had previously served as a kind of dramatic impresario, was commissioned to cause the players to appear before him 'with all such plays, tragedies, comedies, or shows, as they shall have in readiness, or mean to set forth, and them to present and recite before our said servant'.[7] Players who put on satires or political propaganda unpleasing to the government could be imprisoned for sedition, and the texts of plays that had been performed sometimes bear the marks of censorship: the deposition scene in Richard II (1595), for example, is missing from the first three quartos that were published.

Audiences

Because a lot of our descriptions of playhouse audiences derive from puritan pamphlets, City petitions, criminal court records, satirical poems, and the invectives of disappointed playwrights, it is easy to get the impression that playhouse yards were filled with an illiterate rabble containing a large proportion of cutpurses, pickpockets, and whores, and that their galleries were crammed with inattentive 'plush and velvet men' paying court to their mistresses or appearing at the play only to be seen themselves. It would be easy to put that construction upon the following letter of 25 February 1592, from the Lord Mayor to the Archbishop of Canterbury, for example:[8]

> Our most humble duties to your Grace remembered. Whereas by the daily and disorderly exercise of a number of players and playing houses erected within this City, the youth thereof is greatly corrupted and their manners infected with many evil and ungodly qualities by reason of the wanton and profane devices represented on the stages by the said players, the prentices and servants withdrawn from their works, and all sorts in general from the daily resort unto sermons and other Christian exercises, to the great hindrance of the trades and traders of this City and profanation of the good and godly religion established amongst us. To which places also do usually resort great numbers of light and lewd disposed persons, as harlots, cutpurses, cozeners, pilferers, and such like, and there, under the colour of resort of those places to hear the plays, devise divers evil and ungodly matches, confederacies, and conspiracies, which by means of the opportunity of the place cannot be prevented nor discovered, as otherwise they might be.

Yet it is important to remember that the Lord Mayor's description was scarcely disinterested and that in the nature of things it was the disorderly performances that were recorded and not the peaceable ones. Although there is a cutpurse visible in a description of a Fortune audience, its authors, Dekker and Middleton, insist on the attentiveness and prosperity of the spectators:[9]

> Nay, when you look into my galleries,
> How bravely they're trimmed up, you all shall swear
> You're highly pleased to see what's set down there:
> Storeys of men and women, mixed together,
> Fair ones with foul, like sunshine in wet weather;
> Within one square a thousand heads are laid,
> So close that all of heads the room seems made;
> As many faces there, filled with blithe looks,
> Show like the promising titles of new books
> Writ merrily, the readers being their own eyes,
> Which seem to move and to give plaudities;
> And here and there, whilst with obsequious ears
> Thronged heaps do listen, a cut-purse thrusts and leers
> With hawk's eyes for his prey; I need not show him;
> By a hanging villainous look yourselves may know him,
> The face is drawn so rarely: then, sir, below,
> The very floor, as't were, waves to and fro,

And, like a floating island, seems to move
Upon a sea bound in with shores above.

This suggests that if a few depraved spectators were there for the lewdness
of the players' words and gestures, others paid their admission prices to hear
fine poetry and enjoy the rich spectacle. Like Pistol in *Henry V*, some may
have made themselves ridiculous by imitating in their own speech the high
style they heard there, but the Pistols in the audience would at least have
been attentive.

The audience was not, therefore, as some early scholars would have us
believe, an unruly, ignorant mob. Nor is it likely, however, that it attended
to the play in hushed reverence as a modern audience might do. The mere
fact that public playhouse performances generally took place by daylight
meant that the spectators were on show to one another. Gallants took
tobacco as they sat conspicuously on the stage (the habit was established by
1596),[10] orange- and beer-sellers plied their trade before the play began and
possibly during the performance; and certainly complaints about the
distractions of nut-cracking among the audience are fairly common in the
plays. Books and pamphlets were also hawked in the auditoria. There were
few if any reserved seats and the passage quoted above bears testimony to
the pushing and swaying in the yard when it was full.[11] Although plays were
advertised by playbills posted around the town and, occasionally for a new
play, a procession, it is possible that some attended performances without a
certain knowledge of what would be played. On carnival days the playhouses might be taken over and the programme changed at the demand of
the mob: Chambers prints a letter from a Florentine describing how an
audience discontented with the day's offering demanded an impromptu
performance of, probably, *Friar Bacon and Friar Bungay*.[12] Such reports are
exceptions that prove the rule, but Beaumont was able to use the device of
audience taking over the play as the basis of the structure of *The Knight of the
Burning Pestle*. In some respects then the atmosphere in an Elizabethan
public playhouse must have been more like that of a funfair than of
a modern theatre. The players had to draw attention to themselves and
could not count on reverent silence. In *A Midsummer Night's Dream* and
Love's Labour's Lost Shakespeare with great sympathy presents common
players whose performances were 'dashed' by frivolous aristocrats and the
morose Ben Jonson more in seriousness than in fun felt it necessary to
draw up a contract of attention for the audience of *Bartholomew Fair* at the
Hope.

Descriptions of the behaviour of Elizabethan audiences have infected
descriptions of the types of people who attended the playhouses. Besides
mentioning harlots and cutpurses the Lord Mayor in his letter to the
Archbishop stated that 'all sorts in general' frequented the playhouses.[13]
And yet it has been common among theatre historians to argue that the

public playhouses were frequented for the most part by members of the 'lower orders' or 'the working class'.[14] It is in fact extremely difficult if not impossible to ascertain the composition of Elizabethan audiences. The basic demographic information is exceedingly scanty and there are grave dangers of distortion if we allow modern demographic categories to settle on the period. Certainly the Elizabethan distinction between nobility and commoners, a distinction based on caste, cannot be simply translated into modern gradations of class defined as much by income as by birth. Too often the label 'working class' has been applied to Elizabethans who belonged to a spectrum defined by porters and mechanicals at its bottom end, apprentices, artisans, and shopkeepers at its middle, and craftsmen and merchants at its top. Elizabethan society was a pre-industrial society. So too it is naive to postulate a correlation between literacy,[15] taste, or sophistication and social rank: an aristocrat could be depraved or discriminating in judgment, a water-carrier as fond of high rhetoric as inexplicable dumb shows and noise. The academically educated were fascinated by the native wit of the illiterate as the profusion of underworld pamphlets, by Greene and others, reveals. Any generalizations risk foundering on our knowledge that they may hold true for only one playhouse at one period or even for one performance. There does, however, seem to have been a growing distinction between the fare offered and therefore presumably the audience at the playhouses to the north of the City, the Fortune and the Red Bull, which offered a diet of heroic spectacles, and the diet of the Bankside houses which served up plays of intrigue and love. William Turner's *Dish of Lenten Stuff* (unfortunately undatable) puts it thus:[16]

> The players of the Bankside,
> The round Globe and the Swan,
> Will teach you idle tricks of love
> But the Bull will play the man.

In his account of his visit to London in 1599 Thomas Platter describes how one paid for admission to the playhouses:[17]

> And thus every day at two o'clock in the afternoon in the city of London two and sometimes three comedies are performed, at separate places, wherewith folk make merry together, and whichever does best gets the greatest audience. The places are so built, that they play on a raised platform, and every one can well see it all. There are, however, separate galleries and there one stands more comfortably and moreover can sit, but one pays more for it. Thus anyone who remains on the level standing pays only one English penny: but if he wants to sit, he is let in at a further door, and there he gives another penny. If he desires to sit on a cushion in the most comfortable place of all, where he not only sees everything well, but can also be seen, then he gives yet another English penny at another door. And in the pauses of the comedy food and drink

are carried round amongst the people, and one can thus refresh himself at his own cost.

Now although Platter's account makes it clear that one could see a play for only one penny, it does not follow that the majority of the audience was made up of illiterate 'groundlings'. Artisans earned about a shilling a day throughout the period, while soldiers were provided with a daily ration of food that cost about sixpence.[18] This indicates that half the income of, say, a mason might go on food alone and if he had a family to support there would have been little left over for entertainment. Of course some people whose earned income was low might, then as now, have been prepared to spend a large sum on admission to a popular entertainment, but it is unlikely that they could have gone often. Other factors confirm our speculation that the number of poorer people in the audience must have been comparatively small. Harbage deduced that the galleries which were more expensive to enter held in fact twice as many people as the yards[19] and, most important, as Platter noted, plays were performed in the afternoon, a time when wage-earners, the self-employed, apprentices, and purveyors of goods and services would have been labouring at their vocations. Tradesmen as opposed to craftsmen are conspicuously absent from Gosson's invective (in *Plays Confuted*, 1582) against 'the common people which resort to theatres [who are] but an assembly of tailors, tinkers, cordwainers, sailors, old men, young men, women, boys, girls, and such like'.[20] Tailors, like cordwainers (shoemakers), were members of a craft guild, although they were common objects of disdain in proverbs (*v. OED*, 1b). It was probably therefore invective rather than observation that led Gosson to include tinkers in his list. Nor, of course, was admission the only expense in attending the play. To cross the river by boat, the normal manner of reaching the Bankside playhouses, probably cost threepence each way,[21] and if a servant, say, chose to walk out to Shoreditch or round over London Bridge he would have had to take that much more time from his employment. Only on holidays and Sundays, and only then at times when the bans on sabbath performances were not enforced, could such people attend. It seems therefore that the character in *Jack Drum's Entertainment* played by the Children of Paul's in 1600 who praises the private houses because there 'a man shall not be choked with the stench of garlic, or be pasted to the barmy jacket of a beer-brewer' (V.i.) is displaying his own squeamish snobbery and not giving an accurate description of a public playhouse yard. (Admission to Paul's ranged from only twopence to sixpence, which may indicate that admission was regulated there by caste and not by price.)

Nor can we argue easily about audience behaviour from what we know of the social habits of particular groups of the lower orders. It used to be argued that apprentices represented a large and especially unruly part of the audience. Certainly there are records of frays and riots, but these were often

associated with Shrove Tuesday, a customary day of licence when it was the
practice of the apprentices to prepare for Lent by dousing bawds under
water-pumps and taking over and sometimes sacking playhouses. There is a
graphic description of the habit in Gayton's *Festivous Notes upon Don
Quixote* (1654):[22]

> I have known upon one of these festivals, but especially at Shrove-tide,
> where the players have been appointed, notwithstanding their bills to
> the contrary, to act what the major part of the company had a mind to.
> Sometimes *Tamerlane*, sometimes *Jugurtha* [a lost play of about 1600 by
> William Boyle?], sometimes *The Jew of Malta*, and sometimes parts of
> all these; and at last, none of the three taking, they were forced to
> undress and put off their tragic habits, and conclude the day with *The
> Merry Milkmaids* [unknown]. And unless this were done, and the
> popular humour satisfied (as sometimes it so fortuned that the players
> were refractory), the benches, the tiles, the laths, the stones, oranges,
> apples, nuts, flew about most liberally; and as there were mechanics of
> all professions, who fell every one to his trade, and dissolved a house in
> an instant, and made a ruin of a stately fabric.

What is important to remember, however, is that aspects of these revels
reveal puritanical rather than lawless impulses; these ritual cessations of
order implicitly assert the normal rule of law. Nor were apprentices riotous
adolescents of the lowest caste: as Harbage points out, men were not
released from apprenticeship until they had reached the age of twenty-four,
'the sons of unskilled labourers and husbandmen were generally barred
from apprenticeship, and certain guilds insisted upon property qualifications in the parents and educational qualifications in the boy'.[23] Apprentices
therefore were not 'working class' necessarily. Moreover their working
hours would have kept them from the playhouses except on these special
occasions, and as they were given only lodgings and board without wages it
is unlikely that any poor boys from the group could have afforded admission.

It seems therefore that the majority of the audience was, as Ann Jennalie
Cook has argued recently, 'privileged'.[24] Thomas Nashe suggested as much
in *Pierce Penilesse* (1592):[25]

> For whereas the afternoon being the idlest time of the day; wherein men
> that are their own masters (as Gentlemen of the Court, the Inns of the
> Court, and the number of captains and soldiers about London) do
> wholly bestow themselves upon pleasure, and that pleasure they divide
> (how virtuously it skills not) either into gaming, following of harlots,
> drinking or seeing a play: is it not then better (since of four extremes all
> the world cannot keep them but they will choose one) that they should
> betake them to the least, which is plays?

Allowance has to be made here for satirical licence; a more objective account

occurs in a letter of one Philip Gawdy who reports that when the Privy
Council ordered the press gangs into the 'playhouses, bowling-alleys, and
dicing-houses' 'they did not only press gentlemen and serving-men, but
lawyers, clerks, countrymen that had law-causes, aye the Queen's men,
knights, and, as it was credibly reported, one earl.'[26] We are reminded of
how it was increasingly important for men of position to gravitate about the
Court (Harbage refers to 1,500 courtiers in attendance on the Queen[27]), to
maintain houses in London, or to spend long times there attending to
business or legal affairs. We are reminded too that the Bankside playhouses
were almost opposite the Inns of Court where there were approximately
1,000 students in residence, drawn from the more moneyed groups in the
land. These 'young gentlemen who have . . . small regard of credit or
conscience', as the Lord Mayor complained in 1593,[28] were probably the
most influential group in an audience where young adult males were in a
majority. Playhouses were therefore obviously a good place for prostitutes
to solicit, but it is important to remember that women of quality, masked
perhaps, were no less important a group than the whores. In 1580 the Lord
Mayor lamented that the Theatre had attracted 'assemblies of citizens and
their families',[29] and several travellers remark on how in London it was
possible for women to attend the playhouses in safety.[30] In the first Quarto of
Hamlet (1603), 'Gilderstone' implies that audiences at public and private
playhouses were in fact similar if not identical: 'For the principal public
audience that, Came to them, are turned to private plays, And to the
humour of children' (Sig. E2ᵛ).

Preparation and rehearsal

Generalizations based on conjectures about the behaviour and composition
of Elizabethan audiences can therefore shed only a limited light on what it
would have been like to attend a playhouse. (And yet critics often use 'the
Elizabethan audience' as evidence in their arguments. These are almost
invariably circular: they describe one feature of a play, postulate an
audience who would have been pleased by it, and then argue that that
feature was written into the play to 'please the audience'.) Nor do we know
very much about the ways in which the players prepared for their performances: what follows can be based only on inference. The first factor to be
taken into consideration is that the companies worked a repertory system.
As the following extract from Henslowe's diary reveals, the Admiral's Men
performed a fresh play every day, presenting fifteen different plays over
twenty-five playing days:[31]

1596

31 of maye whittsen-mvnday		Rd at pethagores . . . . iij^{li}
1 of June 1596		Rd at chinone of Ingland . . . . iij^s
2 of June 1596		Rd at longshancke . . . . iij^{li}
3 of June 1596		Rd at the blinde beager . . . . xxxxjs
4 of June 1596		Rd at the tragedie of focas . . . . xxxjs
5 of June 1596		Rd at tambercame . . . . xxviijs
7 of June 1596	m^{r}pd	Rd at cracke me this nvtte . . . . xxviijs
8 of June 1596		Rd at wisman of weschester . . . . xxs
9 of June 1596		Rd at the chaste ladye . . . . xviijs
10 of June 1596		Rd at tambercame . . . . xxviijs
11 of June 1596	ne	Rd at 2 pte of tambercame . . . . iij^{li}
12 of June 1596		Rd at Docter fostes . . . . xvij^s
14 of June 1596		Rd at sege of london . . . . xxx^s
15 of June 1596		Rd at pethagores . . . . xxiiij^s
16 of June 1596		Rd at ffocase . . . . xx^s
17 of June 1596		Rd at hary the v . . . . xxvijs
19 of June 1596	m^{r}pd	Rd at j pte of tambercame . . . . xxxvjs
20 of June 1596		Rd at 2 pte of tambercame . . . . xxxvs
21 of June 1596		Rd at Jew of malta . . . . xiijs
22 of June 1596		Rd at focas . . . . ls
22 of June 1596	ne	Rd at troye . . . . iij^{li} ixs
23 of June 1596		Rd at cracke me this nvtt . . . . xijs
25 of June 1596		Rd at the beager . . . . xixs
26 of June 1596		Rd at j pte of tambercame . . . . xxxs
27 of June 1596		Rd at 2 pte of tambercame . . . . xxs

(It is notable that in this month although the new ('ne') plays brought in larger receipts, holidays are not marked by noticeably bigger takings. The £3 taken at *Pythagoras* (lost) on Whit Monday is matched by the takings two days later at *Longshanks* (a revision of Peele's *Edward I*?) and takings on the Sundays, 7, 14, and 21 June, are not consistently higher than on weekdays. Two putative explanations offer themselves: a run of wet Sundays or the absence of those who paid higher prices when the yard might be expected to be full of one-penny groundings. Who can tell?[32]). It has also been calculated that companies added a new play every two weeks during the playing season.[33] This means that there can have been very little time for what we would call 'rehearsal'. We know that the Lord Chamberlain's Men were able to mount a production of *Richard II* at one day's notice on 7 February 1601 at the request of some followers of the Earl of Essex, even though Augustine Phillips, one of the Globe 'sharers', said of the play that it was 'so old and so long out of use that they should have small or no company at it. But at their request [they] were content to play it'.[34] Similarly *The Jew of Malta* was suddenly revived in January 1596, shortly after the trial and execution of the Jewish Dr Lopez, accused of attempting to poison the Queen. Beckerman has reckoned that 'the time between final purchase of the manuscript and the first indication of production extends from three to fifty-one days, the average duration being a little over twenty days'.[35]

What happened between a company's purchase of the manuscript of a play and its appearance in the playhouse? First the company's scribes produced three different kinds of document: a prompt-book[36] for the prompter or, as he was sometimes called, the 'book-holder',[37] parts for the actors, and a 'plot' of the play. The prompt-book or, as it was generally called, the 'book' was often the document sent to the Master of the Revels to be 'seen and allowed' or to the Stationers' Company to be 'entered' if and when the play was to be printed. When the 'book' returned to the playhouse it seems that it was generally the book-holder who supervised rehearsals – the same man who attended to the smooth running of performances. In other words one man filled the now separate offices of director and stage manager. He had assistants called 'stage-keepers'[38] dressed in the blue coats of servants, who looked after properties, prepared 'discoveries', etc. A marginal note in Heywood's *The Captives* (1624) indicates that they could double as supernumerary actors. We can get at least a faint impression of the way the book-holder worked by examining the rehearsal scene in *A Midsummer Night's Dream* (III.i.). There Peter Quince holds the book, indicates from which place the entrances are to be made, and explains to the players their motives for their movements: 'For you must understand he goes but to see a noise that he heard and is to come again' (ll. 81–2). There is no evidence from the Elizabethan period that the book-holder did much more than this, and the prompt-books that survive contain no interpretative notes or character sketches (nor, of course, do modern ones), but confine themselves to entrances and exits and the indication of sound effects. Indeed the book-holder's main function seems to have been to see that things happened on time. A character is thus described in Lewis Machin's (?) *Every Woman in her Humour* (1607?): 'He would sweare like an elephant, and stamp and stare (God bless us) like a playhouse book-keeper when the actors miss their entrance'.[39] There is little evidence that he enjoyed as elevated status in the company – no names of the book-holders of our period have survived.

It is also highly likely that the playwrights had a hand in the preparation of their plays. Jonson certainly did: he gets one of the boys to say in the Induction to *Cynthia's Revels* (1601):

we are not so officiously befriended by him, as to have his presence in
the tiring-house, to prompt us aloud, stamp at the book-holder, swear
for our properties, curse the poor tire-man, rail the music out of tune,
and sweat for every venial trespass we commit.

Tradition has it that Shakespeare, who of course served as a player himself, instructed his fellows in their art. 'John Downes, who was prompter to the Duke of York's Men after the Restoration, relates how, when Betterton played Hamlet, "Sir William [Davenant] (having seen Mr. Taylor of the Blackfriars Company act it, who being instructed by the author Mr. Shakespeare) taught Mr. Betterton in every particle of it"'; and how Davenant was similarly able to act as Betterton's tutor for Henry VIII, for he 'had it from old Mr. Lowen, that had his instructions from Mr. Shakespeare'.[40] Stage directions in the reported text of 3 *Henry VI*, which expand those of the Folio and which reflect a knowledge of historical details found in the source of the play, also suggest that Shakespeare at least 'told the player or tire-man what to do'.[41] Finally there is the testimony of a German, Johannes Rhenanus, who had probably been in England himself in 1611 and who in 1613 published a German adaptation of Tomkis's *Lingua* (1607):[42]

> So far as the actors are concerned they, as I have noticed in England, are daily instructed as it were in a school, so that even the most eminent actors have to allow themselves to be taught their places by the dramatists, and this gives life and ornament to a well-written play, so that it is no wonder that the English players (I speak of skilled ones) surpass others and have the advantage over them.

Even if dramatists played a comparatively small role in rehearsals, the nature of the relationship they enjoyed with the acting companies meant that their writing must have been informed by their knowledge of the way their plays would be mounted. They would have been familiar with the physical layout of particular playhouses and their resources in costumes and properties, and they created at least some of their parts with particular actors in mind.[43] But even the playwrights who were most involved in the production of their plays would not have had the influence on what the audience witnessed that is wielded by a modern director. Audiences tend nowadays for better or worse to expect 'interpretations' of plays: the Elizabethan companies did not draw upon a repertory of 'classics'. At its first performance *Hamlet* was simply enacted and not deliberately interpreted. And although we should not underestimate the physical resources of Elizabethan playhouses, they did not in any way possess the number of technical devices found in even the most modest modern theatre, nor was there available to book-holder or author the expertise in scenic design that a modern director can draw upon.

There is only one surviving example of an actor's 'part' from a public playhouse,[44] that of Edward Alleyn for the title-role of Greene's *Orlando Furioso* (1591). It is written on a number of strips of paper which were then pasted together to form a continuous roll (the French metonym *rôle* gives us our modern 'role' or part). What is most interesting is that it omits all other speaking parts, supplying only two- or three-word cues. There are also a few simple stage directions. Whether or not this is typical of the manuscripts that players worked from we have no way of telling, but its pattern suggests that it was produced in this format so that it could be committed simply and perhaps rather brutally to memory. (Companies may have been chary of distributing complete texts of their plays to their players in order to minimize the risk of unauthorized copying and piratical printing or perhaps the cost of paper and of the services of scriveners kept copying to a minimum.)

The third class of document, the 'plots' of the plays, are single sheets which generally were pasted on to card or thin boards and which obviously hung near an entrance from the tiring-house, presumably near where the book-holder stood. (This was also done in Italy, incidentally, with the *scenarii* for performances in the *commedia dell'arte*.) They record usually the names of players and characters in each particular scene, and obviously served to remind actors of the number and order of their entrances.

What all this evidence suggests is that performance could not have depended on the subtly orchestrated ensemble work that we now expect, but must have been exhibitions of the individual skills of the members of the company, the tire-men who looked after the costumes, the stage-keepers who may have aided the musicians in sound effects – as well as the players themselves. The players' 'parts' suggest that each player can have known little more than his own lines and therefore been much less aware than a modern actor of the effects his fellows were searching for. The 'plots' were probably therefore very necessary reminders. Actors in a modern production, particularly a long run, come to know their entrances and exits well, to feel the rhythm of the play. Elizabethan players must have nervously consulted their plots, found themselves suddenly on stage giving a performance based on their individual skills and depending largely on extemporization to establish contact between their own and others' parts. As we shall see in the next chapter, particular players specialized in particular kinds of roles and acting, but having performed the massive task of committing lines quickly to memory, each player must have drawn heavily on his own repertoire of stock gestures or routines, and when memory failed (in Elizabethan English, when he was 'out'), or when audience demanded, relied on skills of verbal improvization. Elizabethan players probably thought of their task as having to render scenes, rather than create characters, to remember their lines and be in the right spot at the right time to deliver a 'passion' (Elizabethan for a passionate speech) or to perform a piece of business. (The labour of getting it right is suggested in a theatrical image from *King John* (1596), where the Bastard speaks of 'industrious scenes and acts of death' (II.i.375).) It is significant too that the scripts the players used were not printed (although some touring companies may have used Quarto versions of the plays as prompt-books or players' parts[45]). Their manuscripts remind us that their texts did not have the 'stability' of modern printed books, that it is impossible to postulate a definitive version of a lot of

Elizabethan plays,[46] and that 'characters' and even plots were correspondingly fluid. Certainly it is highly unlikely that any Elizabethan performance would be as similar to another as is the case with a modern play enjoying even a modest run.

There are no contemporary accounts of Elizabethan rehearsals, but a poem by a Spanish actor, Agustin de Rojas, the 'Viage entretenido' of 1602, gives us a glimpse of what, allowing for some exaggeration, life may have been like for players in England at the same time:[47]

There is no negro in Spain or slave in Algiers but has a better life than the actor. A slave works all day, but he sleeps at night; he has only one or two masters to please, but when he does what he is commanded, he fulfills his duty. But actors are up at dawn and write and study from five o'clock till nine, and from nine till twelve they are constantly rehearsing. They dine and then go to the comedia; leave the theater at seven, and when they want rest they are called by the President of the Council, or the *alcaldes*, whom they must serve whenever it pleases them. I wonder how it is possible for them to study all their lives and be constantly on the road, for there is no labor that can equal theirs.

Articles of agreement, dated 7 April 1614, between the actor Robert Dawes and Henslowe and Meade suggest a similar regime:[48]

Robert Dawes shall and will at all times during the said term [of three years] duly attend all such rehearsal, which shall the night before the rehearsal be given publicly out; and if that he . . . shall at any time fail to come at the hour appointed, then he shall and will pay to the said Philip Henslowe and Jacob Meade . . . twelve pence; and if he come not before the said rehearsal is ended, then the said Robert Dawes is contented to pay two shillings; and further that if the said Robert Dawes shall not every day whereon any play is or ought to be played, be ready apparelled and – to begin the play at the hour of three of the clock in the afternoon, unless by six of the same company he shall be licensed to the contrary, that then he . . . shall and will pay . . . three [shillings]; and if that he . . . happen to be overcome with drink at the time when he [ought to] play, by the judgment of four of the said company, he shall and will pay ten shillings; and if he shall [fail to come] during any play, having no licence or just excuse of sickness, he is contented to pay twenty shillings . . .

Plays were supposed to begin at two or three o'clock. Sometimes, however, public performances took place considerably later in the afternoon or in the early evening, perhaps to draw in a larger number of wage-earners. A letter from the Privy Council to the Lord Mayor dated 11 April 1582 prays him to 'revoke [his] late inhibition against . . . playing on the said holidays after evening prayer'. The Lord Mayor replied that if he did this it would 'drive the action of [the] plays into very inconvenient time of night specially for

servants and children to be absent from their parents and master's attendance and presence',[49] and a letter of 1594 from the Lord Chamberlain admits
that the players had not been beginning until four o'clock. This implies
that, contrary to the received view, lighting was necessary and may have
been used for theatrical effect in the public playhouses: Chambers notes a
suggestive definition from Cotgrave's *French-English Dictionary* of 1611:
'Falot, "a cresset light (such as they use in playhouses) made of ropes
wreathed, pitched and put into small and open cages of iron"'.[50] And like
the Spanish actors, Elizabethan players may well have had to go on to
engagements to play in the private houses of the great or at Court. There
performances after supper[51] did not begin until ten o'clock and frequently
ended at one in the morning.[52]

Scene building

Given the comparatively brief time that was available for rehearsal it is
probable that the companies agreed on only the boldest of effects, which
doors to use for entrances and exits, basic blockings for the most important
moments of the scenes, cues for the introduction of properties or for
flourishes. Many scenes depended on the construction of symmetrical
tableaux: the Folio's (Shakespeare's) stage direction to *3 Henry VI*, IV.i.6,
reads: '*Flourish. Enter King Edward [attended]; Lady Grey [as Queen];
Pembroke, Stafford, Hastings, [and others]. Four stand on one side and four on
the other.*' Similarly formal groupings are indicated by stage directions in
two Rose plays, *Edward I* (1591) and *Look about You* (1599):[53]

> *the Queen Mother being set on the one side, and Queene Elinor on the other,
> the King sitteth in the middest mounted highest, and at his feet the ensign
> underneath him.*

> *Sound Trumpets; enter with a Herald on the one side, Henry the Second
> crowned, after him Lancaster, Chester, Sir Richard Faukenbridge; on the
> other part, King Henry the son crowned, Herald after him; after him Prince
> John, Leicester; being set, enters fantastical Robert of Gloucester in a gown
> girt; walks up and down.*

As the leading players swept down the stage (the mere size of the stage
demanded bold moves and large gestures) or took up poses for scenes where
they threatened or wooed, the players with smaller parts must have
possessed the skills or the sense to find positions or gestures which
completed the composition of the scene. There were no spotlights to
highlight a leading player: this must have been done by grouping the players
in such a way as to focus the audience's attention where it was required.

There can have been few productions which were able to 'shake down' in the way modern productions do, but Elizabethan performances must have had a compensating freshness. A common phrase meaning to perform a role was to 'discharge a part'. Besides giving an opportunity for bawdy, the words suggest an actor releasing his nervous energy in words and gestures as a weapon releases a missile, even if his talents were channelled with what might seem to us restricting conventions. There were obviously conventions for distraction as is indicated by a stage direction from *Richard III* (II.ii.33): '*Enter the Queen with her hair about her ears*',[54] and in Marston's *The Insatiate Countess* (1610) we find the bald direction: '*Isabella falls in love with Massino*'.[55]

If we approach the plays of Marlowe or Shakespeare's chronicle of Henry VI from this direction rather than looking in them for patterns of imagery or nice indications of 'character' we can see that they depend on scenes that follow one another with a strong architectonic rhythm, on moments that must have been realised by bold visual effects, formal groupings that tend towards tableaux, archetypal personages, frozen moments that would lodge in the spectators' minds. The final sequence of Heywood's *The Silver Age* opens with a direction that shows how important grouping was, in that the playwright was prepared to sacrifice his knowledge of divine hierarchies to visual effect: '*Sound. Enter Saturn, Jupiter, Juno, Mars, Phoebus, Venus and Mercury: they take their place as they are in height*'.[56] For a more extended analysis we might choose I.ii. of *Tamburlaine*, the scene in which we first see the hero. The scene has three such moments, what Brecht was later to call *Gestus* (which I shall translate as 'gest'), a word that means both 'gist' and 'gesture', moments when the visual elements of the scene combine with the dialogue in a significant form that reveals the condition of life in the play.[57] In fact the word 'gesture' has almost this meaning in Elizabethan times. It was a technical term for 'the employment of bodily movements, attitudes, expression of countenance, etc., as a means of giving effect to oratory' (*OED*, 3a). The printer's epistle to the 1590 Quarto of *1 Tamburlaine* notes that he has 'omitted and left out some fond and frivolous gestures, digressing (and in my poor opinion) far unmeet for the matter' – these comic scenes presumably were either written by Marlowe himself or developed with his cognizance. The first gest in this scene is established by the opening stage direction: '*[Enter] Tamburlaine leading Zenocrate, Techelles, Usumcasane, [Agydas, Magnetes], other Lords and Soldiers loaden with treasure.*'[58] It would seem appropriate for Tamburlaine to have made his first entrance through the central opening bringing with him Zenocrate and leading the captured lords. His own followers, Techelles and Usumcasane, may have led in processions of soldiers laden with the 'mails' or treasure chests that are mentioned at l. 138, through two or more side doors – it was played in 1594 at the Rose, where the tiring-house had probably five doors.[59] The

scene contains two wooing sequences, first of Zenocrate, second of Theridamus, emissary of Mycetes the witless King of Persia. Both seem to be won
over by Tamburlaine's 'pathetical' persuasions, but in a typically sardonic
Marlovian moment Tamburlaine casually throws out a dark threat:

You shall have honours as your merits be;
Or else you shall be forced with slavery (255–6)

and it is tempting to conjecture that Tamburlaine's soldiers had moved
around the stage so that they in fact surrounded both Zenocrate and later
Theridamus. This provides a visual frame for the second gest of the scene
when Tamburlaine divests himself of his shepherd's weeds (either a costume of sheepskins or the 'white sheepen cloak' listed in Henslowe's
inventory[60]) and dons his 'complete armour and this curtle-axe' (1.42). The
moment is one that lodged in the spectators' imaginations: his preceding
line 'Lie here, ye weeds that I disdain to wear!' became a catch phrase and
was parodied by Jonson who gave it to Juniper the cobbler in the first scene
of *The Case is Altered* (1597). It is the visual enactment of the player
becoming his part and draws attention to the art of impersonation. It would
be appropriate, therefore, for the soldier who bore in the armour to have
taken up his position down-stage from where Tamburlaine can move back
to deliver his first great declamation:

Zenocrate, lovelier than the love of Jove,
Brighter than is the silver Rhodope,
Fairer than whitest snow on Scythian hills,
Thy person is more worth to Tamburlaine
Than the possession of the Persian crown,
Which gracious stars have promised at my birth . . . (87–92)

Like the previous gest in which Alleyn put on his costume before the
spectators there is no attempt at illusion here: rather Marlowe draws
attention to his own art by deliberate bathos. After Tamburlaine has
delivered his mighty lines Techelles demolishes the moment:

TECHELLES: What now! In love?
TAMBURLAINE: Techelles, women must be flattered:
But this is she with whom I am in love. (106–8)

This suggests that the wooing scene must have been done with formality,
the grouping must have matched the dialogue's switch from ceremony to
comedy.[61]

The second part of the scene is a parallel wooing scene as Tamburlaine
wins Theridamus over to his side. Again it is prepared for by a visual device
as the soldiers flip open the treasure chests to display 'the golden wedges' to
the view of Mycetes' emissary. Theridamus and his followers are magnificently dressed:

Their plumed helms are wrought with beaten gold,
Their swords enamelled, and about their necks

Hangs massy chains of gold down to the waist;
In every part exceeding brave and rich. (124–7)

Tamburlaine being dressed only in steel armour obviously felt that their richness must be visibly matched. There is a second long declamation which ends with demonstration of its own artifice:

And when my name and honour shall be spread
As far as Boreas claps his brazen wings,
Or fair Boötes sends his cheerful light,
Then shalt thou be competitor with me,
And sit with Tamburlaine in all his majesty.
THERIDAMUS: Not Hermes, prolocutor to the gods,
Could use persuasions more pathetical. (206–11)

Possibly the parallels between the two declamations were reinforced by quoting the grouping of the first in the second.

What emerges from this kind of analysis – its details of course can be merely conjectural – is that plays of this sort moved from set piece, or from one gest or formal dramatic image, to another. There are important implications in that once we have realized that the set piece or formal group is a basic element of the Elizabethan play, we are in less danger of the moral reductivism that comes with a concentration on plot, on end-directed action, which deduces a play's meaning simply in moral terms from its resolution. Nor are we tempted to regard the dumb shows, songs, masques, etc., found in the plays as excrescences or 'insets' but rather we recognize them as evidence of the basic mode of Elizabethan drama. As late as 1625 Heywood could write in the prologue to *The English Traveller*:

A strange play you are like to have, for know
We use no drum, nor trumpet, nor dumbshow,
No combat, marriage, not so much today
As song, dance, masque, to bombast out a play.
Yet these all good, and still in frequent use
With our best poets.

In plays with conventions like these there can simply have been no time for the actors to develop the kind of relationship with one another through their roles that allows for naturalistic character portrayal, nor can their energies have been devoted to the collective sustaining of illusion. Rather they must have had a sense of the pattern of their scenes and the non-representational nature of their art meant that the dramatic images they created were organized from concepts rather than being pictures of the real world.

Our hypothesis that Elizabethan drama tended towards the emblematic rather than the realistic is confirmed when we consider that the plays consisted of far more than is represented by the printed words that alone have survived. The rise of the modern intensive study of Renaissance plays coincided with the rise of a kind of drama that is closely related to the novel –

the plays, say, of Ibsen and Chekhov. Such works were set in realist milieux that were established by naturalistic scenery, and their excellence depends largely on the credibility, psychological or social, of their characters. Most educated people find it easy to imagine the kinds of setting these plays require and also find that the plays give up much of their meaning when they are read. Perhaps as a consequence many who have written about the plays of the Renaissance in this century have concentrated their energies on what might be read: stage directions derived from playhouse copy drop into the small print of textual collation (see the New Arden editions of *Titus Andronicus* and *Love's Labour's Lost*) and few editors do much to kindle the visual imagination of their readers although they may reprint the music for the songs. So too one often finds an unconscious prejudice against any delight in the visual. The habit of thought, implanted in the European mind by Aristotle's incidental remarks on spectacle, was further cultivated in England at least by puritan attitudes towards the theatre. In 1582 Gosson lamented in *Playes Confuted in Five Actions* that 'the stateliness of the preparation drowns the delight which the matter affords' and claimed that it was the devil himself that made plays alluring: 'For the eye, beside the beauty of the houses and the stages, he sendeth in garish apparel, masks, vaulting, tumbling, dancing of jigs, galliards, moriscos, hobby-horses, showing of juggling casts.'[62] Merely reading the words, therefore, does not do justice to a body of drama that, as contemporaries put it, had its life in its 'action' and depended for its effect on the 'impurity' of its art. In fact is must have been sometimes very difficult to separate what was 'drama' from other forms of popular entertainment. In 1584 Lupold von Wedel described the bear-baiting in Southwark adjacent to the playhouses thus:[63]

> There is a round building three storeys high, in which are kept about a hundred large English dogs, with separate wooden kennels for each of them. These dogs were made to fight singly with three bears, the second bear being larger than the first and the third larger than the second. After this a horse was brought in and chased by the dogs, and at last a bull, who defended himself bravely. The next was that a number of men and women came forward from a separate compartment, dancing, conversing and fighting with each other: also a man who threw some white bread among the crowd, that scrambled for it. Right over the middle of the place a rose was fixed, this rose being set on fire by a rocket: suddenly lots of apples and pears fell out of it down upon the people standing below. Whilst the people were scrambling for the apples, some rockets were made to fall down upon them out of the rose, which caused a great fright but amused the spectators. After this, rockets and other fireworks came flying out of all corners, and that was the end of the play.

The bear-baiting proper was followed by fireworks and entertainment which, if not arguably a 'play', was in the nature of a jig (see below).

Music and dancing

We might begin our examination of the non-verbal elements of the plays by considering the evidence that survives for the kinds of music that accompanied performances. Music was not 'incidental', expressive of the emotions portrayed, heard by the audience but not by the characters, but provided a dramatic frame and mediating perspective for the action. Plays began with three soundings of a trumpet to herald in many plays the entrance of the black-cloaked Prologue who bowed deeply to the auditory.[64] Trumpets or cornets sounded the flourishes that announced and the 'sennets' that accompanied ceremonial entrances, or the 'tuckets' that were the signals for mounted soldiers to advance, as in I.iii. of *Richard II*, set in the lists at Coventry. Horns were blown to announce messengers as in I.i. of *Edward III* and II.i. of *1 Henry VI*. Many battle sequences were built around these sounds. Drums were sounded for marches, hautboys for the entertainment of guests, pipes for clowns, and the winding of horns established the frequent hunting scenes.[65] Music was a convenient form of dramatic shorthand: III.iii. of *1 Henry VI* provides a good example where Joan Pucelle describes the manoeuvres as the Duke of Burgundy abandons his allegiance to the English Talbot:

> PUCELLE: Your honours shall perceive how I will work
> To bring this matter to the wished end.
> > *Drum sounds afar off.*
> Hark! by the sound of drum you may perceive
> Their powers are marching unto Paris-ward.
> > *Here sound an English march.*
> There goes the Talbot, with his colours spread,
> And all the troops of English after him.
> > *French [a slow] march.*
> Now in the rearward comes the Duke and his:
> Fortune in favour makes him lag behind.
> Summon a parley; we will talk with him.
> > *Trumpets sound a parley.* (27–35)

Three of the first four entrances of *2 Tamburlaine* specify that characters enter '*with drums and trumpets*', a form of words that indicates that musicians accompanied the players onto the stage. (In *Edward I* we find '*Enter the Mayoress of London . . . music before her.*') A dead march was sounded at the end of tragedies like *The Massacre at Paris* and *Hamlet* ('soldiers' music'), and *Coriolanus* (a play full of music), at the funeral of Zenocrate (*2 Tamburlaine*, III.ii.), and at the openings of *Titus Andronicus* and *1 Henry VI*.

Songs of course were frequent although they can easily be overlooked as they were not always printed with the dialogue and their presence can be inferred only from a terse '*song*' or from an allusion in a character's speech. Often authors did not themselves write the words for them but were content to use a well-known air – or else they set their own words to an existing tune. Many players must have been able to sing music in parts: certainly catches and group songs figure large in interludes and there is no reason to suspect that this talent was missing from the commercial playhouses. II.iii. of *Twelfth Night* is improved if Sir Toby and Sir Andrew can sing their catches in tune. Songs could themselves have visual settings as elaborate as one in Heywood's *The Golden Age*:

> *Enter with music (before Diana) six Satyrs, after them all their Nymphs, garlands on their heads, and javelins in their hands, their bows and quivers. The Satyrs sing:*
>
> Hail, beauteous Dian, Queen of shades,
> That dwells beneath these shadowy glades . . .

In Renaissance theory music was held to be an emblem of the harmonic structures of the universe and was often used as a realisation of the relationship between macrocosm and microcosm, a way of portraying mental torment or social disorder. So it is used in the prison sequence just before Richard II's death and in IV.iv. of *Richard III*, where the newly-crowned tyrant enters with a cacophony of drums and trumpets to interrupt the ceremony of the wailing queens. Later in the private playhouses music was commonly played between the acts. Performances in public playhouses seem to have run almost continuously, possibly with pauses between the acts, although two plays of 1590, *James IV* and *The Dead Man's Fortune*, stipulate songs or dances between the acts.[66] In one rather unlikely public playhouse play, *Sejanus* (1603), Jonson stipulates a chorus of musicians after each act – a feature that is suppressed, incidentally, in the Everyman and World's Classics texts of the play. Music in the public playhouses was generally provided by wind and percussion instruments although Henslowe owned, as well as 'iij tymbrells' [tambourine-like instruments], 'iij trumpettes and a drum', 'a trebel viall, a basse viall, a bandore, a sytteren [or cithern, like the bandore which supplied its bass, a guitar-like instrument]'.[67] They may have been used to accompany dumb shows – viols, citherns, and bandores are the instruments used for the first dumb show of *Jocasta* (1566). Musicians and players had separate organisations – they had separate licences from the Revels Office – and it is possible that particular

bands or the municipally-paid 'waits' were hired for particular performances. So we hear in *Sir Thomas More* (1595), 'Where are the waits? Go bid
them play to spend the time a while' (l. 944).

Dancing too was often incorporated into the plays. When the Devils enter
to present Faustus with crowns and rich apparel they dance to delight his
mind before they depart; Joan Pucelle witnesses an elaborate mime of devils
that signals her end in *1 Henry VI*, V.iii, and Heywood's *A Woman Killed
with Kindness*, a Rose play of 1603, calls for a dance of country wenches in its
second scene. Then the music changes to the winding of horns to signal the
hunting scene that follows. Dances were useful for wooing scenes, and
Shakespeare used them thus in *Love's Labour's Lost*, *Romeo and Juliet*, and
Much Ado about Nothing. Players in Shakespeare's histories (but significantly not in Marlowe's more pageant-like plays) had also to perform fights
before spectators, of whom many would have been keen amateurs of the
sport. In 1587 the principal comedian of the Queen's Men, Richard
Tarlton, was allowed as a Master of Fence.[68] The outcome of *Hamlet*
depends upon the outcome of an elaborate fencing-match – some good
modern productions have made the 'action' of the fight mirror the action of
the play as a whole.

Dumb shows, set pieces, and jigs

It had been the practice in academic drama performed at the universities,
the inns of court, and at Court before the public playhouses opened to begin
each act of a play with a dumb show. In the case of *Gorboduc*, the first of
these plays to use this device, the dumb shows prefigured the action of the
ensuing act:[69]

> *First, the music of violins began to play, during which came in upon the stage
> six wild men, clothed in leaves. Of whom the first bare in his neck a fagot of
> small sticks, which they all, both severally and together, assayed with all
> their strength to break; but it could not be broken by them. At the length, one
> of them plucked out one of the sticks, and brake it: and the rest plucking out
> all the other sticks, one after another, did easily break them, the same being
> severed; which being conjoined, they had before attempted in vain. After they
> had this done, they departed the stage, and the music ceased. Hereby was
> signified, that a state knit in unity doth continue strong against all force, but
> being divided, is easily destroyed; as befell upon Duke Gorboduc dividing his
> land to his two sons, which he before held in monarchy; and upon the
> dissension of the brethren, to whom it was divided.*

This description is fuller though no different in kind from those found in
public playhouse plays like Peele's *The Battle of Alcazar* (1589). These

allegorical devices were related to the religious and civic shows of the late Middle Ages, to Royal Entries, City pageants, and Lord Mayor's processions. They were obvious occasions for spectacular moments in plays and provided another kind of dramatic shorthand as dramatists could draw upon the moral learning of iconological encyclopaedias and emblem books as well as on the familiar devices of English heraldry. Certain dramatists, notably Jonson and Chapman, did not use the form, but it is a mistake to assume that Shakespeare was parodying this 'pantomimic' (silent) action in the dumb show in *Hamlet* or that the convention was antiquated by the turn of the century. Shakespeare used a kind of dumb show to open Acts I and III of *1 Henry VI* and also in his last plays; they were used extensively in Heywood's *Ages*, and are found in plays by Jonson's protégé, Richard Brome, in the 1630s. They may have sometimes served as sops to the groundlings: they are so described by Puttenham in 1589, whose description of classical practice was probably based on contemporary knowledge (witness his reference to the non-classical 'vices'):[70]

> between the acts when the players went to make ready for another, there
> was great silence, and the people waxed weary, then came in these
> manner of counterfeit vices, they were called *Pantomimi*, and all that
> had before been said, or great part of it, they gave a cross construction
> to it very ridiculously.

Perhaps these were the kinds of 'graced deformities' that the printer said he had excised from *Tamburlaine*. Inferior dramatists found them useful for compressing their often rambling narratives. Marlowe like others often called for elaborate dumb show entrances. III.i. of *2 Tamburlaine*, for example, begins thus:

> *Enter the Kings of Trebizon and Soria, one bringing a sword and another a*
> *sceptre; next Natolia [Orcanes] and Jerusalem with the imperial crown;*
> *after Callapine, and after him [Almeda and] other lords. Orcanes and*
> *Jerusalem crown him and the other give him the sceptre.*

Music probably accompanied the entrance and the procession may have passed two or three times about the stage, as was common in the classical tragedies.[71] The moment comes after another emblematic scene, that of the death of Zenocrate:

> *The arras is drawn, and Zenocrate lies in her bed of state; Tamburlaine*
> *sitting by her; three Physicians about her bed, tempering potions;*
> *Theridamus, Techelles, Usumcasane, and the three sons [Calyphas,*
> *Amyras, and Celebinus].*

The tableau thus discovered is a mute emblem of pathos as Tamburlaine moves forward to join the lords and deliver his lament before his queen dies to the sound of music. The scene ends with Tamburlaine re-entering the discovery space and the arras drawn closed. Marlowe may well have drawn directly on the allegoric conventions of the dumb show for some of his most famous scenes. The chariot drawn by kings, for example, may have been inspired by the first dumb show in *Jocasta* which had been reprinted in 1575 and 1587, although it could equally derive from Italian *trionfi*. The animals listed in Henslowe's inventory may have been employed to draw chariots in triumphant entries.[72] It has been suggested that Tamburlaine's chariot may have entered into the yard of the playhouse[73] and that he here represents the Triumph of Fortune;[74] when he comes in in V.iii., again in his king-drawn chariot, however, he shows the pain-wracked body of the dying man that he is, signifying the Triumph of Death. After alighting from the chariot he may have turned to point to his vacant seat:

> See where my slave, the ugly Monster Death,
> Shaking and quivering, pale and wan for fear,
> Stands aiming at me with his murdering dart,
> Who flies away at every glance I give,
> And when I look away, comes stealing on.
> Villain, away, and hie thee to the field! (V.iii.67–72)

It is a simple but most effective piece of visual irony.

Dumb shows are simply extended examples of the visual emblems that are so important in Elizabethan drama. Entrances in particular often established an informing image for the ensuing scene. Stock properties such as torches had two functions when carried on to the stage: to reveal to the audience that the action is taking place by night, but also to suggest that the bearer is in the dark, uncognizant of his fate. So Hieronimo is shown bearing a long torch in the engraving of the titlepage of the 1615 edition of *The Spanish Tragedy* (see Plate 12), which shows the opening of II.v., the moment when Hieronimo discovers the body of his murdered son (the stage direction reads '*Enter Hieronimo in his shirt etc.*'). Similarly Othello enters 'with a light' to strangle Desdemona. The moment 'quotes' Iago's entrance eighty lines before; both men wittingly and unwittingly are turning light and order to darkness and chaos. Earlier in *3 Henry VI*, Keepers enter in III.i. with cross-bows to hunt the driven deer, the fleeing King himself. The entrance of players in masks often prefigures confusion as in *Romeo and Juliet* and *Much Ado about Nothing*. A final example of this kind of 'visual metonym' is provided by those scenes in which devils offer men daggers or halters to tempt them to the sin of sins, despair: Macbeth's dagger is a late instance of this.

One of the few extended accounts of a performance of an Elizabethan play that has come down to us is provided from the recollections of one R. Willis who saw a now lost play called *The Cradle of Security* at Gloucester about 1570. The morality play needed only the simplest of stages, but the meaning of the action which obviously included dumb shows was, as I have argued, generated by the use of emblematic costumes and properties:[75]

In the city of Gloucester the manner is (as I think it is in other like corporations) that when players of interludes come to town they first attend the Mayor to inform him what nobleman's servants they are, and so to get licence for their public playing; and if the Mayor like the actors or would show respect to their lord and master he appoints them to play their first play before himself and the aldermen and common council of the city; and that is called the Mayor's play, where every one that will comes in without money, the Mayor giving the players a reward as he thinks fit to show respect unto them. At such a play, my father took me with him and made me stand between his legs as he sat upon one of the benches where we saw and heard very well. The play was called *The Cradle of Security*, wherein was personated a king or some great prince with his courtiers of several kinds, amongst which three ladies were in special grace with him; and they keeping him in delights and pleasures drew him from his graver counsellors, hearing of sermons, and listening to good counsel and admonitions, that in the end they got him to lie down in a cradle upon the stage, where these three ladies joining in a sweet song rocked him asleep that he snorted again, and in the meantime closely conveyed under the cloths wherewithal he was covered a vizard like a swine's snout upon his face, with three wire chains fastened thereunto, the other end whereof being holden severally by those three ladies, who fall to singing again, and then discovered his face that the spectators might see how they had transformed him, going on with their singing; whilst all this was acting, there came forth of another door at the farthest end of the stage two old men, the one in blue with a Sergeant at Arms, his mace on his shoulder, the other in red with a drawn sword in his hand, and leaning with the other hand upon the other's shoulder, and so they two went along in a soft pace round about by the skirt of the stage, till at last they came to the cradle when all the court was in greatest jollity, and then the foremost old man with his mace struck a fearful blow upon the cradle; whereat all the courtiers with the three ladies and the vizard all vanished; and the desolate prince, starting up bare-faced and finding himself thus sent for to judgement, made a lamentable complaint of his miserable case, and so was carried away by wicked spirits. This prince did personate in the moral, the Wicked of the world; the three Ladies, Pride, Covetousness, and Luxury, the two old men, the End of the World, and the Last Judgement. This sight took such impression in me that when I came towards man's estate, it was as fresh in my memory, as if I had seen it newly acted.

The dumb shows and set-pieces I have described are those for which there is evidence in the printed texts of the plays that are extant. It is probable, however, that printed stage directions record only a fraction of the spectacular business in Elizabethan performances, for there is considerable evidence outside the printed texts that audiences enjoyed many dances, songs, farcical and satiric routines which have simply not survived. These entertaining interludes which often had little or nothing to do with the story of the play were often referred to by contemporaries as 'jigs'. The word is almost impossible to define: a jig could be a song, a ballad in dialogue form, a burlesque of tradesmen or women, or a dance performed to drum or music.[76] We find a description of such an insert in *The Pilgrimage to Parnassus* (1599):[77]

> *Enter Dromo, drawing a clown in with a rope*
>
> CLOWN: What now, thrust a man into the commonwealth, whether he will or no? What the devil should I do here?
>
> DROMO: Why, what an ass art thou? Dost thou not know a play cannot be without a clown? Clowns have been thrust into plays by head and shoulders ever since Kempe could make a scurvy face, and therefore reason thou shouldst be drawn in with a cart rope.
>
> CLOWN: But what must I do now?
>
> DROMO: Why if thou canst but draw thy mouth awry, lay thy leg over thy staff, saw a piece of cheese asunder with thy dagger, lap up drink on the earth, I warrant thee, they'll laugh mightily. Well, I'll turn thee loose to them, either say somewhat for thyself, or hang and be *non plus*.
>
> CLOWN: This is fine in faith: now, when they have nobody to leave on the stage, they bring me up, and which is worse tell me not what I should say. Gentles, I dare say you look for a fit of mirth, I'll therefore present unto you a proper new love letter of mine to the tune of 'Put on the smock a Monday', which in the heat of my charity I penned, and thus it begins:
>
> 'O my lovely Nigra, pity the pain of my liver: that little gallows Cupid hath lately pricked me in the breech with his great pin, and almost killed me thy woodcock with his birdbolt. Thou hast a pretty furrowed forehead, a fine leacherous eye, methinks I see the bawd Venus keeping a bawdy house in thy looks, Cupid standing like a Pander at the door of thy lips.' – How like you masters, has any young man a desire to copy this, that he may have *forma epistolae conscribendae*? Now if I could but make a fine scurvy face I were a king. O nature, why did'st thou give me so good a look?
>
> *[Re-enter Dromo, with Philomusus and Studioso]*
>
> DROMO: Give us a voider here for the fool. Sirrah, you must begone, here are other men that will supply the room.
>
> CLOWN: Why, shall I not whistle out my whistle? Then farewell gentle auditors, and the next time you see me I'll make you better sport.

Texts reveal how such set pieces were inserted into plays: what they seldom record is the habit of ending performances with a jig. English players in Europe were particularly famous for their singing and dancing skills and one of the things that most impressed the Swiss traveller, Thomas Platter, during his visit in autumn 1599 were the jigs that followed a performance of a Julius Caesar play at the Globe:[78]

> After dinner on the 21st September, at about two o'clock, I went with my companions over the water, and in the straw-thatched house [*streüwine Dachhaus*] saw the tragedy of the first Emperor Julius with at least fifteen characters very well acted. At the end of the comedy they danced according to their custom with extreme elegance, two in each group dressed in men's and two in women's apparel.

Most accounts of the jigs, however, derive either from the puritan enemies of the playhouses and so stress their lewdness or were written by playwrights who, while striving to create refined and academically respectable forms of drama, were forced to admit the popularity of such entertainments – even in the private playhouses and right until the middle of the seventeenth century. In 1615 'I.H.' in his *This World's Folly* inveighed against the 'squeaking out of those . . . obscene and light jigs, stuffed with loathsome and unheard-of ribaldry, sucked from the poisonous dugs of sin-swelled Theatres . . . I will not particularise those . . . Fortune-fatted fools . . . whose garb is the toothache of wit, the plague-sore of judgement . . . who are fain to produce blind Impudence [in margin, 'Garlicke' – a popular actor][79] to personate himself upon their stage, behung with chains of garlic, as an antidote against their own infectious breaths, lest it should kill their oyster-crying audience.'[80] In the famous prologue to *Tamburlaine*, Marlowe repudiates the 'jigging veins of rhyming mother wits' and yet the printer's epistle reveals that in performance the play contained episodes of this kind. Even in 1632 one of the characters in Shirley's *Changes* notes that many gentlemen:[81]

> Are not, as in the days of understanding,
> Now satisfied without a jig, which since
> They cannot, with their honour, call for after
> The play, they look to be served up in the middle.

Sometimes the habit of ending a play's action with a dance or a song as in *Much Ado*, *Twelfth Night* (did Feste's song accompany a dance by the company?) or the Bergomask dance at the conclusion of Pyramus and Thisbe gives some intimation of this convention of a terminal jig, perhaps refined on these occasions; on other occasions the evidence is more difficult to uncover. Despite its several complex textual problems, the epilogue to *2 Henry IV* indicates that that play ended with a dance. Dekker's satirical passage in *A Strange Horse Race* (1613) is therefore supported by more dispassionate testimony:[82]

As I have often seen, after the finishing of some worthy tragedy or catastrophe in the open theatres that the scene after the epilogue hath been more black (about a nasty bawdy jig) than the most horrid scene in the play was: the stinkards speaking all things, yet no man understanding any thing.

It is even conceivable, therefore, that at the conclusion of *King Lear* the King's Men performed a jig.

There may have been further 'action' after the jig in that it seems that some of the most verbally dextrous clowns, Tarlton and Wilson among others, were in the habit of giving improvised verses or 'themes', based on some idea tossed to them from the audience.[83] There may have then been an announcement of what the next performance was to be,[84] after which the company may have knelt in prayer for their patron[85] or more probably for the sovereign and the estates.

In his prologue for *Midas* (1589), admittedly a Paul's play, Lyly seems therefore to speak for all dramatists: 'If we present a mingle-mangle, our fault is to be excused, because the whole world is become an hodge-podge'.

3 · Players and playing

Playhouse economics

Although the Elizabethan theatrical companies bore the names of noble families, their financial organization was quite independent of their aristocratic patrons. Before the construction of the playhouses, London drama had been dominated by boy companies attached to schools or religious institutions, and by small groups of adult players who acted more or less regularly in the City's inns or in the halls of the nobility for occasional performances. Payments for performances by the boys at Court and elsewhere went to the master who had schooled them; what could be gathered from the inn audiences was presumably split among the players. The capital investment in playhouses together with large stocks of costumes and properties, however, necessitated a more sophisticated financial structure. Evidence from the diary of Philip Henslowe, who had a close financial relationship with the Admiral's and Lord Worcester's Men, as well as from a number of legal documents reveals that the main companies at least were owned by a syndicate of their leading players. Each company had about five or ten 'sharers' who, in return for investing capital in the company, took their profits by dividing among themselves the receipts from one part of the house, first the yard, later the galleries.[1] Shares in companies could be bought, sold, bequeathed, or divided among several individuals. The rest of the takings went to the owner of the playhouse and to support the rest of the organization: the tailors and tire-men who had care of the costumes, the book-holder and stage-keepers, and the gatherers – as well as the hiremen and the boys. For before he could acquire the status (or the capital) of a sharer, a player often progressed through two stages analogous to the degrees found in most Elizabethan trades, that of apprentice and that of hireman or journeyman. Actors did not, however, form a craft guild and the fiction of feudal patronage meant that boys had the status of servants to full members of the company. 'Hirelings' played minor parts and were paid a weekly salary or might be taken on for a particular performance. The

articles of agreement between Henslowe and several players have survived:
I reprint the memorandum for the playwright Thomas Heywood who
bound himself to play at the Rose for two years:[2]

> Memorandum that this 25th of March, 1598, Thomas Heywood came
> and hired himself with me as a convenant servant for two years by the
> receiving of two single pence according to the statute of Winchester and
> to begin at the day above written and not to play anywhere public about
> London not while these two years be expired but in my house if he do
> then he doth forfeit unto me by the receiving of these two pence forty
> pounds . . .

That the players' companies bore some similarity even if they did not bear
the name of a craft guild appalled the puritans and City fathers who opposed
them,[3] and their rapid rise to prosperity drew much satirical comment. A
passage from the Parnassus plays aptly contrasts their social with their
economic status:[4]

> But is't not strange, these mimic apes should prize
> Unhappy scholars at a hireling rate?
> Vile world, that lifts them up to high degree,
> And treads us down in groveling misery,
> England affords those glorious vagabonds,
> That carried erst their fardels on their backs,
> Coursers to ride on through the gazing streets,
> Sooping it in their glaring satin suits,
> And pages to attend their masterships.
> With mouthing words that better wits have framed,
> They purchase lands, and now esquires are named.

Elizabethan companies were small – at least in comparison to the massive
cast lists. The lists of characters that appear in the printed texts of some of
the late morality plays note, as a selling point, that they might be played by a
handful of men and a couple of boys. Thomas Preston's *Cambises*, for
example, possibly played by Leicester's Men about 1561, had thirty-eight
roles that could be played by six men and two boys and its titlepage indicates
how the parts could be divided. Thomas Platter was impressed when he saw
fifteen players employed at the performance of the Julius Caesar play[5] –
Shakespeare's version has thirty-five named parts and also requires 'extras'.
So although the surviving plots indicate that up to twenty-six players were
on occasion employed,[6] companies obviously were in the habit of using
actors to play more than one part each, of doubling. Although the leading
actors in a play took only one role, even sharers might have to take on six or
seven.[7] It seems that on some occasions stage-keepers might be used for
supernumeraries or 'mutes'.[8] The convention of doubling roles was not (and
is not) confusing to audiences although often playwrights anticipated
difficulties by announcing entrances in advance or by firmly naming

characters immediately they entered: the first acts of *The Jew of Malta* and *Richard II* provide good examples. Changes of character could be easily indicated by a quick change of cap and gown, or of beards (or by using the reversible cloak mentioned in *The Devil is an Ass*): even the amateurs in *A Midsummer Night's Dream* had 'your straw-colour beard, your orange-tawny beard, your purple-in-grain beard, or your French-crown-colour beard' (I.ii.84–5). A rustic could be created by the adoption of south-western dialect, a convention used from about 1553.[9] It is difficult to know, however, whether companies regularly made a virtue of necessity as Peter Brook did in his 1970 production of *A Midsummer Night's Dream*. Then he doubled the parts of Theseus and Oberon, Hippolyta and Titania, Puck and Philostrate and was thus able to make an effective theatrical demonstration of the unity of the play's action. In fact doubling provides an agreeable demonstration of a player's versatility.

Acting styles

Acting is notoriously difficult to describe and an attempt to reconstruct the acting styles of Elizabethan players is bound to founder on the shoals of fragmentary evidence and untenable generalization. As the sixteenth century drew to its close, well-known passages in the plays of Shakespeare and others contrast melodramatic huffing with a more modulated and temperate technique, but Shakespeare was simply attempting to define quality in acting, not a more modern style, and there is no reason to believe that the ham actors he was berating were the last survivors of a disappearing generation. Certainly the more bombastic passages in Marlowe and his contemporaries must have been temptations to what Nashe called 'ruff raff roaring, with thwick, thwack thirlery bouncing',[10] and there are several parodies of what the anonymous author of *The Puritan*, a Paul's play of 1606, epitomized in his portrait of 'a stalking, stamping player, will raise a tempest with his tongue, and thunder with his heels' (III.v.84).[11] Within each company, moreover, there was probably a wide variety of styles of acting. It is a common intellectual temptation to attempt to impose the patterns of reason on the complexities of art, and those scholars who have sifted through the references to players and orators in plays and pamphlets, or through Elizabethan treatises on psychology, in order to formulate one monolithic theory of Elizabethan acting forget that they are in danger of postulating playhouses filled with marionettes. Our contemporary experience of theatregoing tells us that a production can indeed be enhanced by a group of actors who use a range of styles to establish a range of different characters – indeed each 'character' by definition is established by a different 'style'. Those modern companies which have drilled their members into the adoption of uniformly formalist or naturalist styles for the presentation of Elizabethan drama inevitably, if they persist with their programmes, are greeted with more boredom than enthusiasm.

What kinds of generalizations, then, or even what kinds of discussion, are possible about Elizabethan acting? Audiences of any age demand performances that bring realities to mind and some players must have based their art on their powers of observation and of mimicry. In the first (Italian) version of *Every Man in his Humour*, Jonson has a character describe how another had disguised himself with complete success:

> 'Sblood, man, he had so writhen himself into the habit of one of your poor Disparviews here, your decayed, ruinous, worm-eaten gentlemen of the round: such as have vowed to sit on the skirts of the city . . . and have translated begging out of the old hackney pace to a fine easy amble, and made it run as smooth off the tongue as a shove-groat shilling; into the likeness of one of these lean Pirgo's had he moulded himself so perfectly, observing every trick of their action, as varying the accent, swearing with an emphasis. Indeed, all with so special and exquisite a grace, that (hadst thou seen him) thou wouldst have sworn he might have been the Tamburlaine or Agamemnon on the rout. (III.ii.)

Implicit in this passage, however, is the assumption that the player will imitate not simply the individual but the species, that his art consists of selecting particular elements of behaviour and excluding what is not relevant to the author's design. The final theatrical metaphor (revised in the English version to 'sergeant-major, if not lieutenant-colonel to the regiment' (reminds us too that the player is in fact likely to imitate types that are themselves 'theatrical', exemplifying either the eccentric humours of comedy or the moments of grandiloquent passion in tragedy. An actor therefore may remind us as much of traditions of playing as of our 'real' experience or, as Jonson again put it,

> poet never credit gained
> By writing truths, but things like truths well feigned.
> (second Prologue to *The Silent Woman*)

How then do we explain the fact that Elizabethan players were praised by their contemporaries for their 'naturalness'? We might start by reminding ourselves that Elizabethan connotations of 'natural' were very different from either the romantic meaning of the adjective which defines it by opposition to 'artificial' or the modern meaning which derives it from naturalism, that late nineteenth-century movement in the arts which sought to uncover the laws governing human behaviour or what had been shrouded by the demands of artistic decorum or social gentility. Certainly the Renaissance did not entertain the modern opposition between what was artificial or formal on the one hand and what was real or natural on the other.

Art was Nature's handmaid, what Sidney called 'second nature', and poets play frequently with the paradoxes that the best art is the most natural and that nature follows the dictates of art. Elizabethan players, as we have seen when examining the organization of their companies, would have thought of themselves as possessing skills like those of any other profession or craft guild: they would not have thought of themselves as separated from their fellows by the possession of a particular sensibility. Nashe's brusque instructions to his players in the prologue to *Summer's Last Will and Testament* (1592) have the tone of a master's words to his hirelings: 'this I bar, that none of you stroke your beards to make action, play with your codpiece points, or stand fumbling on your buttons when you know not how to bestow your fingers. Serve God and act clearly.'[12] The players' task, as they conceived it, was to employ these skills to create a fit style for the matter of their plays. Like all their contemporary artists they realised the principles of decorum.

An age like the present, out of sympathy with 'rules' of art, is apt to think of 'decorum' as having to do with social niceties, with plays that exhibit the manners of the upper orders of society and which are peopled with characters who tend towards stereotypes. It is important to realize that for Renaissance artists decorum was an enabling rather than restrictive principle. In other words players relied not just on the skills they acquired during their apprenticeship but on theory. And one of the first things the awareness of the rhetorical principle of decorum enabled dramatists to do was to differentiate styles of speech. We may see this development by contrasting an interchange between Mistress and Servant (A.) in Medwall's early Tudor interlude, *Fulgens and Lucrece*, where the styles of the two characters are interchangeable, with a passage from Richard Edwards's Court play *Damon and Pithias* of 1565:

A: Fair mistress liketh it you to know
    That my master commends me to you?
LUCRECE: Commendeth you to me?
A: Nay, commendeth you to him.
LUCRECE: Well amended, by Saint Sim.
A: Commendeth he to you, I would say,
    Or else you to he, now choose ye may
    Whether liketh you better;
    And here he sendeth you a letter –
    God's mercy I had it right now.
    [To the audience]
    Sirs, is there none there among you
    That took up such a writing?
    I pray you, sirs, let me have it again.
LUCRECE: Ye are a good messenger, for certain,

But I pray you, sir, of one thing,
Who is your master? tell me that.
A: Master, what call ye him? perdie ye wot
Whom I mean well and fine . . . (II.316–33)

The Edwards passage is a scene between the two noble heroes and a hangman:

GRONNO: Damon, thou servest the gods well today, be thou of comfort;
As for you, sir, I think you will be hanged in sport;
You heard what the king said: I must keep you safely,
By cock, I will: you shall rather hang than I.
Come on your way.
PITHIAS: My Damon, farewell, the gods have thee in keeping.
DAMON: Oh my Pithias, my pledge, farewell; I part from thee weeping,
But joyful at my day appointed I will return again,
When I will deliver thee from all trouble and pain.
Stephano will I leave behind me to wait upon thee in prison alone,
And I whom fortune hath reserved to this misery will walk home.
Ah Pithias, my pledge, my life, my friend, farewell.
PITHIAS: Farewell, my Damon.
DAMON: Loth I am to depart, sith sobs my trembling tongue doth stay.
Oh music, sound my doleful plaints when I am gone my way.
GRONNO: I am glad he is gone, I had almost wept too. Come, Pithias,
So God help me, I am sorry for thy foolish case.
Wilt thou venture thy life for a man so fondly?
PITHIAS: It is no venture; my friend is just for whom I desire to die.
GRONNO: Here is a mad man, I tell thee. I have a wife whom I love well,
And if ich would die for her, 'chould ich wear in hell:
Wilt thou do more for a man than I would for a woman? (ll. 1050–71)

Despite some unintentional lapses the dialogue between the two friends is in a deliberately high style while the comic hangman speaks plainly (and to the audience in the last speech) and is given a west country accent. In fact we owe to Edwards's prologue to this play an important description of this aspect of the playwright's and player's art:

In comedies, the greatest skill is this: rightly to touch
All things to the quick, and eke to frame each person so
That by his common talk you may his nature rightly know:
A roister ought not preach, that were too strange to hear,
But as from virtue he doth swerve so ought his words appear.
The old man is sober, the young man rash, the lover triumphing in
joys,
The matron grave, the harlot wild and full of wanton toys.
Which all in one course they in no wise do agree:
So correspondent to their kind their speeches ought to be.

Which speeches well pronounced, with action lively framed,
If this offend the lookers on, let Horace then be blamed,
Which hath our author taught at school from whom he doth not
    swerve,
In all such kind of exercise decorum to observe. (ll. 14–26).

The lines anticipate Hamlet's advice to the players: suiting the action to the word, the word to the action is in fact not a plea for 'naturalness' but for art.

We can see how false is the definition of acting in terms of opposition between realism and formalism in another context. Among the prime documents for those that hold that Elizabethan acting was formal[13] are two treatises by John Bulwer, the *Chirologia* and the *Chiromania* published together in 1644. Bulwer attempts to catalogue the stock hand gestures of ancient orators as they had been listed by Quintilian and others and as they had been 'most strangely enlarged by actors, the ingenious counterfeiters of men's manners'.[14] The works are illustrated by charts of hand gestures. If we were to take his statement about the origins of these gestures literally, it would be easy to postulate an Elizabethan style of acting that is 'gestic', related to modern mime; and yet it is misleading to imagine these gestures being used extensively in drama that depends so much on its verbal art. The point is made neatly by a character called Common Sense in an academic morality from Trinity College, Cambridge, Thomas Tomkis's *Lingua*. Comedus is reciting the prologue to Plautus' *Menaechmi* but is interrupted by Phantastes who wants the addition of gesture or 'action'.

PHANTASTES: Pish, pish, this is a speech with no action. Let's hear
    Terence: *Quid igitur faciam*, etc.
COMEDUS: *Quid igitur faciam? non eam? ne nunc quidem, Cum arcessor
    ultro?*
PHANTASTES: Fie, fie, fie, no more action! Lend me your bays. Do it
    thus. *Quid igitur*, etc. *He acts it after the old kind of pantomimic action.*
COMMUNIS SENSUS: I should judge this action, Phantastes, most absurd;
    unless we should come to a comedy, as gentlewomen to the
    Commencement, only to see men speak.
PHANTASTES: In my imagination 'tis excellent; for in this kind the hand,
    you know, is harbinger to the tongue, and provides the words a
    lodging in the ears of the auditors. (IV.ii.)

The implications are that 'gestic' acting was used in dumb shows, and perhaps for some moments of the highest passion – Marston's parodies of heroic romance, *Antonio and Mellida* and *Antonio's Revenge*, make great fun of the convention, possibly deriving from public playhouses, of players lying on the ground to express grief – but that this was used only sparingly. In fact it is probable that many of the gestures Bulwer illustrates would not be recognized as 'formal' even by a modern audience: a hand held up with open palm forward, hands pressed together at the fingers' ends are the 'natural' gestures for admiration or supplication respectively. Without a knowledge of the degree to which Elizabethans gesticulated in real life – a knowledge which we cannot now acquire – it is impossible to define how the gestures of life were selected and exaggerated by the actors of the time.

Modern realist drama assumes that the persons imitated are particular individuals who might have lived at particular times: Renaissance drama, like classical drama, imitated types or universals. Aristotle had written:[15]

Poetry . . . is a more philosophical and a higher thing than history: for poetry tends to express the universal, history the particular. By the universal I mean how a person of a certain type will on occasion speak or act, according to the law of probability or necessity; and it is this universality at which poetry aims in the names she attaches to the personages.

Likewise Renaissance dramatists did not assume that they were imitating simply historical figures: as we have seen, visual devices were emblematic rather than naturalistic and medieval kings wore basically Renaissance costumes. Mid-sixteenth-century plays sometimes have allegorical and historical characters in the same action: Death the Mower appears at the end of *Edward II*, and even Shakespeare continued to use personifications in his choruses. In printed texts generic designations, 'King', 'Braggart', 'Clown', etc., sometimes supplant proper names in the speech prefixes. Likewise in Spenser's *Faerie Queene* characters now seem to be individuals acting naturally, now allegoric personages whose actions are dictated by their roles. Certainly Shakespeare felt that it was the player's task to realize the type rather than the individual. When Hamlet looks in the mirror held up to nature he expects to see not individuals but personifications: the player must 'show Virtue her own feature, Scorn her own image, and the very age and body of the time his form and pressure' (III.ii.20) – 'form' here derives from Aristotle's 'formal cause', that on-driving power that impels something to realize its essence. Again Hamlet feels that the good player becomes the very figure of the emotion proper to his character, here 'the distracted lover':

Is it not monstrous that this player here,
But in a fiction, in a dream of passion,
Could force his soul so to his own conceit
That from her working all his visage wanned;
Tears in his eyes, distraction in's aspect,
A broken voice, and his whole function suiting
With forms to his conceit? (II.ii.544–50)

It has been argued that the appearance of the word 'personate' about 1600 – 'Whom do you personate?' asks Alberto in the Induction to *Antonio and Mellida* (1599) – is indicative of an assumption that drama is turning to the depiction of individuals, characters with a particular 'identity' or inner self.

Yet the word did not at that period lose the connotations it derived from its etymology (from the Latin *persona*, a mask) of the generic and the feigned. It did not imply singularity.

In practice this means that modern actors attempting Renaissance parts might try to banish from their minds the notions of character that are associated with naturalistic drama, the common modern assumption that personality can be best described by depth metaphors, stripping away surfaces to find a hidden source of energy, that 'character' that determines all actions. The reply to Alberto's question is 'Piero, Duke of Venice', which elicits the instruction:

> O, ho; thus frame your exterior shape
> To haughty form of elate majesty
> As if you held the palsy-shaking head
> Of reeling chance under your fortune's belt . . . (ll. 7–10)

Marston's insistence on the 'exterior shape' reminds us that characters may be built not from a theory of an individual's psychology but from without: from a costume, a catch phrase like Armado's 'let that pass' (*Love's Labour's Lost*, V.i.94ff.), or the famous 'Tu quoque' of the Jacobean clown, Thomas Greene, or from a physical mannerism. Biting the lip was a stock sign of passion, biting the thumb – 'putting the thumb-nail into the mouth, and with a jerk (from the upper teeth) make it to knack' – expressed defiance.[16] Burbage seems to have found a neat way of epitomizing the nervousness of *Richard III*, regicide and villain:[17]

> Gallants, like Richard the usurper, swagger,
> That had his hand continual on his dagger.

Even when Elizabethans speak of what we might call 'identification' between spectator and player, they do this not in the context of situation and highly particularized characters but in terms of the player's art of distilling the actions proper to his part. So Thomas Heywood wrote in 1608:[18]

> What English blood, seeing the person of any bold Englishman
> presented, and doth not hug this fame, and hunnye [talk sweetly] at his
> valour, pursuing him in his enterprise with his best wishes, and as being
> wrapt in contemplation, offers to him in his heart all prosperous
> performance, as if the personator were the man personated? So
> bewitching a thing is lively and well-spirited action that it hath power to
> new-mould the hearts of the spectators, and fashion them to the shape
> of any noble and notable attempt. What coward, to see his countrymen
> valiant, would not be ashamed of his own cowardice? . . .

Forty years later, in his epistle to the readers of the Beaumont and Fletcher Folio of 1647, the dramatist James Shirley describes how 'you may here find passions raised to that excellent pitch, and by such insinuating degrees, that you shall not choose but consent and go along with them, finding yourself at last grown insensibly the very same person you read; and then stand admiring the subtle tracks of your engagement'. Although both Heywood, whose description is part of a moral defence of drama, and Shirley, whose encomium is part of a praise of the wit and variety of his dramatic predecessors, feel tempted to imply an identity between player and character and spectator and character respectively, both are equally insistent that the audience does not lose sight of the player's skill and thus of a distinction between the person represented and the person representing. Audiences were aware of two levels of action: that which was imitated and the spoken and physical gestures of the imitation. Revivifying an old Platonic image, players commonly referred to themselves as 'shadows', insubstantial no-things compared with the 'matter' of their plays.

Plays and games

We can see then that the empathy Heywood and Shirley describe is for the player and not the character. It is different from the reactions that are generally posited for modern 'real life stories' although it may be similar to the empathy a spectator feels for a skilled player in a football match. For Elizabethan plays were closely related to games. Modern contexts of verisimilitude, defined by congruence of dramatic action to real or imagined life at particular moments, are misleading. Instead therefore of attempting to forge a logical relationship between the two different categories of life and art, we can direct ourselves to the examination of the conventions of our one category of behaviour, playing. As Nashe and Shirley make clear, verisimilitude comes from a recognition of the player's skill and energy, his ability to cut a figure, establish a concentrated image hard in outline. Energy (in its rhetorical sense of vigour of expression, what Puttenham called a 'goodly outward show' imposed on what works 'a stir to the mind'[19]), clarity, intellectual engagement are the appropriate criteria of excellence. In folk-plays characters drew attention to the personation: when Friar Tuck says, 'Am not I a jolly friar, For I can shoot both far and near', the 'I' designates the player and not the character.[20] The anonymous dramatist wanted to kindle the audience's awareness of the play as play. So Lording Barry wrote in the prologue to *Ram Ally* (1608) that the players' task was

to show

> Things never done, with that true life
> That thoughts and wits should stand at strife
> Whether the things now shown be true,
> Or whether we ourselves now do
> The things we but present.

The modern tendency for an actor working in naturalist theatre to subordinate his own personality and body movements to those of the particular character he is imitating would not fit the demands of an Elizabethan playhouse. 'Liveliness', a common Elizabethan term of praise, does not mean 'lifelikeness' but rather describes a spirited or inspired personation of what is fitting.

Plays had historical as well as categorical relationships with games. The customary Elizabethan word for actor is 'player', and Elizabethan plays draw upon the traditions of popular and aristocratic sports and revels. A printed text of *c.*1560 gives us 'The Play of Robin Hood, very proper to be played in May Games'.[21] The Bankside playhouses lay right by the bear-baiting rings and were associated with them by the City fathers and doubtless by many members of their audiences. The first Blackfriars playhouse had been used as a fencing school. Tudor interludes draw upon folk forms: impersonations, slapstick combats, verbal 'flytings', bawdy anecdotes, the pageants of the Midsummer shows, as well as on traditional seasonal games of Robin Hood and St George. The devils with squibs and crackers in their tails, so popular in the public playhouses come, like fools and clowns, from the 'dramatized life' of the community. Conversely popular public playhouse plays like *The Spanish Tragedy*, *Edward II*, and *Pericles* incorporate the pageantry of aristocratic tournaments. It is important to remember that within the one play folk figures often appear alongside personages characteristic of 'aristocratic' genres, especially the romance. In a medieval work like *Sir Gawayn and the Green Knight* we find both boisterous physical contests and passages of high moralizing, and Greene's *James IV* (1590) opens with an induction with which Oberon King of the Fairies confronts 'Bohan, a Scot, attired like a Redesdale man' – probably a wild-looking man from the Scotch borders. He pours invective scorn upon the Fairy King, who promptly charms his sword that it might not be drawn from its sheath. Peele's *Old Wives Tale* of the same year has an induction in which appear three pages called Antic, Frolic, and Fantastic – their names conjure up the extravagances of community revelry. The noble knights and ladies, the magicians, wild men, and comic servants that inhabit plays of this sort have their origins in old tales, dreams, and games, and it is futile to place them on any scale that starts from a notion of realism. Like Spenser, Marlowe is as closely related to these elements of popular English culture, what Christopher Sly calls 'household stuff',[22] as he is to the high Renaissance culture, the history, theology, and moral philosophy he read at Cambridge. Actors who have to personate characters in this type of play, therefore, have no problem in establishing the credibility of those they portray. The archetypes they embody belong already in the popular imagination, and the excellence of a performance will depend upon a player's or a company's ability to realize the appropriate conventions. As Vindice in *The Revenger's Tragedy* (1606) remarked tersely, 'When the bad bleeds, then is the tragedy good' (III.v.205).

As a particular example we might examine the few traces that remain in the text of the kind of performance that Edward Alleyn might have given in one of the most celebrated roles in the period, Barabas in *The Jew of Malta* (1589). The form of the story enables us to regard the play as a tragedy and yet we look in vain it for any indications of the hero's conscience (or consciousness) or indeed any of the high matter that neo-classical criticism has led Europe to expect in this genre. (For this reason the play, like most of Marlowe's works, was scarcely performed between the closing of the playhouses and this century.) This play derives its energy not from the hero's individuality but from his conventionality. Marlowe undoubtedly knew the actual writings of Machiavelli, but chose instead to introduce the piece with a prologue who represents the popular bogy-man 'Machevell' who had entered English consciousness through anti-Catholic invectives. The 'Machiavellian' villain Barabas is accordingly a pantomime villain. Alleyn probably wore a red wig, as actors playing Judas had traditionally done, and almost certainly a large false nose, like those worn by representations of Jews in Italian carnival: Ithamore says, 'I have the bravest, gravest, secret, subtle, bottle-nosed knave to my master' (III.iii.9–10) and later (IV.i.23) jocularly calls his master 'Nose' to his face. In Rowley's *A Search for Money* (1609) a servant is said to have 'a visage like the artificial Jew of Malta's nose'. In II.iii. Barabas intersperses his conversation with Lodowick with cynical asides direct to the audience, and the broad farce of the scene in which he appears disguised as a musician (IV.iv.) depends upon the audience enjoying the fun of the game:

BELLAMIRA: A French musician! Come, let's hear your skill.

BARABAS: Must tune my lute for sound, twang twang first. (ll. 29–30)

Likewise Pilia-Borza probably wore an outsize moustache like a rogue in a nineteenth-century melodrama. Clifford Williams's decision to give the nuns outrageously large headpieces in his 1964 production was therefore an appropriate one. The farce does not prevent the play being a painful demonstration of the way in which those who treat life as a ruthless game to be won may threaten those who attempt to live by the rules of society. Marlowe adds to the fun by showing that Malta is itself corrupt: the Christians are no better than the Jews and so the play acquires a specific satirical edge. Alleyn's acting must have been both a comic performance and a frightening demonstration of the power of an unscrupulous tactician.

Two years later Robert Greene produced another outsize part for Alleyn, the title role in *Orlando Furioso*. The plot is insignificant; the episodes allow the hero to brag in war and languish in love until jealousy turns him mad. Between bouts of ranting and railing he pulls the leg off an innocent shepherd and uses it to beat back the 'Duke of Aquitaine and Soldiers' (II.i.). Later he breaks a fiddle over the head of its owner before a witch charms him to sleep to cure his distraction. When he awakes he slaughters an evil magician and Angelica his love is restored to him. With its spectacle, music, dances, kitchen humour, and feigned combats the play derives from folk games and tales and is the precursor of modern pantomime.

Games that call on a player's performing skills can appear in scenes that seem most naturalistic, scenes that would seem to depend on exact mimicry. As an example we might take Launce's first scene with his dog in Act II of *The Two Gentlemen of Verona* (1593). Launce speaks prose, his dog is an emblem of naturalness in the play, and the account of Launce's hysterically weeping family seems to set off the fine sentiments and noble dolours that afflict Proteus and Valentine. And yet the scene calls for the player to mount a kind of puppet-show using his shoes for his parents, his staff for his sister, his hat for the maid.

On a more complex level we might examine a much neglected scene in *Richard II* (V.iii.), the scene in which the Duke of York comes to the newly crowned Bolingbroke to beg the death of his own son Aumerle whose treachery he has just discovered. His wife enters presently to crave mercy for Aumerle. From that moment until Bolingbroke grants the pardon the scene is written in comic couplets:

YORK: So shall my virtue be his vice's bawd,
　And he shall spend mine honour with his shame.
　As thriftless sons their scraping fathers' gold.
　Mine honour lives when his dishonour dies,
　Or my shamed life in his dishonour lies.
　Thou kill'st me in his life; giving him breath,
　The traitor lives, the true man's put to death.
DUCHESS [*within*]: What ho! My liege, for God's sake, let me in!
BOLINGBROKE: What shrill-voiced suppliant makes this eager cry?
DUCHESS: A woman, and thy aunt, great King – 'tis I.
　Speak with me, pity me, open the door;
　A beggar begs that never begged before.
BOLINGBROKE: Our scene is altered from a serious thing,
　And now changed to 'The Beggar and the King'.
　My dangerous cousin, let your mother in:
　I know she is come to pray for your foul sin.
　[Aumerle unlocks door during York's speech]
YORK: If thou do pardon whosoever pray,
　More sins for this forgiveness prosper may.
　[Enter Duchess]
　This festered joint cut off, the rest rest sound;
　This let alone will all the rest confound. (ll. 67–86)

'The Beggar and the King' is probably an allusion to the ballad of King Cophetua and the Beggar-maid but the passage is a reminder that fighting for the crown has to do not only with the fate of the nation but with the pattern of fairy stories. Bolingbroke had appeared back on England's coasts as a beggar seeking his patrimony and by a combination of guile and good fortune had been granted more than his expressed wish – the kingdom, in fact. The scene also anticipates the troubles that Bolingbroke will have with his own unthrifty son, the roistering Prince Hal, thus reducing him to a comic mirror for fathers.[23] The motif of beggar and king as well as the riddle of 'setting the word itself against the word' are repeated some eighty lines later in King Richard's speech before his death:

> thoughts of things divine are intermixed
> With scruples, and do set the word itself
> Against the word . . .
>
> Thus play I in one person many people,
> And none contented. Sometimes am I king;
> Then treasons make me wish myself a beggar,
> And so I am . . . (V.v.12–14, 31–4).

The scene indicates a type of acting, allusive, slightly posed, in which the mighty actions of the great might be seen as the strutting and fretting of characters who are only too aware that their roles have taken over their personalities. Players in these mirror scenes or ritual games must recreate the figures or gests of those they reflect to make the point that tragic aspirations in the theatre of the world appear as comic pretensions. (Marlowe achieved this same double perspective by his habit of ending his mighty speeches with lines of deliberate bathos.)

Boy players

Given, then, the inevitable degree of stylization in a drama that was as much related to the patterns of games and revels as it was to the patterns of workaday life, what were the conventions that would seem most unusual to a modern spectator were he to be transported back to an Elizabethan performance? First perhaps would be the rapid pace and continuity of the plays: intervals seem to have been introduced only in private playhouses, possibly because candles had to be frequently trimmed.[24] The pace enabled playwrights to use juxtaposition techniques to the full, to add unobtrusively telling techniques to the showing techniques of mimetic drama. Second was the use of boy players for women's as well as juvenile roles. In fact, as anyone who has seen a modern production in which all the parts are taken by males can testify, problems of disbelief do not occur, as few plays make a claim for pure showing or complete naturalism. The boys joined playing companies between the ages of ten and thirteen and played boys' parts until they were about twenty – not twenty-four as it used to be believed.[25] We must not therefore imagine piping choirboys but mature youths whose voices may not have broken until they were fifteen or sixteen (assuming the onset of puberty to have been considerably later than it is now). Even the youngest boy players were professionals in the sense that they devoted all their time to their craft, and in an age in which one of the chief entertainments at Court had been music and acting by troupes of boys there were traditions of high attainment. The popularity of the boys' companies that were established in the first decade of the seventeenth century in indoor private playhouses – Hamlet's 'little eyases' – is further testimony to their skills, and it may be conjectured that the plays they presented are a final exploitation of the mannerism, an inherent contrast between content and form, that we have seen to be typical of popular drama. It is difficult to believe, however, that on occasions the boys did not provoke a more immediate appeal, flaunt their sexuality and enjoy their travesty roles to the delight of their audiences and the outrage of moralistic members of the community. Shakespeare at least once seems to refer disparagingly to the boys when Cleopatra imagines herself captive and forced to watch a pageant depicting her own life:

> Antony
> Shall be brought drunken forth, and I shall see
> Some squeaking Cleopatra boy my greatness
> I'th'posture of a whore. (V.ii.216–19)

Yet she is referring more to the libel that will be done to her character than to the inability of young players to embody her greatness. Shakespeare would simply not have written her part or, in the 1590s, those of Joan of Arc and Margaret of Anjou if he had not known of young players who could rise to the occasion.

The few female roles in the plays of Marlowe and Greene, on the other hand, are far less demanding, being examples of beauty or pathos (Zenocrate, Queen Isabella) – or theatrical viciousness (Bellamira). A passage from II.i. of *A Looking Glass for London and England* suggests that in heroical romances boys were expected to do little more than wear gorgeous gowns and wigs and recite their lines. The ladies have entered '*in all royalty*':

> ALVIDA: The beauties that proud Paris saw from Troy,
>   Mustering in Ida for the golden ball,
>   Were not so gorgeous as Remilia.
> REMILIA: I have tricked my trammels up with richest balm,
>   And made my perfumes of the purest myrrh:
>   The precious drugs that Egypt's wealth affords,
>   The costly paintings fetched from curious Tyre,
>   Have mended in my face what nature missed.
>   Am I not the earth's wonder in my looks?

ALVIDA: The wonder of the earth, and pride of heaven.
REMILIA: Look, Alvida, a hair stands not amiss;
    For women's locks are trammels of conceit,
    Which do entangle Love for all his wiles. (18–30)

(Obviously this 'iconic' style would not have been appropriate to comedy – *The Comedy of Errors* and *The Taming of the Shrew* were produced within four years of Greene's play.) Costumes appropriate to this scene must have restricted natural movements and dictated stylized gestures – a help to young players. The large number of climactic scenes in which women appear mad or distracted is probably due to the fact that the stylized playing they demand was more accessible to boys than was naturalism. 'Breeches parts' (boys playing girls playing boys) became common only after the turn of the century, presumably because of the developing skills of the boy players. One of the prototypes and best of these parts, Shakespeare's Joan of Arc in *1 Henry VI*, demands both gestic and naturalistic playing. She probably wore a blonde wig as a Venerean figure – she was 'black and swart before' (I.ii.84) – and her role demands the wiliness and energy that we associate with major male roles.

Make-up and costumes

The passage from Greene is one of the few pieces of evidence of the use of make-up by Elizabethan public players. Encouraged by the example of the ageing Queen, Court ladies had begun to paint their faces in the 1590s – the practice is satirized in III.ii. of Marston's *Antonio and Mellida* – and the boy players presumably followed suit. Cosmetics, including white lead, were certainly available, but there is very little known about whether the adult players used make-up. If they did, it was probably only for the boldest effects, to create moral types and not for niceties of character. Ghosts' faces were whitened with flour and David Bevington detected two examples of cosmetics being applied on stage as symbols of corruption: 'In *Marriage of Wit and Wisdom* [1568] . . . Wantonness and Idleness blacken Wit's face as he lies asleep. When in *Three Ladies of London* [1581] Conscience falls from her state of moral purity, the stage directions specify "*Here let Lucre open the box, and dip her finger in it, and spot Conscience' face*".'[26] On the other hand there is plenty of evidence for the use of false beards, either for emblematic scenes as in *The Golden Age* where we find '*Enter Saturn with hair and beard overgrown*',[27] or as the most convenient and quick way to effect a disguise. Beards seem to have been glued rather than hooked on,[28] but audiences used to doubling may have been easily able to accept the simplest of disguises and even enjoy the quick-change of a new hat and cloak and an obviously false beard.

If the disguising of the face was crude by modern standards of naturalism, the disguising of the body, the costumes worn by the players, represented true examples of Elizabethan magnificence. Henslowe's inventory of apparel (1602) indicates their lavishness:[29]

1 A scarlett cloke wth ij brode gould Laces: w^t gould buttens of the sam downe the sids

2 . . . A scarlett cloke Layd [the] downe w^t silver Lace and silver buttens . . .

His papers indicate their great value and his accounts reveal that he spent more on costumes than on properties and could spend more on a single costume than on the script for a play. The richness of the players' appearance is referred to in puritan attacks and travellers' reports. So Platter in 1599:[30]

The comedians are most expensively and elegantly apparelled, since it is customary in England, when distinguished gentlemen or knights die, for nearly the finest of their clothes to be made over and given to their servants, and as it is not proper for them to wear such clothes but only to imitate them, they give them to the comedians to purchase for a small sum.

Not all costumes, however, were inherited in this way for some were obviously made for specific plays. Henslowe's inventory contains a list of what he calls 'Antik sutes' which besides 'a red velvett hors mans cote' itemises 'daniels gowne' and 'will somers cote':[31] a play of *Daniel in the Lion's Den* was performed in Nördlingen by English players in 1604,[32] and there may have been a revival of Nashe's *Summer's Last Will and Testament* before the Queen in 1600.[33] Presumably 'antik sutes' also included costumes for allegorical personages like those who appear in the dumb shows we have already examined. The costume of Rumour 'painted full of tongues' who is prologue to *2 Henry IV* is of this kind.

As there was no attempt to represent a particular place on the playhouse stages, so there was seldom any attempt to represent a particular time in the players' dress. Costume in fact was a language, a system of signs, whose meanings derived from its own codes and not from congruence with reality. The engraving of Alleyn as Tamburlaine shows him bravely dressed, and if the cut of his costume is meant to be 'Scythian' it corresponds to an Elizabethan notion of exoticism and not to any knowledge of what the natives of those parts actually wore (Plate 9). Henslowe's 1598 inventory specifies the richness and not the fashion of his clothes: it mentions his 'cotte with coper lace' and his 'breches of crymson vellvet'.[34] Two generations later a playwright was to remember these years as an age of

doublets with stuffed bellies and big sleeves,
And those trunk-hose which now our life doth scorn.

(Heywood, Epistle to 1637 edition of *The Royal King*, 1602)

1 Detail from 'The View of the Cittye of London from the North towards the South', an engraving found in the manuscript journal of Abram Booth (*c.* 1599). Library of the University of Utrecht

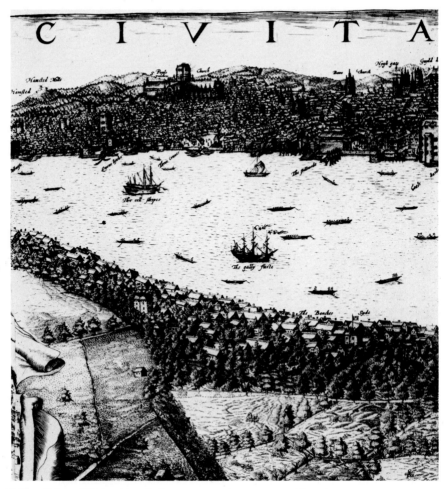

2 Detail from 'Civitas Londini', an engraved panorama of London by John Norden (1600). Royal Library, Stockholm

3 *(opposite)* Details from J. C. Visscher, 'Londinum Florentissima Britanniae Urbs' (Amsterdam, 1616). British Museum

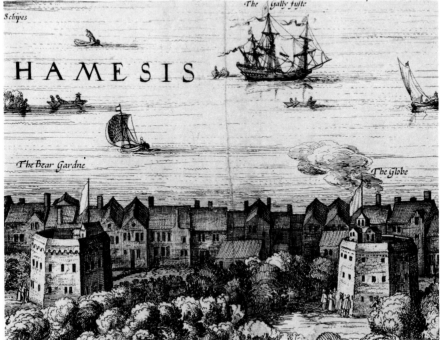

4 Detail from Wenceslaus Hollar, 'Long View of London'
(*c.* 1642). British Museum (the labels for the 'Beere bayting'
and 'The Globe' are transposed)

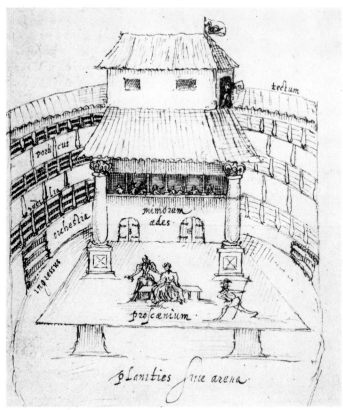

5 A sketch of the Swan (1596) by Arnoldus Buchelius after a
drawing by De Witt. Library of the University of Utrecht

6 Detail from Pieter Brueghel the Younger's 'Village Fair'. Auckland City Art Gallery (the book-holder is standing behind the curtain)

7 Fludd's *Theatrum Orbis,* from his *Ars Memoriae* (1623). Folger Shakespeare Library

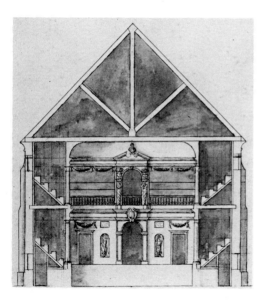

8 Plans by Inigo Jones (for the
conversion of the Cockpit in
Drury Lane in 1616?).
Worcester College, Oxford

The engraving bears the encircling inscription: TAMERLANES TARTARORVM IMPER. POTENTISS. IRA DEI ET TERROR ORBIS APPELATVS OBIIT AN° 1402

LAWRANCE IOHNSONN. SCVLP:

9 Edward Alleyn as Tamburlaine, from Richard Knolles's *A Generall Historie of the Turkes* (1603). British Library

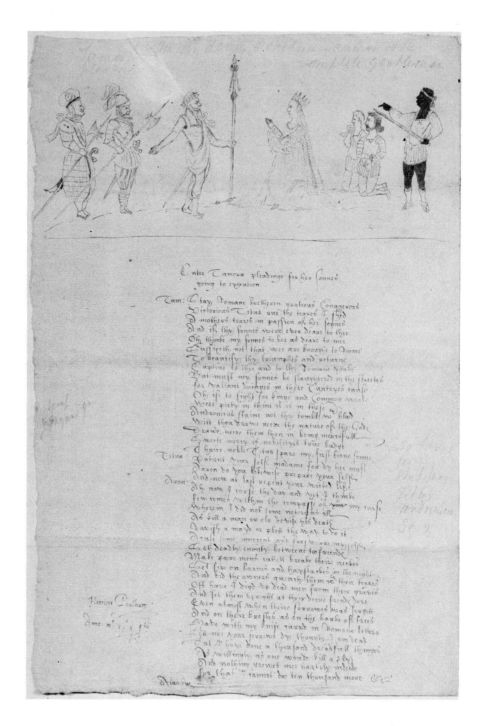

10 Drawing of Titus Andronicus, attributed to Henry Peacham (*c.* 1595). Library of the
Marquess of Bath

The picture here set down
within this letter. T.
A right doth shew the formes
of Tharlton vnto the shap

When hee in pleasaunt wise
the Counterfet expreste
of Clowne w coote of russet
and sturtups w v reste, hem.

Whose merry many mad,
when he appeard in sight
The graue and wise as well as
at him did take delight, rude.

The partie nowe is gone,
and closlie clad in claye,
Of all the Iesters in the land,
he bare the praise awaie.

Now hath he plaid his pte,
and sure he is of this.
If he in Christe did dieto liue
with him in lasting blis.

11 John Scottowe, Portrait of Richard Tarlton (1588?). British Library

12 Title-page to the 1615 edition of *The Spanish Tragedy*. British Library

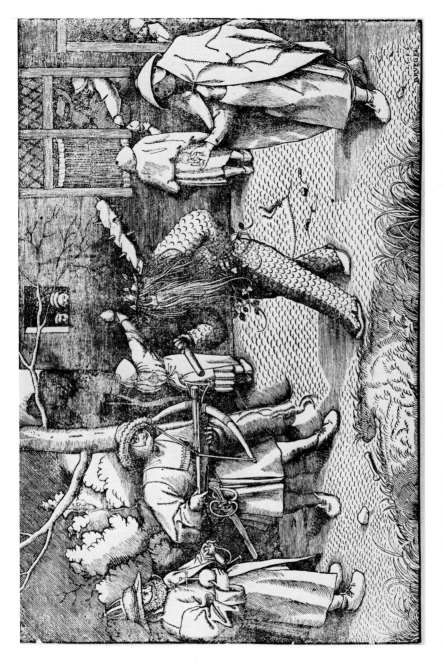

13 Pieter Brueghel the Elder, 'Mascarade D'Ourson et de Valentin'. Bibliothèque royale, Brussels

14 Title-page to the 1624 edition of *Doctor Faustus*. British Library

The Peacham drawing does show some attempt at Roman costume for Titus, but the soldiers are clearly wearing Elizabethan costumes (Plate 10).[35] Similarly there are references in *Woodstock* to medieval shoes with long pointed toes. The inference we might draw is that occasionally a sort of 'costume property' might have been added to a standard Elizabethan costume. Money was certainly spent on elaborate dress for those who played leading roles, but these garments were used to define the natures of those that wore them rather than mark the period of the play. The scarlet of Tamburlaine and the frieze of Woodstock are obviously emblematic of their natures. Minor characters were costumed out of the company's stocks – there can have been no question in the Elizabethan repertory system of finding a uniform style for each production. Many parts required conventional or vocational costumes: characters of high degree wore robes with heraldic or ecclesiastical emblems, the ceremonial dress of the present rather than fancy dress from the past. Kings wore crowns, devils wore horns, doctors' gowns were of scarlet, lawyers' gowns of black, rustics and clowns wore 'startups' (boots that reached to mid-calf), allowed fools wore long coats of motley woven of coarse wool and particoloured green and yellow 'in the weave of the material and not in the cut of the coat';[36] virgins wore white, prologues wore black with a crown of bays, ghosts wore leather pilches[37] (garments made of skins dressed with hair), shepherds wore white coats and carried staff and bottle, sailors wore canvas suits, servants blue coats or slops. Henslowe's inventory lists 'a robe for to goo invisibell',[38] presumably something like the 'shape [costume] invisible' worn by Ariel in *The Tempest* (IV.i.185). Faustus went invisible with a simple girdle (III.ii.17–18). Other costumes were those found in popular chapbooks: as Baskerville pointed out, 'the fact that the ragged garb indicated for daemonic figures at an early period in the term ragman was used in Shakespeare's time for both rogue and goblin is evident from Forman's description of Autolycus as "the Rog. that cam in all tottered like coll pixci".'[39] Colle- or Colt-pixies were hobgoblins which led horses astray into bogs (*OED*). Obviously such costumes served a useful function in identifying characters quickly as they entered.

Players wearing costumes of this kind would have had no difficulty in presenting themselves to their spectators as characters from allegory. In V.iii. of *A Looking Glass for London and England* the prophet Jonas watches while a serpent devours the vine that formed the arbour under which he was resting. The spectacle may have been effected by drawing the arbour back into the discovery space from which it had been thrust out, a dragon's mouth having been set up behind the doors in the meanwhile. A late Red Bull play, the anonymous *The Two Noble Ladies* (1622), depicts the drowning of two soldiers who were dragging away a young woman. She is rescued by a young hero, and the soldiers' lines: 'What strange noise is this –

Dispatch, the tide swells high' are accompanied by the stage directions: '*Thunder. Enter two Tritons with silver trumpets. The Tritons seize the soldiers . . . The Tritons drag them in sounding their trumpets.*'[40] Battles too were sometimes done with an almost equal degree of symbolism, as in V.i. of *3 Henry VI* where no fewer than five armies with drum and colours cross the stage in a passage of sixty lines of dialogue. Players thus dressed could equally take part in scenes of pure naturalism, scenes that they shared with animals. The stage directions in III.ii. of *Woodstock* leave us in no doubt that the 'spruce courtier' from Richard II's court actually enters on horseback, possibly into the playhouse yard. Whether horses were used in I.iii. of *Richard II* or whether the players used hobby-horses as they had done in a court play *Paris and Vienne* (1572) – and as they did in John Barton's 1974 production at Stratford – there is no way of knowing.[41] Finally we might conjecture that this mode of costuming affects our notion of stage soliloquy. As a character was not fixed in a particular time or place by setting or dress, a player did not have to adopt the nineteenth-century convention of treating soliloquies as if they were moments at which a character was talking to himself. Instead he might as it were talk 'through' the costume directly to the audience. The opening soliloquy of *Richard III* demands direct address; it is a skilled piece of rhetoric in which the character attempts to justify his villainy by sophistical reasoning. The soliloquies of Benedick in *Much Ado* are much funnier if they are delivered directly to the audience, and Peter Brook in his 1978 production underlined the debilitating honesty of Antony by having him tell the audience the truth directly in the soliloquies of Act IV.

Clowns and tragedians

We have seen how conditions of performance and certain elements in literary theory combined to produce an acting style different from that modern audiences are familiar with in today's highly directed and much rehearsed productions of Renaissance plays or in contemporary drama which is often based on naturalistic assumptions. A third factor was the personalities of the players themselves. Then as now spectators went to the theatre to see well-known players in famous roles: pleasure at such perform-ances comes not from mere recognition but from a more conscious admira-tion of the familiar player's skills and perhaps from awakened memories of his past performances. The first Elizabethan player to achieve real fame was the clown Richard Tarlton. He flourished as a member of the Lord Chamberlain's and Queen's Men from the 1570s until his death in 1588. Tarlton's descendants are to be found in clubs and music halls today: he began with an appearance distinctive enough to cause laughter when he merely appeared. He was of squat build with curly hair, a squint, and a squashed nose (Plate 11). He made art out of the folk forms of his time which he incorporated into the jigs that made him famous. But he was most celebrated for his extemporal wit. He would cap interruptions from the audience with a jest, make up verses to compliment the Queen before whom he often played, or return the insults thrown at him from the crowd in the playhouses – probably in order to tap this very wit. An example is given in Tarlton's Jests:[42]

At the Bull in Bishopsgate Street where the Queen's Players oftentimes played, Tarlton coming on the stage, one from the gallery threw a pippin at him. Tarlton took up the pip, and, looking on it, made this sudden jest:

Pip in, or nose in, choose you whether,
Put yours in, ere I put in the other.
Pippin you have put in: then, for my grace,
Would I might put your nose in another place.

His stock role was that of a rustic clown, and in the preface to *Tarlton's News* (1590) the ghost of the comedian is presented as appearing to the author 'attired in russet, with a buttoned cap on his head, a great bag by his side, and a strong bat in his hand, so artificially attired for a clown as I began to call Tarlton's wonted shape [costume] to remembrance'.[43] Obviously he appeared as much as himself as the 'characters' that he played.

Another anecdote from *Tarlton's Jests* reveals how he could exploit his fame – and reminds us of the knockabout elements in Elizabethan comedy:[44]

At the Bull at Bishopsgate was a play of Henry the Fifth [*The Famous Victories*, not Shakespeare's play], wherein the judge was to take a box on the ear; and because he was absent that should take the blow, Tarlton himself, ever forward to please, took upon him to play the same judge, besides his own part of the clown: and Knell then playing Henry the Fifth hit Tarlton a sound box indeed, which made the people laugh the more because it was he; but anon the judge goes in, and immediately Tarlton in his clown's clothes comes out and asks the actors what news: 'O', saith one, 'hadst thou been here, thou shouldest have seen Prince Henry hit the judge a terrible box on the ear.' 'What, man,' said Tarlton, 'strike a judge?' 'It is true, yfaith,' said the other. 'No other like,' said Tarlton, 'and it could not be but terrible to the judge, when the report so terrifies me, that me thinks the blow remains still on my cheek that it burns again.' The people laugh at this mightily: and to this day, I have heard it commended for rare; but no marvel, for he had many of these.

The Stage-keeper in the Induction to *Bartholomew Fair* remembers one of his famous comic routines:

you should ha' seen him ha' come in, and ha' been cozened i' the
cloth-quarter, so finely! And Adams [a fellow Queen's Men player], the
rogue, ha' leap'd and capered upon him, and ha' dealt his vermin about,
as though they had cost him nothing. And then a substantial watch to ha'
stolen in upon 'em, and taken 'em away, with mistaking words, as the
fashion is, in the stage-practice. (39–45)

A passage from the bad Quarto of *Hamlet* (1603) reveals both how clowns
would stuff their routines with 'gag', crosstalk and catch phrases, but also
how the best jests were extemporized in the manner of which Tarlton was
obviously a master:

HAMLET: Let not your clown speak
   More than is set down; there be of them, I can tell you,
   That will laugh themselves to set on some
   Quantity of barren spectators to laugh with them
   Albeit there is some necessary point in the play
   Then to be observed: O, 'tis vile, and shows
   A pitiful ambition in the fool that useth it.
   And then you have some again that keeps one suit
   Of jests, as a man is known by one suit of
   Apparel, and gentlemen quotes his jests down
   In their tables, before they come to the play, as thus:
   'Cannot you stay till I eat my porridge?' and 'You owe me
   A quarter's wages', and 'My coat wants a cullison [badge]',
   And 'Your beer is sour' and, blabbering with his lips
   And thus keeping in his cinquepace of jests,
   When, God knows, the warm clown cannot make a jest
   Unless by chance, as the blind man catcheth a hare:
   Masters tell him of it. (Sig. F1ᵛ–F2ʳ)

And yet it is a mistake to think that the literary sophistication of plays like
Hamlet drove such popular figures from the stage. In fact Shakespeare
created in one of his last plays, *The Winter's Tale*, the part of Autolycus
which calls for the kind of performance that the great Elizabethan clowns
were able to give. The other renowned Elizabethan clown was William
Kempe, famous for his jigs as well as for his feat of dancing a morris from
London to Norwich. His name has crept in to the speech prefixes of *Romeo
and Juliet* (IV.v.) and *Much Ado* (IV.ii.) so that we know that he played
Peter in the one play and Dogberry in the other. He is introduced as a
character in *2 Return from Parnassus* to instruct a budding actor and is given
a virtuoso piece of chop-logic on the duty the ignorant owe to their
superiors. It is safe to conjecture that such players were type cast and that
playwrights wrote parts with their particular skills in mind.

The same cannot be said of the great tragic players of the day. The first of
these, and the first player to achieve a great social success, was Edward

Alleyn who founded Dulwich College and left a fortune to maintain it. He was the creator of Marlowe's greatest parts, of Tamburlaine, Barabas, and Faustus. He probably played Orlando in Greene's *Orlando Furioso* and possibly Hieronimo in *The Spanish Tragedy*.[45] He was tall, of commanding presence, and when he appeared as the Genius of the City in the coronation procession of 15 March 1604 he was commended for his 'excellent action' and 'well tuned audible voice'.[46] He lived until 1626 but retired from the stage about 1605. He did after that date, however, maintain his financial investments in the theatre – he owned the Fortune. Alleyn played roles that give little sense of the ebbs and flows of character's consciousness. The personages are created from without and participate in scenes that are often tableaux, 'speaking pictures', as emblems were designated in contemporary criticism. His skills must therefore have lain in his capacity for speaking verse and in a kind of 'action' that must have been devoted to the creation of gests hard in outline, attitudes that captured the essence of the role. At its worst this style must have approached what Jonson remembered as 'scenical strutting and furious vociferation'; at its best spectacle could, in the words of Dekker in the Prologue to *The Whore of Babylon* (1606), 'reach the mystery'.[47]

His successor in the esteem of the public, the great Richard Burbage, was, early in his career (1584?–1619), playing similar parts. He too played Hieronimo and also Richard III but then was the first Hamlet, Lear, and Othello. From a modern point of vantage these latter roles seem to demand a more modulated acting style and offer more room for 'interpretation', for particular vocal delivery or for the insertion of pieces of business that give specific definition to the part. Burbage was indeed celebrated for his Protean qualities and a famous elegy describes his capacity for suiting his part to the life:[48]

> He's gone and with him what a world are dead,
> Which he revived, to be revivèd so.
> No more young Hamlet, old Heironimo,
> Kind Lear, the grievèd Moor, and more beside,
> That lived in him, have now for ever died.
> Oft have I seen him leap into the grave,
> Suiting the person which he seemed to have
> Of a sad lover with so true an eye,
> That there I would have sworn he meant to die.
> Oft have I seen him play this part in jest,
> So lively, that spectators and the rest
> Of his sad crew, whilst he but seemed to bleed,
> Amazed, thought even then he died in deed.

Yet he played his most pathetical parts 'in jest' – it is notable that both Alleyn and Burbage played parts that demand a sardonic wit (Tamburlaine and Hamlet are examples): both were capable of standing apart from their roles and may have been more similar than is sometimes imagined. They may have *looked* very different as the old Tudor padded costumes were replaced by the 'nicer' clothes of the Jacobeans that fitted the body more closely. In fact, however, Burbage may have drawn on the formal techniques of Alleyn when he played Hieronimo as well as the skills of mimicry and quick wit and action that are demanded by the parts he took in Jonson's comedies: he was certainly not type-cast in parts like Hamlet.

Shakespeare, Marlowe – and Brecht

It is from *Hamlet* in fact that we get one of the most illuminating glimpses of the acting techniques of the 1590s. It comes in the speech that the Prince imperfectly remembers when he first encounters the players. It matches the style and subject of Marlowe's *Dido Queen of Carthage*:

> The rugged Pyrrhus, he whose sable arms,
> Black as his purpose, did the night resemble
> When he lay couched in the ominous horse,
> Hath now this dread and black complexion smeared
> With heraldry more dismal; head to foot
> Now is he total gules, horridly tricked
> With blood of fathers, mothers, daughters, sons,
> Baked and impasted with the parching streets,
> That lend a tyrannous and damned light
> To their lord's murder. Roasted in wrath and fire,
> And thus o'er-sized with coagulate gore,
> With eyes like carbuncles, the hellish Pyrrhus
> Old grandsire Priam seeks . . .
>   Anon he finds him
> Striking too short at Greeks; his antique sword,
> Rebellious to his arm, lies where it falls,
> Repugnant to command. Unequal matched,
> Pyrrhus at Priam drives, in rage strikes wide;
> But with the whiff and wind of his fell sword
> Th'unnerved father falls. Then senseless Ilium,
> Seeming to feel this blow, with flaming top
> Stoops to his base, and with a hideous crash
> Takes prisoner Pyrrhus' ear. For, lo! his sword,
> Which was declining on the milky head
> Of reverend Priam, seemed i'th'air to stick.
> So, as a painted tyrant, Pyrrhus stood

And, like a neutral to his will and matter,
Did nothing.
But as we often see, against some storm,
A silence in the heavens, the rack stand still,
The bold winds speechless, and the orb below
As hush as death, anon the dreadful thunder
Doth rend the region; so, after Pyrrhus' pause,
A roused vengeance sets him new a-work;
And never did the Cyclops' hammers fall
On Mars's armour, forged for proof eterne,
With less remorse than Pyrrhus' bleeding sword
Now falls on Priam . . . (II.ii.446–86)

The first thing that we might notice about this is that Shakespeare is giving us yet another perspective upon Hamlet the revenger, another 'figure' to set beside those of Laertes and Fortinbras. If Shakespeare intended some element of parody or burlesque it is subservient to what Coleridge described as 'the substitution of the epic for the dramatic',[49] as Hamlet contemplates a man who, after pausing in his revenge, fell to his task with cold-blooded resolution. But what features of Marlowe's dramaturgy are defined here? First we have an example of playwriting in which character is rendered almost wholly from outside. The audience concentrates on the role being played and is scarcely inward with any motive or cue for action. Pyrrhus is a living emblem, a bejewelled and grotesque icon whose nature is defined by his appearance. He is a construct of art not an imitation of nature, the summation of the tradition embodied in the allegories of Spenser, the incarnation of the *idea* of a tyrant, a nightmare monster.

Marlowe's characters were frequently dressed as emblems. Their symbolic costumes contributed to the meaning of the play and provided the audience with an intimation of its outcome. As we have seen, Tamburlaine lays by his shepherd's weeds and dons a suit of armour and a curtle-axe, 'adjuncts' or tokens that anticipate his career as a scourge and slaughterer, and Doctor Faustus wore a cross and surplice to register the degree of his unorthodoxy. But the fullest description of a Marlovian character comes, not surprisingly, from a poem rather than a play since in the poem the author describes in words what was immediately seen by the audience in the playhouse. It is the description of Hero we find at the beginning of *Hero and Leander*, a passage, we may note, in the very mode of the description of Pyrrhus:

The outside of her garments were of lawn,
The lining purple silk, with gilt stars drawn;
Her wide sleeves green, and bordered with a grove
Where Venus in her naked glory strove
To please the careless and disdainful eyes

Of proud Adonis, that before her lies;
Her kirtle blue, whereon was many a stain,
Made with the blood of wretched lovers slain.
Upon her head she ware a myrtle wreath,
From whence her veil reached to the ground beneath:
Her veil was artificial flowers and leaves,
Whose workmanship both man and beast deceives.
Many would praise the sweet smell as she past,
When 'twas the odour which her breath forth cast;
And there for honey bees have sought in vain,
And, beat from thence, have lighted there again.
About her neck hung chains of pebble-stone,
Which, lightened by her neck, like diamonds shone.
She ware no gloves; for neither sun nor wind
Would burn or parch her hands, but to her mind,
Or warm or cool them, for they took delight
To play upon those hands, they were so white.
Buskins of shells, all silvered, usèd she,
And branched with blushing coral to the knee;
Where sparrows perched, of hollow pearl and gold,
Such as the world would wonder to behold:
Those with sweet water oft her handmaid fills,
Which, as she went, would cherup through the bills.
Some say, for her the fairest Cupid pined,
And, looking in her face, was strooken blind.
But this is tue; so like was one the other,
As he imagined Hero was his mother . . . (ll. 9–40)

Hero is 'all art': there is nothing in the description to give us her 'character' but only details that define her role. The references to Venus and to the blood-stained kirtle prefigure the story of Leander, the elaborateness of the costume complete with mechanical buskins (admittedly it is unlikely that any boy player ever wore such things) matches the hyperbolic description of her person. The bathos – the bees that plagued her lips and the Gilbertian feminine rhyme that ends the quotation – keeps Marlowe quite aloof from his subject. Hero has been frozen into significance and the story can proceed without dallying around the inward life of the character and can concentrate on the comedy of the tragedy. Everything is directed towards the consolidation of Marlowe's vision, nothing is superfluous. As Hamlet reported when he was thinking about the Pyrrhus play, 'I remember one said there were no sallets in the lines to make the matter savoury, nor no matter in the phrase that might indict the author of affection; but called it an honest method, as wholesome as sweet, and by very much more handsome than fine' (II.ii.435ff.).

The most interesting part of the Pyrrhus speech, however, a part that shows how brilliantly Shakespeare was defining his own art against that of Marlowe, comes when Shakespeare makes Pyrrhus delay, cuts short the action of his sword-stroke:

So, as a painted tyrant, Pyrrhus stood
And, like a neutral to his will and matter,
Did nothing. (II.ii.474–6)

Shakespeare has in fact isolated one of the most salient features of Marlowe's dramatic technique, his habit of interrupting the action, displacing its course, so that new perspectives or 'speaking pictures' are quickly built up, often focusing on a frozen gesture like the one that Shakespeare describes. The 'painted' image of the tyrant is an eidetic image that will etch itself into the consciousness of the spectators, cause them to both wonder at the art that so captured the savagery of Pyrrhus and think about the morality of slaughter and revenge. Shakespeare was to expand the technique – so many of his scenes depict interrupted ceremonies.[50]

We can see the technique at work if we analyse the opening of *Edward II*. First we see Gaveston jetting it with joy as he reads a letter from Edward his minion that has summoned him back to England. His dreams of passion and power are interrupted by a tableau of three Poor Men: 'Why, there are hospitals for such as you' sums up his reaction, and he returns to dream upon the wanton masques and entertainments by which he means to 'draw the pliant King which way I please' (l. 52). This vision of high Renaissance art, pleasant in its way, is in turn interrupted by the entrance of the King and his lords engaged in dreary self-seeking power squabbles. The only touch of loyalty or affection in the sequence comes when Gaveston comes forward to embrace his lord.

Marlowe is using theatrical techniques that are now familiar to cinema audiences, montage techniques, in fact. Many dramatists have formalized the spectacular elements of their plays in an attempt to make them strange, wondrous, frightening, or emblematic of social or moral values. They have played word against spectacle, have broken dramatic sequences into memorable images (it is worth remembering here that 'image' in Elizabethan English designates a statue rather than a painting) or into gestural patterns that might be viewed from alternative and clearly defined moral positions by the spectators. Walter Benjamin gives us a succinct account of how Brecht found a way through interruption to a new kind of unity:

The task of the epic theater, according to Brecht, is not so much the development of actions as the representation of conditions. This presentation does not mean reproduction as the theoreticians of Naturalism understood it. Rather, the truly important thing is to discover the conditions of life. (One might say just as well: to alienate [*verfremden*] them.) This discovery (alienation) of conditions takes place through the interruption of happenings. The most primitive example would be a family scene. Suddenly a stranger enters. The mother was just about to seize a bronze bust and hurl it at her daughter; the father was in the act of opening the window in order to call a policeman. At that moment the stranger appears in the doorway. This means that the stranger is confronted with the situation as with a startling picture: troubled faces, an open window, the furniture in disarray. But there are eyes to which even more ordinary scenes of middle-class life look equally startling.

This passage is followed by a passage on 'The Quotable Gesture':[51]

'Making gestures quotable' is one of the substantial achievements of the epic theater. An actor must be able to space his gestures the way a type-setter produces spaced type. This effect may be achieved, for instance, by an actor's quoting his own gesture on the stage. Thus we saw in *Happy End* how Carola Neher, acting a sergeant in the Salvation Army, sang, by way of proselytizing, a song in a sailors' tavern that was more appropriate there than it would have been in a church, and then had to quote this song and act out the gestures before a council of the Salvation Army. Similarly, in *The Measure Taken* the party tribunal is given not only the report of the comrades, but also the acting out of some of the gestures of the comrade they are accusing. What is a device of the subtlest kind in the epic theater generally becomes an immediate purpose in the specific case of the didactic play. Epic theater is by definition a gestic theater. For the more frequently we interrupt someone in the act of acting, the more gestures result.

Brecht's technique is like Marlowe's technique:[52] just as the audience is getting used to the roll of the mighty line it is interrupted – by bathos often, or by the entrance of a new kind of character – and the spectators are forced to take stock. The spectacle is suddenly ionized or, to change the metaphor, arranges itself into an icon. In the subplots of Elizabethan plays clowns must have quoted the gestures of the leading characters. This kind of acting makes particular demands upon the player: he cannot be naturalistic but must do two things, play the character and define the role, that is, comment by gesture or inflexion on what he is doing as he does it. In this he could draw upon the audience's knowledge of himself: a great player like Alleyn could assume not simply that his audience had come to see Tamburlaine but to see Alleyn playing Tamburlaine. The 'star system' was part of the play.

Speaking the speech

In conclusion, what might the speaking of verse have sounded like? This is the most elusive feature of Elizabethan performances. It is possible that the great feats of memory that Elizabethan players were called upon to perform encouraged them to fix at points in long speeches somewhat mannered cadences to serve as mnemonic devices. Certainly the way in which catch phrases from the stage passed into the common language or were parodied suggests that lines like 'Hieronimo, go by' or 'Eyes, no eyes, but fountains filled with tears' were delivered in a manner fairly remote from the rhythms of common speech. It is also probable that Elizabethan players were more conscious than modern ones of the rhetorical structures of their speeches. The opening soliloquy of Richard III, for example, is structured as an enthymeme, the rhetorician's equivalent of the logician's syllogism. It falls into three parts, two premises reducible to 'Only lovers prosper in times of peace' and 'I am not shaped to be a lover' and a conclusion with its corollary 'Therefore in these times I cannot prosper' so 'I am determined to be a villain' (l. 30). A player may well have emphasized the turns of the argument, marked at line 14 by 'But I . . .' and at line 28 by 'And therefore . . .' more than his modern counterpart. So too the rhetorical figures, especially anaphora – the pronoun 'I' is repeated three times early in the line – serve both as mnemonic device and as a measure of dramatic rhythm. But it is unlikely that the best Elizabethan players adopted the habit of exercising what must have been pleasant well-trained voices in cadences that displayed their own virtuosity rather than the sense of the line – a vice that in the 1970s beset Shakespearean actors who were perhaps reacting against the tendency in the decade before to suppress any indications that a lot of Elizabethan drama was written in verse. Hamlet's request to the players to 'speak the speech . . . trippingly on the tongue' and his deprecatory gestures towards the 'mouthing' of common players suggests that he was advocating the use of what is now called 'sustained tone', a technique of verse-speaking in which the breath is exhaled gently and continuously as opposed to being released in intense puffs. In Chapman's children's play, *The Widow's Tears* (1605), it is asked of a player, 'Has not his tongue learned . . . to trip o'th' toe' (III.ii.17–18). The metaphor suggests a musical delivery. Later in *The Actor's Remonstrance* (1634) the pitfalls of this technique, degeneration into sing-song, are suggested: 'we will not entertain any comedian that shall speak his part in a tone as if he did it in derision of the pious'.[53] After the Restoration, Flecknoe remembered Burbage as an actor who could become his character, 'wholly transforming himself into his part, and putting off himself with his clothes, as he never (not so much as in the tiring-house) assumed himself again until the play was done.' And yet this identification was attained not by the player imagining the emotional life of the character and submerging his own personality therein but by having recourse to skills which would enable him to realize the role he had undertaken. Flecknoe continues his description thus:[54]

there [was] as much difference between him and one of our common actors as between a ballad-singer who only mouths it and an excellent singer, who knows all his graces, and can artfully vary and modulate his voice, even to know how much breath he is to give to every syllable. He had all the parts of an excellent orator (animating his words with speaking, and speech with action) his auditors being never more delighted than when he spoke, nor more sorry when he held his peace; yet even then, he was an excellent actor still, never falling in his part when he had done speaking; but with his looks and gesture, maintaining it still unto the height, he imagining *Age quod agis* only spoke to him . . .

Musical delivery would not, of course, have been appropriate for the shouts and cries of battle scenes, or for citizen comedy which is deliberately based upon the patterns of common speech. Yet the Elizabethans had no knowledge of a 'classic' drama: all their plays were written by contempor-aries and the idea of inventing a 'ritualistic' style to cloak some ancient masterpiece while saving their 'natural' talents for the personation of 'real' characters would have been incomprehensible to them. Instead their art depended upon the fusion of skill with spontaneity, the timeless forms of art with the pressures of the present, their capacity for memorizing a part with their gift for extemporization. We cannot know for certain exactly how they performed, and it would be fruitless for a modern company to attempt to recreate the conditions of an Elizabethan band of players as a preliminary to the productions of Renaissance plays: no twentieth-century actor could improvise Elizabethan English. And yet might there not be patterns in the organization of the Elizabethan troupes and the dramaturgy of their plays which might help some contemporary players to realize a drama with some of the liveliness of theirs?

Part Two

Plays

4 · *The Spanish Tragedy*: architectonic design

When he wrote *The Spanish Tragedy* Thomas Kyd not only found a theme that kindled the imagination of his audiences but devised a form that fully and spectacularly utilized the resources and conventions of the popular playhouses of the 1590s. Revenge is a perennial theme in popular literature: in Christian cultures it combines the lure of what is forbidden by religion and society with expectation, surprise, and the suspense of the hunt. It can, moreover, like Kyd's play, exploit the fascination with obsession, madness, and violence that for centuries filled ballads and chapbooks until they were replaced by popular newspapers and films. The play was also topical: like Shakespeare's Henry VI plays and Marlowe's *Edward II*, Kyd's work grew out of the strengthening Renaissance sense of national identity: it dramatized the state of a nation, in particular the way its destinies are shaped by politics, the specific personalities and actions of its rulers. (Lorenzo is the first 'Machiavellian' figure in English drama.) Spain was a Catholic country, England's arch-enemy, a country whose armada had attempted an invasion of England at about the time the play was probably written (see below). Kyd created a sequence of dramatic images that displayed both the magnificence and the ephemerality of a secular and, to the Elizabethans, a totalitarian power, and was thus able to appeal to the chauvinism of native protestants just as Shakespeare did in his dramatization of the defeat of the French in *1 Henry VI*. He mustered the support a mass audience will give to a heroic individual who sets himself against a network of contrivance and corruption – the number of references to the play or affectionately parodic quotations from it show that it occupied the collective consciousness of the Elizabethans in the way that the James Bond films did for a much later generation.

Kyd along with Marlowe and the young Shakespeare had a sense of basic stagecraft that far exceeded that of their predecessors. Kyd's distinctive contribution was his sense of theatrical space. He used the two levels of the stage and gallery, the discovery space, and scenic properties, like the arbour in this play, in an economical and assured way, a way that enabled him not only to dramatize narrative but to create with visual devices as well as words the consciousness of his characters. He exploited the visual frames provided by elements of the tiring-house façade in a manner analogous to that of a film director today, bringing objects and dramatic tableaux into a field and focus shared by both character and spectator. He was able to give the plebeian members of the audience a sampling of the dramatic fare served up at Court – masques, dumb shows, and magniloquent declamations. He domesticated the learned and modernized the antique, even as he incorporated into the play the elements of street theatre and clownage of Pedringano's gallows scene. While attending scrupulously to the design of his plot, he built up archetypal images by using the conventions of dream, and worked towards subconscious layers of response by composing strong speech rhythms familiar in folk forms like ballads, using language as a kind of music, as well as by creating a strong visual pattern of repeated theatrical images.

Kyd was one of the first to learn how the physical arrangement of stage and tiring-house, the spatial relationship between players and spectators, made possible that combination of history and tragedy, the particular and the universal, that gives the popular drama of the Renaissance its distinctive resonances. Medieval drama was anachronistic and timeless: it made no attempt to emphasize the historical truth of its stories but concerned itself with morality and religious symbol. Its scenic devices and costumes were allegorical, its concerns were ethical, and players switched from dramatic dialogue to direct exhortatory address to the audience. Renaissance drama too used non-illusionistic properties and costumes, but the transition from *décor simultané*, playing spaces equipped with mansions that stood unmoved throughout the action (as in *The Castle of Perseverence*), to an empty space (on which similar devices if used might be displayed in sequence as the play unfolded) made possible the writing of plays concerned with time and change, with history. (Mansions could, as we have seen, be introduced into history – as with the tents on Bosworth Field at the end of *Richard III* – to universalize the predicament of the hero.) Although there was no physical division between audience and players in the popular playhouses, the elevation of the stage did create a special world, a world apart, and in this play Kyd seems not to have infringed its boundaries, his sense of the identity of 'Spain', by direct address to the audience. Moreover Kyd, like Marlowe and Shakespeare, found that the sheer size of the new permanent stages and the enlargement of the dramatic companies enabled him to dramatize the fates of nations rather than individuals, and the flexibility of theatrical conventions of time and space enabled him to realize particular moments in the kingdoms of men rather than the eternal presence of the kingdom of God. Particular moments of time and place could be fixed by indications in the dialogue, while the ethical status or freedom of the characters would be revealed by their position in relationship to the tiring-house façade. To put the matter in the crudest terms, personages with a propensity to evil might emerge from the cellarage, those that were not free to prosper, because of their evil actions or the superior power of contriving adversaries, stood beneath the gallery whence they might be regarded with compassion or contempt by classical deities or earthly potentates.

The achievement of *The Spanish Tragedy* was of course to be soon surpassed. It was quickly parodied by dramatists whose verse was more flexible and sophisticated and who could thereby create characters with a greater degree of individuality than any in Kyd's play, as well as scenes that opened on to wider areas of experience than that of the claustrophobic Iberian courts so obviously painted in primary moral colours. Yet that iconic, gestic style, the procession of 'painted tyrants' retained its hold on popular audiences and for some thirty years, from the time of its composition through the first decades of the seventeenth century, *The Spanish Tragedy* was one of the most successful plays of its age.

It must have been in existence by 14 March 1591–2, when Henslowe recorded a performance of 'Jeronymo' at the Rose by Strange's Men and could conceivably have been written shortly after 1582, the date of publication of Watson's *Hecatompathia* which includes a sonnet imitated by Kyd at the opening of II.i. The most judicious review of the problems of dating the play seems to me to be that of Philip Edwards in his introduction to his Revels edition, and he proposes 1590.[1] This uncertainty means that we are unable to work out with any confidence whether the play influenced or was influenced by the works of Marlowe and Shakespeare. What we can demonstrate, however, is that Henslowe's diary indicates that between 1592 and 1597 it was the third most popular play in the repertories of the companies with which he was associated: only *The Jew of Malta* and the lost play *The Wise Man of West Chester* were performed more frequently.[2] After 1597 it is impossible to date any specific performances although the eleven editions of the play up to 1633 bear testimony to its enduring popularity. (Edwards suggests, however, that the seventeenth-century reprints testify to literary interest rather than theatrical revivals.) As well as being performed at the Rose, the fact that the play was the property of Strange's Men means it may have been acted at the Cross Keys Inn, the Theatre, and at Newington Butts. When it became the property of the Admiral's Men it must have been played at the Fortune and if, as seems highly probable, the Induction to *The Malcontent* (1604) and the Elegy on Burbage we examined in Chapter 3 indicate that Burbage played Hieronimo, the play was probably performed by the King's Men at the Curtain, the Globe, and even the second Blackfriars. These are only the London productions: there is evidence from Dekker's *Satiromastix*, IV.i. (1601) that Jonson appeared in it on a provincial tour,[3] and there is a German version which may have been performed on the continent by English players.⁴ (After this period no professional productions are recorded until the play was performed at the Citizens' Theatre in Glasgow in 1978.⁵) Any account of the play's staging therefore can merely define problems and not propound solutions. Although as I have argued it is easy to overemphasize the differences rather than the similarities between the various stages available in London's popular playhouses, some early performances must have taken place without the benefit of a gallery above or a cellarage beneath the stage, so that we must not be too dogmatic about even the most basic blocking of some of the most crucial scenes.

The popularity of the play meant that there were many productions, and these are recorded in variant states of the text. We know that in 1601 and 1602 Henslowe advanced money to Ben Jonson for 'adicians in geronymo'⁶ and in Pavier's edition of 1602 we find five additional passages. The fact that their style is rough and in no way Jonsonian has led editors either to conjecture an earlier revision, possibly for the revival of 1597, or to surmise that the text of the new passages was corrupted by inaccurate and piratical reporting – although there is no reason why Jonson should not have written a sturdy imitation of Kyd's style. Not only has their provenance been suspected but some scholars have thought that these scenes are in fact replacements – as additions they would make the play over-long – modernizations of antiquated material. I shall use these as a first example of the different kinds of evidence which reveal how contemporaries or near-contemporaries reached to Kyd's dramaturgy.

The most revealing as well as the most extensive is the fourth, which is printed between III.xii. and III.xiii. (It may be a replacement for III.xiii. – the similarity of the names of the old man, Bazulto, and the painter, Bazurdo, suggested this hypothesis to the German critic, Schücking.) The importance of the scene lies in Hieronomino's discussion with the painter.

> HIERONIMO: Bazardo! afore God, an excellent fellow! Look you sir, do you see, I'd have you paint me in my gallery, in your oil colours matted, and draw me five years younger than I am – do you see, sir, let five years go, let them go like the marshal of Spain – my wife Isabella standing by me, with a speaking look to my son Horatio, which should intend to this or some such like purpose: 'God bless thee, my sweet son', and my hand leaning upon his head, thus sir, do you see? May it be done?
>
> PAINTER: Very well, sir.
>
> HIERONIMO: Nay, I pray mark me, sir. Then sir, would I have you paint me this tree, this very tree. Canst paint a doleful cry?
>
> PAINTER: Seemingly, sir.
>
> HIERONIMO: Nay, it should cry: but all is one. Well sir, paint me a

youth, run through and through with villains' swords, hanging upon this tree. Canst thou draw a murderer?

PAINTER: I'll warrant you, sir: I have the pattern of the most notorious villains that ever lived in all Spain.

HIERONIMO: O let them be worse, worse: stretch thine art, and let their beards be of Judas his own colour, and let their eye-brows jutty over: in any case observe that. Then sir, after some violent noise, bring me forth in my shirt, and my gown under mine arm, with my torch in my hand, and my sword reared up thus: and with these words:

What noise is this? who calls Hieronimo?

May it be done?

(ll. 117–42)

The paintings he desires are paintings of the moments of high feeling he has enacted and the scene is a digression apologetical for the nature of the play. When Lamb inserted it in his *Specimens* he was probably reacting to it as an example of the Romantics' predilection for painterly poetry – *ut pictura poesis* – but it is more than a flowering of the unknown author's invention. Like the analogous scene between the Painter and Timon in *Timon of Athens* it suggests that we have to do with a species of pageant play, a parade of great theatrical emblems calling for bold gestic acting, 'speaking looks', as characters move towards the brink of caricature. Scenes of passion and violence or, to use important words from the play, 'league and love' (I.v.4), are juxtaposed, and thus became themselves the structuring elements of the drama rather than the plot and intrigue that bind them together. As the Ghost declares in the final scene of the play, 'These were spectacles to please my soul' (IV.v.12).

The other additions amplify the subtitle of the 1615 edition, 'Hieronimo is mad again', although the first and fourth additions contain one other element that is worthy of note. In III.vii. Hieronimo receives from the Hangman Pedringano's letter of confession. After reading it he reflects that he had been unable to believe what had been contained in an earlier letter, the letter that had dropped from Bel-Imperia's place of imprisonment. Hieronimo has just witnessed a macabre scene in which Pedringano goes jestingly to his death, confident until the last moment that the Page's box contains his reprieve. Now Hieronimo reflects:

Now may I make compare, 'twixt hers and this,

Of every accident; I ne'er could find

Till now, and now I feelingly perceive,

They did what heaven unpunished would not leave. (III.vii.53–6)

What the dramatist is implying is that one set of evidence or experience is not enough for belief, or, as Hieronimo calls it, 'feeling perception'. In this play scenes will repeat situations or gests, bringing the audience to the point where it would accept not only the validity of the player's art as a plausible form of experience but the reality of situations that are strange or improbable. Kyd's method of composition, then, is based on analogy, on the creation of *figurae*, and the architectonic arrangement of these gives the play its strong dramatic rhythm.[7]

Further evidence for this notion of scenic structure comes from entries in the *Stationers' Register* and the expanded titles (the forerunners of modern 'blurbs') on the titlepages of early editions, pages that were sometimes pasted up on posts about the city as advertisements. The entry of 6 October 1592 reads: 'A book which is called the Spanish Tragedy of Don Horatio and Bel-Imperia' and the titlepage for the first six editions reads in part: 'The Spanish Tragedy, Containing the lamentable end of Don Horatio, and Bel-Imperia: with the pitiful death of old Hieronimo.' The 1615 edition adds the subtitle and the woodcut depicting one of the most memorable images of the play (Plate 12). Hieronimo bears his torch towards the arbour where the body of his son is hanging. Behind him is Bel-Imperia and behind her in a black mask is Lorenzo with drawn sword. What is notable about these descriptions is that they do not imply only a single hero but see the tragedy as that of a family or dynasty, and suggest that what would sell the play would be a reminder of those great *scenes* in the play that had caught the imagination of the audiences. Like audiences at operas now who anticipate with pleasure favourite arias or pieces of spectacle, the Elizabethans did not see the play only through the eyes of the hero or assume that it was shaped about his consciousness. Rather it was for them a sequence of performed actions. Indeed Kyd may be said to have gained his effect by adding theatrical action to the long declamatory sequences developed by the academic dramatists and English Senecans; to have, in effect, created the 'scene' as the elemental dramatic unit. Without *The Spanish Tragedy* for a model, Shakespeare would not have written a play like *Richard III* in which so many scenes are based around a simple bold incident – or gest – of the kind we have described.

The Spanish Tragedy, then, is a Renaissance artefact, dependent for its effect on the bold architectural symmetry of its dramatic form and the statuesque massiveness of its characters: *Hamlet* belongs to the more painterly modes of Mannerism or the Baroque; details are not always informed by their coherence with a simple design, its climaxes are expressive of fine emotion, and its artful perspectives created by an elaborate series of dramatic analogies open on to spaces filled with realistically presented life, like the scenes with the players and gravediggers. No one could forget that Laertes and Ophelia are brother and sister: who remembers that Lorenzo and Bel-Imperia have the same relationship? Instead therefore of looking for touches of 'felt life' in a play which is impervious to that sort of analysis, I shall be concentrating on the bold movements of its dramatic rhythm and the hard outlines of its theatrical images.

Kyd was remembered by contemporaries not only for the high relief of his scenic construction but for his language. It is easily recognizable as rhetorical in that he often employs the boldest and simplest of the figures of sound: isocolon, or repetition of clauses of approximately the same length, parison, parallel placing of corresponding grammatical units of these clauses, and paramoion, similarity of sound in the parallel clauses. Kyd, who took these academic devices into the popular playhouses, sought from the declamation of his lines a musical and emotional effect. There is a sure sense of simple rhythms in Kyd, and his sound patterns, even if they tend towards the hypnotic, are a compelling part of his dramatic climaxes.[8]

It might be claimed that the rolling rhythms and surging movements of the speeches lead only to mannerism and monotony. Kyd himself gives a description of his manner when Hieronimo claims he wants

<blockquote>
stately-written tragedy,
   Tragedia corthurnata, fitting kings,
   Containing matter, and not common things. (IV.i.159–61)
</blockquote>

Actors prating and braving on buskins (*corthurnata*) cannot hold an audience's attention for long. Yet the declamatory style and high manner of action and gesture that must have marked contemporary productions did not prevent audiences finding their own kind of emotional appeal or lifelikeness in the play. Boas quotes[9] an interesting testimony from the opening scene of Thomas May's *The Heir* (1620):

> ROSCIO: Has not your lordship seen
>   A player personate Hieronimo?
> POLYMETES: By th'mass, 'tis true. I have seen the knave paint grief
>   In such a lively colour that for false
>   And acted passion he has drawn true tears
>   From the spectators. Ladies in the boxes
>   Kept time with sighs and tears to his sad accents
>   As he had truly been the man he seemed.

This ceremony of passion, at once exotic and 'true', seems to have worked precisely by means of the dramatic rhythms I have described.

But Kyd was not remembered just for the loftiest of his sentiments, the grandiloquence of his conceits, what the Wife in *The Knight of the Burning Pestle* called 'huffing parts' (Ind. 73). 'What outcries pluck me from my naked bed?' (II.v.1) might have become a catch phrase, a comedian's invitation to an audience to laugh, but other simpler lines remained in people's minds: the seeming artlessness of Castile's lament, 'It is not now as when Andrea lived' (III.xiv.111) is remembered by Jonson in plays as late as *The Staple of News* (1626) and *The New Inn* (1629). 'Hieronimo beware: go by, go by' (III.xii.31) became the 'stock phrase to imply impatience of anything disagreeable, inconvenient, or old-fashioned'.[10]

Like that of all his contemporaries, Kyd's art is self-conscious in that it

draws attention to its own method. In his conversation with Bazulto
Hieronimo describes an extreme of passion that demands bravura playing:

> Thou art the lively image of my grief:
> Within thy face, my sorrows I may see.
> Thy eyes are gummed with tears, thy cheeks are wan,
> Thy forehead troubled, and thy mutt'ring lips
> Murmur sad words abruptly broken off,
> By force of windy sighs thy spirit breathes,
> And all this sorrow riseth for thy son:
> And selfsame sorrow feel I for my son.
> Come in old man, thou shalt to Isabel,
> Lean on my arm: I thee, thou me shalt stay . . . (III.xiii.162–71)

We may deduce from the 'theatricality' of this that Kyd made no attempt to
pretend that the action of the play was not taking place on the stage. 'Lively'
as we saw in Chapter 3, means energetic, hard in outline. Moreover Kyd
calls, as we shall see, for two players to act the part of spectators, looking
down from above to the action on the stage below. For them the play is 'real'
in that Andrea is satisfied by the acts of revenge that take place, but,
paradoxically, it is also a dream. So we hear at the end of the Ghost's speech
as he describes Proserpine:

> Forthwith, Revenge, she rounded thee in th'ear,
> And bade thee lead me through the gates of horn,
> Where dreams have passage in the silent night.
> No sooner had she spoke but we were here,
> I wot not how, in twinkling of an eye. (I.i.81–5)

There were two gates of sleep in the underworld: through those of ivory,
false visions emerged, through those of horn, true visions. The figure recurs
ironically when Hieronimo, after hearing the outcries at his son's murder,
reasons: 'I did not slumber, therefore 'twas no dream' (II.v.5). The device is
another way of creating the familiar Elizabethan conceit that what is strange
may yet be true, inviting actors to play out the play's conventions with
confidence.

A second device that sets the play firmly within the structure of theatrical
art is apparent in the opening speeches. Following classical example, Kyd
introduced narrative into his plays, and characters are thus called upon to
act as prologue and choruses. Moreover these narratives do not simply use
the third person but employ the device of *prosopopeia* or impersonation. As
in some of Brecht's theatre, a player acting one character has to impersonate
another. So Andrea, narrating his journey to the underworld, tells of his
meeting with the infernal judges, Minos, Aeacus, and Rhadamanth:

> To whom we sooner gan I make approach,
> To crave a passport for my wand'ring ghost,
> But Minos, in graven leaves of lottery,

Drew forth the manner of my life and death.
'This knight,' quoth he, 'both lived and died in love,
And for his love tried fortune of the wars,
And by war's fortune lost both love and life . . .' (I.i.34–40)

Beyond the symmetrical stylization of the verse we notice a deliberate use of archaic formulae ('quoth he') and, more interesting perhaps, self-dramatization as Andrea refers to himself as both 'I' and 'my . . . ghost'. As was characteristic of popular drama, the player remains distinct from the character he plays; he is therefore called upon to tell as well as to show, to indicate by physical gesture and inflexion of voice his and the author's attitude to the genre that is created and to the mode of theatrical illusion.

With regard to the literary dimension of the play, Kyd was bringing to a popular audiences elements of the highest and most aristocratic genres, the epic and the romance. Andrea has ventured in the footsteps of epic heroes through the underworld, Pedringano plays the servant go-between in the love affairs of Bel-Imperia. Kyd was making accessible to the people by his dramatization what had been available only to the most literate. The lines of Latin that stud the play would have been pleasingly familiar to the judicious, exotic fare for the general. They are also related to the conventions of Renaissance emblem books in which a Latin motto was illustrated by an engraving and amplified by verses in the vernacular. Again there is a similarity to Brecht's dramaturgy: the Latin tags or passages resemble the captions he put on stage to turn image to emblem.

Kyd even gave Hieronimo a fourteen-line Latin dirge to recite (II.v.) as he contemplates suicide after the death of his son. Perhaps these lines were there simply to please those with a taste for rhetorical declamation but they also point towards an interesting if not wholly successful experiment with dramatic language. In IV.i. Hieronimo promises the court that the play of Soliman and Perseda will be performed in sundry tongues:

Each of us must act his part
In unknown languages,
That it might breed the more variety.
And you, my lord, in Latin, I in Greek,
You in Italian, and for because I know
That Bel-Imperia hath practisèd the French,
In courtly French shall all her phrases be. (IV.i.172–8)

Although 'variety' was a quality to be striven after – according to the rhetoricians (*OED*, 2c) – 'that it may breed the more variety' is a lame and queer explanation, especially as, according to custom, a 'book' of the play had to be handed to the King as the highest personage present that he at least might follow the action. When we come to the text of the play within the play, however, we find the following note appended:

> *Gentlemen, this play of Hieronimo in sundry languages, was*
> *thought good to be set down in English more largely,*
> *for the easier understanding to every*
> *public reader.* (IV.iv.10)

There are several possible explanations for this: (1) Kyd in fact intended that the play be performed in English; (2) we can take the note at its face value and conjecture that the publisher had the foreign tongues translated for his readers; or (3) that the English version represents a revision by Kyd after puzzlement in the playhouse, or else intervention by another hand, perhaps the author of the additions. After the play within the play, however, the text reads;

Here break we off our sundry languages

And thus conclude I in our vulgar tongue (IV.iv.74–5)

which makes the second conjecture at least plausible. Why, though, should Kyd have essayed this strange device? Perhaps the play was in several languages so that it would appear as though the performers did not know exactly what was afoot, but in performance the device might have a different effect. I have suggested that one of Kyd's great fascinations was for memorable speech-rhythms and cadence and it is possible that he was trying to see whether he could employ a theatre language that would, to the unlettered at least, communicate by its mere sound. Anyone who has enjoyed a performance of a Greek play without knowing the language knows, to his surprise perhaps, how this can happen. The story of Soliman and Perseda is simple enough, after all, to be communicated through mime. What an audience who did not understand the dialogue would experience would be the ritual shape of this inset action and perhaps thereby the mythic dimension of the whole play.[11] It is the culmination of a movement from the pronounced narrative elements of the opening of the play, through the manifest dramatic conflicts and on-stage violent action of the middle, towards a species of music that suggests that the action includes more than merely the characters, that it creates its own mythic order.

Before attending to the unfolding action of the play it is necessary to examine further one final component, Kyd's use of specific dramatic emblems or speaking pictures. These occur with a regular rhythm throughout the play. We see Balthazar marched captive between Lorenzo and Horatio, the Portuguese Viceroy leaving his throne and throwing himself to the ground in grief, the court at a banquet (*cf.* the banquet in *Cambises*, 965–1042) watching Hieronimo's masque of the English champions, Alexandro bound to the stake to be burnt, the hanging of Pedringano, Hieronimo with poniard and rope contemplating suicide, the mad scenes, and the great dumb show in which nuptial torches are dowsed in blood. They need little comment but should not be dismissed as mere pandering to a vulgar taste for inexplicable dumb show and noise. As we have seen, they can serve as structural devices:[12]

> The scenes may remind the audience of a cause and effect relationship: Hieronimo, cutting down the lifeless body of his son (II.v.), and Isabella, cutting down the arbour itself (IV.ii.). The scenes may be in ironic contrast: Hieronimo applauded as the master of the 'device', the show concerning past military exploits, by which the court is entertained in Act One, and Hieronimo applauded for the bloody show of 'Soliman and Perseda' in which Balthazar, Lorenzo, and Bel-Imperia meet death before the eyes of the uncomprehending court ('*King.* Well said, old Marshal, this was bravely done!' IV.iv.68.)

These relationships could have been made by quoting the blocking of the scenes in question. They have also a general effect, for these and many of the other scenes of the play are both artificial, and, for the Elizabethans, examples of the shows of their 'real' world. They have their origins in the pageantry of the court, the street dramas of executions, the illustrations to theological and moral tracts. They are images or icons that combine the everyday and the fictional, the real and the artificial, and which, by this combination, achieve their particular dramatic, eidetic effects. Only recently, through the work of Brecht and Artaud, have dramatic critics been able to react without condescension or embarrassment to the basic satisfaction this kind of popular show can provide. *The Spanish Tragedy* had a subtitle, 'Hieronimo's mad again'; later *Philaster* was to be commonly known by its subtitle, 'Love lies a-bleeding', which was illustrated on its titlepage with a woodcut depicting the Country Gentleman looking proudly upon the wounded princess with Philaster disappearing through the woods. These 'naive' images are the stuff of popular drama.

In 1599 was printed an anonymous domestic tragedy, *A Warning for Fair Women*, acted by the Lord Chamberlain's Men, rivals to Henslowe's company, which contains a parodic Induction, a contest between Tragedy, History, and Comedy, that gives us some clues about the appearance and use of the stage in plays like *The Spanish Tragedy*. (Compare Love, Fortune, and Death who appear in the Induction to *Soliman and Perseda*, a play of about 1590 sometimes attributed to Kyd.) First, as we have seen was customary, the sides of the stage were hung with black:

> The stage is hung with black; and I perceive
> The auditors prepared for tragedy. (ll. 82–3)

Second, Comedy's parody of a tragic performance gives some suggestions as to stylized costumes and ostentatious visual and sound effects:

> How some damned tyrant, to obtain a crown,
> Stabs, hangs, empoisons, smothers, cutteth throats;
> And then a Chorus too comes howling in,

> And tells us of the worrying of a cat,
> Then of a filthy whining ghost,
> Lapt in some foul sheet or a leather pilch,
> Comes screaming like a pig half-sticked,
> And cries, '*Vindicta*, revenge, revenge';
> With that a little rosin flasheth forth
> Like smoke out of tobacco pipe, or a boy's squib;
> Then comes in two or three like to drovers,
> With taylor's bodkins stabbing one another,
> Is not this trim? Is not here goodly things? (ll. 50–62).

The Ghost in fact probably wore a fine silver leather 'pilch' or jacket – in *The White Devil* there is a stage direction '*Enter Bracciano's Ghost, in his leather cassock and breeches*' (V.iv.123) – with a whitened face and, conceivably, a crown – Henslowe listed 'j gostes crown' in 1598.[13] We learn of the make-up from a passage in Thomas Rawlins's *The Rebellion* (1636), where four tailors decide to present *The Spanish Tragedy* before the King of Spain:

> 1: Who shall act the Ghost?
> 3: Why marry that will I – I Vermin.
> 1: Thou dost not look like a Ghost.
> 3: A little players' deceit [and] flour will do't. (V.i.)

Perhaps Kyd was drawing on theatrical memories when a couple of years after writing *The Spanish Tragedy* he has his heroine Cornelia from the play of that name (1594) describe a ghost:

> And lo (me thought) came gliding by my bed
> The ghost of Pompey, with a ghastly look,
> All pale and drawn-fallen, not in triumph borne
> Amongst the conquering Romans, as he used,
> When he (enthronized) at his feet beheld
> Great Emperors fast bound in chains of brass;
> But all amazed, with fearful hollow eyes,
> His hair and beard deformed with blood and sweat,
> Casting a thin coarse linsel [shroud] o'er his shoulders,
> That (torn in pieces) trailed upon the ground;
> And (gnashing of his teeth) unlocked his jaws,
> (Which slightly covered with a scarce-seen skin)
> This solemn tale he sadly did begin . . . (III.i.75–87)

Ghosts had to evoke the popular delights of awesomeness or fright: it is said of a character in Randolph's *Hey for Honesty* (1627):

> By Jeronymo, her looks are as terrible as
> Don Andrea or the Ghost in Hamlet. (II.iv.)

Revenge had appeared thus in the second dumb show to *The Misfortunes of Arthur*, a Gray's Inn play of 1588 that was played before the Queen at Greenwich:

After the which there came a man bare-headed, with black long shagged hair
down to his shoulders, apparelled with an Irish jacket and shirt, having an
Irish dagger by his side and a dart in his hand.

And in the anonymous *Locrine*, of doubtful date (1591?) and unknown
auspices, Ate (or Revenge) appears thus:

Enter Ate, with thunder and lightning all in black, with a burning torch in
one hand, and a bloody sword in the other hand . . . (Sig. A3ʳ)

Locrine bears the marks of an amateur academic production, but it is likely
that Kyd adopted the dramatic iconography of these early classical imitations for the popular theatre. Revenge almost certainly wore an antic and
spectacular costume of black, was probably clad in armour and bore a
sword, and may even have brought in a blazing torch at his first entrance.
His black was matched by the costumes of the bereaved: the mourning
Viceroy wears black in I.iii. –

Let Fortune do her worst,
She will not rob me of this sable weed (19–20)

and presumably Hieronimo donned black after the death of his son.

The hero must have worn a cloak and ruff as well. In *The Alchemist* Face
advised Drugger:

Thou must borrow
A Spanish suit: hast thou no credit with the players?
Hieronimo's old cloak, ruff, and hat will serve. (IV.vi.69–71)

The cloak probably enhanced the melodramatic scenes of madness: Dekker
suggests as much in his lampoon of Jonson (Horace) in *Satiromastix* (I.ii.):

TUCCA: Scorn it, dost scorn to be arrested at one of his old suits?
HORACE: No Captain, I'll wear anything.
TUCCA: I know thou wilt . . . for I ha'seen thy shoulders lapt in a
player's old cast cloak . . . and when thou ran'st mad for the death of
Horatio, thou borrow'dst a gown of Roscius the stager, (that honest
Nicodemus) and sentst it home lousy, *responde*, didst not?

One detail of old Hieronimo's appearance that seems to have caught the
attention of contemporaries was that his hair was white. So the discovery of
Horatio is described in the ballad of *The Spanish Tragedy*:[14]

And finding then his senseless form,
The murderers I sought to find,
But missing them I stood forlorn,
As one amazèd in his mind,
And rent and pulled my silvered hair,
And cursed and banned each thing was there.

Minor characters like Pedringano may have been played by 'character'
actors of distinctive appearance – probably one of the company's clowns or
possibly the pale and strikingly thin actor John Sincklo. So Lazarotto is

described in *The First Part of Hieronimo* (which may be an imitation of *The Spanish Tragedy*):[15]

> I have a lad in pickle of this stamp,
> A melancholy, discontented courtier,
> Whose famished jaws look like the chap of death:
> Upon whose eyebrows hangs damnation;
> Whose hands are washed in rape, and murders bold. (i.113–17)

As for the acting style, it must have matched the formality of the play's visual elements. The 'lively images' that Kyd sought to create came not from a modulated natural style of playing, but from conventions that we should now associate with opera and melodrama. The style was parodied by the next generation of dramatists. So Marston in a boys' play, *Antonio's Revenge*, depicts the most famous scene in Kyd's play:

> PANDULPHO: Would'st have me cry, run raving up and down
> For my son's loss? Would'st have me turn rank mad,
> Or wring my face with mimic action,
> Stamp, curse, weep, rage, and then my bosom strike?
> Away, 'tis apish action, player-like. (I.ii.312–16)

In *Antonio and Mellida* the hero tries to get his page to express a lively image of his grief in song, a parody perhaps of the painter scene in Kyd:

> I pray thee sing, but sirrah, mark you me,
> Let each note breathe the heart of passion,
> The sad extracture of extremest grief.
> Make me a strain; speak groaning like a bell
> That tolls departing souls.
> Breathe me a point that may enforce me weep,
> To wring my hands, to break my cursed breast,
> Rave and exclaim, lie groveling on the earth,
> Straight start up frantic, crying, 'Mellida' . . . (IV.i.139–47)

The wits might have scorned these quaint actions but audiences enjoyed them. As Hamlet says, it was 'an honest method, as wholesome as sweet, and by very much more handsome than fine' (II.ii.435–8). It was an art of silhouette, not of detail, of assertion, rather than wit or fine irony.

After the third sounding of the trumpet the play begins – in a very operatic manner. Possibly as in Jonson's *Catiline* (1611), where we find the stage direction '*A darkness comes over the place*' (l. 313), the entry of the Ghost and Revenge in well-equipped playhouses was accompanied by smoke billowing from the stage trapdoor. A cannon ball was rolled in a trough to give a thundrous sound and flashes of lightning were produced by igniting the pieces of rosin mentioned in *A Warning for Fair Women*. It is also probable that before the entrance there were heard low moans of 'Revenge, Revenge'. Cries of 'Revenge' or 'Vindicta' were the stock in trade of ghosts in revenge plays (see *Locrine*, etc.); the specific evidence comes from Act III of *The Poetaster* (1601) where, after burlesquing Balthazar's lament (II.i.9ff.), described as 'King Darius' doleful strain', Tucca has the two Pyrgoi cry alternately '*Vindicta, Timoria*'. Dekker in *The Seven Deadly Sins of London* (1606) speaks of a debtor wishing to be buried at his creditor's door 'that when he strides over him he might think he still rises up (like the Ghost in *Jeronimo*) crying "Revenge!"'[16]

The quotation from Dekker also suggests that in the public playhouses the first entry was through the trap. Hamlet's father's ghost '*cries under the stage*' (I.v.148); Envy, the first character to appear in *Poetaster*, '*arises in the midst of the stage*', and in *Titus Andronicus* Tamora, disguised as Revenge, sends word to Titus that she is 'sent from below' (V.ii.3). These characters come from the part of the playhouse associated with devils – like the devils in *Doctor Faustus*. Their entry may therefore have stamped them as evil scourges of the realm.

It is reasonably certain that at the Rose performances the Ghost and Revenge then mounted to the gallery above the stage to view the tragedy unfold;[17] in provincial performances or performances in great halls they could somewhat less effectively have sat at the side or the rear of the stage, perhaps between the entrance doors. Sly watches *The Taming of the Shrew* from aloft; in the 'plot' for another Rose play, *The Battle of Alcazar*, we find, as part of the direction for a dumb show, '*Enter aboue Nemesis*;'[18] and the 'argument' for a lost play of *Meleager* of about 1580 reads in part:[19]

> Actus 1 . . . The Lords, standing in doubt of the unfortunate sequel of
> so unhappy a beginning, are appointed by Melpomene to sit as Chorus
> over the stage to view the end of every accident, to explain the same of
> every Act . . . the Lords aforesaid being Chorus showeth that for want
> of reverence to the Gods their wrath will not be appeased without
> revenge &c.

There are various possibilities as to how the two figures made their ascent. The first is that they entered the tiring-house at the end of the first scene, probably to the rolling of drums (as in *Alcazar*, l. 288), to reappear aloft, a grim presence as the trumpets sounded for the opening of the second scene – compare the Folio stage direction to *Titus Andronicus* I.i.233: '*A long Flourish till they come downe.*' The second possibility is that there was a staircase set against the façade up which they might make a stately ascent during their final lines: 'i payer of stayers for Fayeton' is listed among the Rose properties.[20] Basilisco and Piston '*go up the ladders*' to the gallery to watch tilting in Kyd's(?) *Soliman and Perseda*, I.iii.180. In *James IV*, a Queen's Men play, Bohan invites Oberon at the end of the Induction: 'Gang with me to the gallery, and I'll show thee the same in action by guid fellows of our country-men', and there is a similar direction in *Alphonsus King of Aragon*. A third possibility is that the mechanism for raising and lowering thrones might this time have carried a platform that could have been lowered into the trapdoor. It could then have been raised to stage level from the 'underworld' bearing the two players who could then have returned to it to be carried up to the gallery. (The crane would have had to be rolled back towards the tiring-house wall.) Another Rose play, Greene and Lodge's *A Looking Glass for London and England*, contains a stage direction that indicates that characters could be lowered to the gallery: '*Enter, brought in by an Angel, Oseas the Prophet, and let (Q3: set Q1) down over the stage in a throne.*' (Compare 'th' gallery, in which the throne should descend' in the Epilogue to Lovelace's lost play, *The Scholars* (1649).[21]) Oseas seats himself in the gallery and from there he watches and comments on the ensuing action. The Ghost and Revenge may likewise have stepped off the platform to take up their seats. An oriel 'window' like that depicted in the Fludd engraving would have been an ideal place for them and left the two sides of the gallery for the concealment of Lorenzo and Balthazar and possibly for the King during the final masque: at V.iii.49 of *Antonio's Revenge*, a parody of this kind of play, we find the stage direction '*While the measure is dancing, Andrugio's ghost is placed betwixt the music-houses*' [of the gallery]. The throne could then have descended again for the King in I.ii. Alternatively, it could have stood on the stage from the beginning of the performance, and indeed an empty throne would have been a good emblem of the vanity of human power, the precarious glory of those who will be destroyed by Revenge.

In *Soliman and Perseda*, sometimes attributed to Kyd although very different metrically from *The Spanish Tragedy*, a triple chorus of Love, Fortune, and Death leave at the beginning and enter at the end of each act. In *The Spanish Tragedy*, however, unless it was being performed in curtailed form by a small travelling group of players, there is no doubt but that the grim duo of Ghost and Revenge remain on stage and visible aloft throughout the play. Like the Devils who appear aloft to watch Faustus' final agony, they are a mute chorus on the action. Their presence there does not signal to the audience that they *control* the action but, for example in III.xiii. (a scene equivalent to Faustus' attempt to decide between good and evil), where Hieronimo enters with a book and vacillates between biblical and Senecan injunctions towards patience on the one hand and covert contrivance on the other, the presence of Revenge makes us know what Hieronimo's choice will be.[22] It is a very simple device for creating dramatic irony. The implications are that all references to Fortune in the play are partly ironical: she has been banished the stage as men's natures take them towards revenge.

Kyd, it seems to me, is not addressing himself primarily to the morality of revenge – the author of the German version of the play changed the name of the protagonist to Maligno, which does not fit *The Spanish Tragedy* as I perceive it. Accounts of this and other 'revenge plays' that attempt to get us to adopt one attitude rather than another towards the 'hero' by marshalling the numerous writings of moral theologicans and philosophers against revenge are not attentive to the responses created by this frame which surrounds the action on the stage. As Berowne says in the overhearing scene of *Love's Labour's Lost*:

Like a demigod here sit I in the sky,
And wretched fools' secrets heedfully o'er-eye. (IV.iii.77–8).

A demigod cannot control but may look down with a measure of compassion or contempt on the antics of poor mortals whose actions are based partly on moral deliberation, partly on their compulsive responses to the contradictions with which they find themselves faced.

I.ii. serves partly to further the exposition of the story, partly to present the audience with a procession of the images of conflict which are such important constituents of the play. After a stately entrance the King installs himself on his throne, surrounded by his court, and the General proceeds to recite his battle narrative. As its outcome has already been revealed in the first scene, we can attend to the ceremony of this dramatic aria, epic declamation rolling with climaxes built up by rhetorical repetition to its conclusion:

When he was taken, all the rest they fled,
And our carbines pursued them to the death,
Till Phoebus waning to the western deep,
Our trumpeters were charged to sound retreat. (I.ii.81–4)

Audiences presumably enjoyed such narratives; *Edward III*, for example, is full of them. There follows a formal and symmetrical exchange of properties: a chain for the General's performance (both as warrior and player) and a treaty promising concord for the King. Immediately, however, this moment of security and 'frolic' (l. 96) is disturbed by a tucket sounded afar and by the staging of the first of the play's dumbshows, almost certainly given to a lavish musical accompaniment:

The army enters. Balthazar between Lorenzo and Horatio, captive.
KING: A gladsome sight, I long to see them here.
They enter and pass by. (I.ii.109–10)

Balthazar *between* Lorenzo and Horatio is an ominous figure of discord as is confirmed in the latter's squabbling for Balthazar's ransom in the second half of the scene. But it also gives the audience a brave and presumably pleasing show. The stage directions that have come down to us are unusual in that two 'entrances' are marked in quick succession. What these and the dialogue suggest, I think, is a combination of the two movements that are generally indicated by references to 'going about' and 'passing over' the stage.²³ The procession would enter the 'cave' of the yard, the area between the '*orchestra*' or Lords' rooms in the side galleries and the stage, move to

steps at the nearer front corner, march across the stage, descend the
opposite steps, and exit by the other 'cave'.[24] The movement neatly
establishes the customary double perspective for the audience: the players
enter the yard, making the audience feel they are 'there', actually present for
the show, but they then mount the playing space from which the audience is
physically and aesthetically detached. Kyd, it seems, introduced the epic
declamations that follow in order, in the words of Coleridge's description of
the Pyrrhus speech in *Hamlet*, to give 'such a reality to the impassioned
dramatic diction'[25] of the later dialogue.

I.iii. introduces the subplot, the intrigues at the court of Portugal. This is
easy to criticize on the grounds that it is superfluous to the demands of the
story, but indeed it is an important part of the action, both thematically and
dramatically. Although the events in Spain end in bloody confusion, it can
be argued that the *Spanish* tragedy turns about codes of honour. Balthazar
re-establishes himself after the humility of his capture by negotiating for the
hand of his adversary's lady, Bel-Imperia and Hieronimo revenge themselves for the deaths of their loved ones. In *Portugal*, however, we witness a
truly Machiavellian struggle simply for power: as Villuppo confesses later:

> For, not for Alexandro's injuries,
> But for reward, and hope to be preferred,
> Thus have I shamelessly hazarded his life. (III.i.94–6)

and there seems to be an echo of Machiavelli's question, 'whether it is better
to be loved or feared' (*The Prince*, ch. xvii) as well as his recognition of the
part played in human affairs by Fortune (ibid., ch. xxv etc.) in the Viceroy's
reflections at the middle of the play, the opening of Act III:

> So striveth not the waves with sundry winds
> As fortune toileth in the affairs of kings,
> That would be feared, yet fear to be beloved,
> Sith fear or love to kings is flattery. (i.8–11)

Just as he may have introduced the epic to heighten the dramatic, so Kyd
may have placed this sordid power struggle, owing no allegiance to any
virtue, even an ambivalent virtue like Revenge, to complement the tragedy.
A modern director might dress the Portuguese in, say, black, white, and
grey to suggest the way this subplot shadows a main action peopled by actors
wearing the customary brilliant costumes of the Elizabethan players – no
evidence of course exists that the Elizabethans themselves did anything like
this.

I.iv. gives us our first sight of Bel-Imperia, although we have been
explicitly told (I.i.10) that she and Andrea were lovers. Her name suggests
her nature: she is beautiful and accustomed to making men her 'servants' or
lovers. We should imagine a Venerean figure like those from Marlowe and
Peele we examined in Chapter 3, a boy wearing a costume as rich and iconic
as those worn by the Queen in the paintings that date from the end of her

reign. She asks for an account of the death of Andrea, for us now the third account of the same battle. An audience can in fact stand this kind of repetition: there is a kind of rhythm in the dramatic narrative that instils a sense of ritualized conflict and violence, a sense that is going to be shattered in the hugger-mugger slayings of the end of the play. But there is no reason why this time the audience should not be heeding the actions of Bel-Imperia rather than the words of Horatio during his speech. She feasts on him with her eyes and impulsively bestows upon Horatio the scarf, the love token Andrea had won in her honour. The gest is a kind of kiss of death and the stage device may be echoed as Hieronimo later takes the bloody scarf from Horatio's body – both pledges bring death. Horatio leaves with a measure of graceful embarrassment, possibly making a lingering exit as he and his love exchange loving glances.

A modern response to the scene may be that Bel-Imperia's conversion from Andrea to Horatio is precipitate and smacks of shallowness of character or of dramatic contrivance. Certainly there is contrivance, but Bel-Imperia and Horatio's love for each other is the *donnée* of the play, and Kyd builds the scene artfully. First we may note that this is the first time that we hear the full circumstances of Andrea's death. Andrea, it turns out, was brutally slaughtered by Balthazar after he had been unhorsed:

> But wrathful Nemesis, that wicked power,
> Envying at Andrea's praise and worth,
> Cut short his life to end his praise and worth.
> She, she herself, disguised in armour's mask
> (As Pallas was before proud Pergamus),
> Brought in a fresh supply of halberdiers,
> Which paunched his horse and dinged him to the ground.
> The young Don Balthazar with ruthless rage,
> Taking advantage of his foe's distress,
> Did finish what his halberdiers begun,
> And left not till Andrea's life was done. (I.iv.16–26)

The personification of Nemesis reminds us of the grim spectators of the scene, but the particularity of the description[26] must have its effect on Bel-Imperia who finds, of course, immediately after Horatio's exit, her privacy invaded by the man she now thinks of as the murderer of her first lover. At this moment Kyd inserts his first passage of *stichomythia* or line-for-line dialogue into the play. It is brilliantly placed and is no mere mannerism; indeed it allows for a kind of naturalism as Bel-Imperia reacts with sardonicism and then passionate sarcasm as the man she detests plays court to her. When she learns that the murderer is to be guest of honour at the ensuing banquet her private hatred turns to public disdain. She lets fall her glove, figuratively in fact throws down the gauntlet, which Horatio *'coming out, takes up'* (l. 99.1). It is a conventional gesture, a bold gesture accessible to a boy player of feminine will subverting Balthazar's masculine assumption of superiority. It too can provoke a 'real' response – in her brother. The reviewer of the Glasgow production reports that the gest of 'the dropped glove registered powerfully as a challenge to Lorenzo, who caught the couple *in flagrante delicto* and mutilated Horatio's hanged body horribly'.[27] League is threatened by love, public security by this tense disturbance.

The rest of the scene reverts to public ceremony, a banquet at which Hieronimo presents a 'masque' of Knights and Kings, something similar to the show of Kings in *Macbeth*. (It is called a masque although there is no dance.) Its function is in part to prepare us for the later fatal show of *Soliman and Perseda*: Balthazar remembers this when he commands the second (IV.i.6off.). The stage direction, '*Enter the Banquet, Trumpets, the King and Ambassador*', gives no indication whether the table set with imitation sweetmeats and fruit and the chairs of state were brought out by players and stage-keepers, 'thrust out', or even elevated through the trap. (This might have been done in *The Tempest*, III.iii.51, where '*with a quaint device the banquet vanishes.*') Meals or banquets are rituals of fellowship, community, harmony: they can take place at the end of a comedy as in *Bartholomew Fair* and *The Taming of the Shrew* or be interrupted by tragic portents as in *Macbeth*. Here the banquet is associated with a show which with its patriotic renderings of English victories in Spain and Portugal suggests confidence and triumph, and with its dumb show of Knights capturing Kings foreshadows the play's resolution. The dumb show may have been done with formal 'mimic' action, for music re-enters the play with the drummer beating out a simple rhythm (we can compare the drum that is played during the dumb show of *Soliman and Perseda*, II.i.190–231 and the remark in *Satiromastix*, 'The watch-word in a masque is the bold drum'),[28] although the players, skilled in the martial arts, may have equally well given a show of their fencing skills while Hieronimo played the customary role of 'trunchman' or interpreter. Kyd imported into the popular playhouses from ritual tilting the device of hanging up shields decorated with allegoric devices and mottos or *imprese*. (There was a gallery hung with such shields at Whitehall which was described in 1584 and still in existence in Pepys's time.[29])

The bonds are now forged of love and league, words which, like 'prattle' and 'practice' in *Othello*, serve as *Leitmotifs* for the play. Act II opens with a scene of intrigue followed by two short scenes which hasten the pace of the play towards its first climax, the murder of Horatio in the bower. Like so many scenes in the play, II.i. is symmetrical: two longish laments from Balthazar frame an image of violence where Lorenzo offers to kill Pedringano, go-between for Horatio and Bel-Imperia. II.ii. is symmetrical with I.iv. in that in the earlier scene Bel-Imperia had drawn Horatio into a confession of his loyalty and love and now she holds back, oppressed by a sense of danger and a longing for security. Looking forward, the dialogue between Bel-Imperia and Horatio is a kind of preliminary recitative to the great love duet in the bower. But ominous notes are audible as Balthazar surveys them from aloft. The stage directions are not clear as to when he appears above and whether Lorenzo and Pedringano are with him. Probably the easiest solution is for all three to appear above at line 6,[30] but the alternative would be to allow Lorenzo and Pedringano to remain below as 'interpreters' of their dramatic show. The device is simple and effective as Balthazar and Lorenzo echo and reverse the lovers' lines:

BEL-IMPERIA: But whereon dost thou chiefly meditate?

HORATIO: On dangers past, and pleasures to ensue.

BALTHAZAR: On pleasures past, and dangers to ensue.

BEL-IMPERIA: What dangers and what pleasures dost thou mean?

HORATIO: Dangers of war, and pleasures of our love.

LORENZO: Dangers of death, but pleasures none at all. (II.ii.26–31)

A score or so years later Monteverdi was to use a similar device in his opera *Il Ritorno d'Ulisse in Patria*, where the bass voice of Nettuno punctuates the parts of two lovers although they, unlike the audience, are unaware that he is present. If, as I have suggested, the Ghost and Revenge are seated in a central 'room' above the stage, the villains must be to one side. Alternatively Kyd may have built up a spatial emblem with the Ghost and Revenge occupying one of the side galleries and the villains facing them across the stage – if we accept Rhodes's reconstruction of the Rose with a concave tiring-house.[31] In either case there is a kind of irony in that here the mortals are playing gods, looking down on an action which they will control by their intervention.

In that scene love threatens league, in the next league threatens love as the dynastic machinations of Spain and Portugal put the bond between Bel-Imperia and Horatio in jeopardy. Presumably the scene between King and Ambassador could be set as a slow walk from one entrance to the other. It was probably framed by two tuckets, and the second would cover the appearance of the bower or arbour, setting for one of the play's great set pieces, the love duet of Bel-Imperia and Horatio. The engraving on the 1615 titlepage shows an arched trellis covered with stylized leaves and just wide enough to contain Horatio's hanged body. Yet it must have been a little wider for the lovers to sit side by side. This means that it could have come up through the trap as a bower does in Act II of another Rose play, *A Looking Glass for London and England*: '*The Magi with their rods beat the ground, and from under the same rises a brave arbour.*' Another uncertainty is whether a tree was in fact used: Isabella refers to it as a 'fatal pine' in IV.ii.7, although the stage direction calls for her to '*cut down the arbour*'. In *A Warning for Fair Women*, '*suddenly riseth up a great tree between*' (l. 1264) two adulterous lovers which is cut down on stage as an emblem of destroyed chastity. Alternatively it could have been thrust out from a door, or one of the discovery alcoves could have been used. (It is highly unlikely that it stood on stage as an unused 'mansion' until this point of the action.)

This scene in the arbour is splendidly sensuous. Like Ovid in Chapman's erotic poem *Ovid's Banquet of Sense* (1595), the lovers move through the senses of sight, hearing, touch, taste (the kiss) towards the erotic climax established by the customary pun on 'dying' (l. 48), here horribly poignant as Lorenzo and the disguised villains enter immediately to hang Horatio in the arbour. (He probably wore a harness to which a rope could be clipped behind his head – hangings are common on the Elizabethan stage and probably posed no technical problems.) The scene works by a subtle combination of expectation and surprise: the earlier wooing scene had been overlooked by the conspirators, here they enter suddenly and without warning. The villains go out through one side door, Hieronimo appears opposite.

Hieronimo's entrance in his nightshirt carrying a torch imprinted itself on the Elizabethan imagination. It must have been an image as widely known as some cinema posters today. The equally famous line, 'What outcries pluck me from my naked bed', is the first line in a speech that methodically leads him to the recognition of his son's body. Shakespeare may have had the moment in the back of his mind when he wrote a similar speech for Imogen who thinks she has come upon the body of her lover Posthumus in *Cymbeline*. Hieronimo cuts Horatio down from the bower, and his lamentations are augmented by those of his wife who turns his lament into a duet. They half raise his body while Hieronimo speaks his Latin dirge over it, at the same time putting his sword to his breast as he contemplates suicide, and then he bears the body away, having removed a blood-stained handkerchief as a token of grief and revenge, and then thrown away his sword. These images need no comment: they are the stuff of popular ballads but also of high art, similar even to the end of *Lear* when Lear enters from another hanging with Cordelia dead in his arms. The stage picture will be painfully repeated at the end of Act IV:

> *The trumpets sound a dead march, the King of Spain mourning after his brother's body, and the King of Portingale bearing the body of his son.*

Act III develops this pattern of symmetrical stage imagery. It opens with the scene in which the Viceroy sounds a lament for the 'unfortunate condition of kings' (III.i.1), which reminds us that the scene we have just witnessed is an emblem of the vanity of all men's lives. In the second part of the scene we see Alexandro falsely accused and bound to a stake (perhaps one of the stage columns) as faggots are brought for his death by burning. His absolute trust in heaven and his composure as the faggots are prepared create an important gest to set against the lamentation of Hieroniono that we have just witnessed. And yet no audience can have expected a real fire to be kindled in the playhouse: the establishment of his innocence by news that Balthazar is alive in Spain can therefore have come as no surprise. Yet again therefore we have a paradoxical stage image of 'artificial truth'. The scene is ironically placed between two hangings: one of the innocent Horatio and the second, five scenes later, of Pedringano. Similar preparations are made on the stage for that second execution, but there the audience knows full well that Pedringano will in fact be turned off the hangman's box as the Page has revealed that the coffer which is supposed to contain the reprieve (III.v.) is in fact empty. The bitter gallows humour of Pedringano, derived it would seem from a well-known *lazzo* in *commedia dell'arte*, is akin to the 'eldritch' humour[32] of *Doctor Faustus* and the 'quaint' devices of death in Webster: it is testimony to a world so beset by evil that the only reaction is laughter.

In scene ii Hieronimo's aria for the wearisome condition of humanity, 'O eyes, no eyes, but fountains filled with tears', is interrupted by a letter written in blood that is dropped from the gallery. There is no indication that Bel-Imperia actually appears, but she is obviously 'aloft' on the same level but presumably in a different 'room' from the Ghost and Revenge. Thus Kyd economically makes us aware that the impulse to revenge is human and not supernatural in origin. The Ghost and Revenge have a function that relates more to the form than the moral of the play: they are a perpetual reminder of the course the action will take. In *Hamlet*, by contrast, the hero is prompted to revenge by being possessed of knowledge hidden from the court of Denmark. Where Hamlet ponders the morality of revenge, Hieronimo seeks only to confirm what Bel-Imperia's letter had revealed:

> Now see I what I durst not then suspect,
> That Bel-Imperia's letter was not feigned,
> Nor feignèd she, though falsely they have wronged
> Both her, myself, Horatio and themselves.
> Now may I make compare, 'twixt hers and this,
> Of every accident; I ne'er could find
> Till now, and now I feelingly perceive,
> They did what heaven unpunished would not leave. (III.vii.49–56)

Having got to this point of recognition, Kyd has a double task. He must dramatize the counter-contrivance, the plots against the plotters, and also show the natures of the characters as they cope with their grief. His method becomes even more pictorial and much of the rest of the act is a *montage*, a series of scenes concentrating generally on one character who usually brings on a token property or appears as part of an emblematic tableau. So Isabella comes on in III.viii. bearing herbs which cannot cure her lunacy and she runs mad. We can take a hint for the performance of Isabella's mad scene from a choric speech in Kyd's *Cornelia*:

> Weep therefore, Roman dames, and from henceforth
> Valing your crystal eyes to your fair bosoms,

Rain showers of grief upon your rose-like cheeks,
And dew yourselves with springtides of your tears.
Weep, ladies, weep, and with your reeking sighs
Thicken the passage of the purest clouds,
And press the air with your continual plaints.
Beat at your ivory breasts, and let your robes
(Defaced and rent) be witness of your sorrows.
And let your hair, that wont be wreathed in tresses,
Now hang neglectly, dangling down your shoulders
Careless of art or rich accoutrements,
That with the gold and pearl we used before
Our mournful habits may be decked no more. (V.417–30)

Isabella's rich court robes would have been replaced by a loose and torn smock, her tied-up hair and headpiece replaced by a long flowing wig, the conventional stage symbol of distraction. In contrast Bel-Imperia appears at a window aloft, calm and constrained to patience, a tableau that serves as prelude to III.x., where she proudly maintains her integrity in the face of her brother's hypocrisy. Then, in an ironic duet with Balthazar that echoes her love duet with Horatio, she utters her sense of foreboding, that ends with a cryptic Latin couplet which emblematizes her and allies her with Hieronimo in the minds of the audience. Most of the rest of the act is a series of 'lively images' of Hieronimo's grief. In III.xi. he enacts by leaving and re-entering the stage by several doors the perilous journey through the torments of hell that he describes to two bemused Portingales. In III.xxi. he enters with poniard and rope, the conventional properties of the would-be suicide. These he casts away as he had previously cast away his sword; mustering his sanity to petition the King for justice, he is thrust aside by the now prospering Lorenzo. His famous aside, 'Hieronimo, beware: go by, go by', marks a turning point in the play as he now turns to what Bacon called the 'wild justice' of private revenge.

In his distraction he takes to digging down to hell with his dagger to bring back his mutilated son; in III.xiii. he brings on a book of Seneca as he deliberates on how to take arms against his sea of troubles. Petitioned himself by three citizens and an Old Man for redress of their wrongs, he draws out his bloody napkin and tears the papers of all save the Old Man whose cause is the portraiture of his. The stage direction gives the hint of a stark image of fury and distraction:

Exeunt all but the Old Man. Bazulto remains till Hieronimo enters again, who, staring him in the face, speaks. (III.xiii.132)

III.xiv. returns us to the court. Even though Kyd, like all dramatists, can render an individual's consciousness only from without, we now feel that the stage reality has become what Hieronimo sees. The formal and controlled scenes that fill the remainder of the act, the meeting between Spain and

Portugal to confirm their league, the scene where Lorenzo allays Castile's suspicions about him, another attempt by Balthazar to confirm his love are, as Hieronimo says, mere 'devices' (III.xiv.117), forms of a world that will end like a dream in the great confusion of the end of the play. So although the sequence ends with a final gest of Hieronimo brandishing his sword of revenge, it is fitting that the Ghost should find that Revenge has gone to sleep during this portion of the play. This can be explained as S. F. Johnson explains it in terms of the iconology of revenge. He quotes from Tymme's translation of Calvin's *Commentaries on Genesis* (1578):[33]

> But first Moses teacheth, that God for a while fared as though he had
> not seen them, to the end he breaking off the work begun by the
> confusion of tongues, might the more evidently declare his judgement.
> For he doth oftentimes so bear with the wicked, that as one asleep he
> doth not only suffer them to take many wicked things in hand; but also
> he maketh them rejoice at the success of their wicked enterprises, that at
> the last he make their fall the greater . . . But he meaneth that God
> showed himself a revenger little by little.

But perhaps the sleeping figure can be explained in dramatic terms. The Ghost's frantic cries to Revenge to 'awake' uncover the strata of comedy that have broken to the surface in this Act in the antic behaviour of Pedringano and Hieronimo. Even a presiding deity is oblivious to the tide running against him, and the laughter engendered is again the laughter of despair. When Revenge presents the spectacular stage show of Hymen god of weddings clad in black over his customary saffron robe, and seizing the nuptial torches at the head of the procession and quenching them in blood – all this probably accompanied by 'broken music' – we realize that this hellish vision is now the reality. As Revenge says, 'Thus worldlings ground, what they have dreamed upon' (III.xv.18). We are prepared for the fiction of the ending of the play, aware that as Nashe contemptuously but acutely pointed out, Kyd has 'thrust Elysium into hell.'[34]

Act IV works swiftly towards a double climax: the first round of killings which occurs 'within' the play of *Soliman and Perseda* and the second round that takes place in the 'real world' of the Spanish court. We have thus an economical demonstration of the way life imitates art as much as art imitates life and the strangeness of the fiction becomes plausible. As Hieronimo says to the villains:

> Assure you it will prove most passing strange
> And wondrous plausible to that assembly. (IV.i.84–5)

Hieronimo instead of being a mere marshal now takes control: we note the disturbing mixture of crazed passion and precision in his megalomania, as well as his pathos in the midst of horror. The first two scenes of the Act are as usual symmetrical: in the first Hieronimo has seemingly recovered his composure and with Bel-Imperia's prompting proceeds to plan his act of revenge. This is the play within the play which is described as the two antagonists enter to join them. In the second his wife appears distraught and in another tableau scene cuts down the arbour. (If this had stood on the stage throughout the action since the bower scene she thus clears the stage; if not, it was doubtless thrust upon especially for this scene.[35]) Her pathos and frenetic suicide is set in contrast with Hieronimo's studied and resolute calm as he busies himself with preparing the stage for the climax. The strange stage direction, 'Enter Hieronimo; he knocks up the curtain' (IV.iii.1), indicates that Hieronimo hangs a curtain over one of the entrances or discovery spaces. This enables the tableau to be prepared for revelation after the show. Certainly this was the method of discovery used in the German version:

> Er geht geschwind, zeicht sein Todten Sohn vnter dem aussgang all mit Blut am Leib gezeichnet herfür. (VI.197.1)

How precarious his control is, however, is revealed by the compulsive meditation on revenge that ends the scene – banging his head on the stage would be an action to accompany the manic repetition of revenge. As there was no indication in the previous scene of how Isabella left the stage – either staggering off after inflicting her fatal wound or carried off by stage-keepers – Hieronimo might come across her body after he has completed his activity and carry it off himself without exclamation or surprise.

There has been some controversy over whether the Court is seated aloft or on stage to witness Soliman and Perseda.[36] If the members are aloft they must be in one of the side galleries so that they can see the central discovery space. If they sit on stage it is possible that a mansion or tent with a curtain was used for the discovery.[37] If a throne or state had stood on stage throughout the play, it could be used in the show as a further reminder of the strangeness of life and the plausibility of art.

The show proceeds with the first set of killings strangely muted – the text at any rate does not indicate that the victims reveal to the stage audience that they are in fact mortally wounded. This is Kyd's contrivance to emphasize the great scene of pathos as Hieronimo draws the curtain to reveal his son and then tells his own tale to the stage audience. For them this is news: for the playhouse spectators the return to narrative, after so much 'action', begins an effective and symmetrical closing of the play. The son's body is presumably exposed on a bier and when Hieronimo runs back to the discovery space to hang himself he might reach down a noose from above that bier in order to compose a tableau mort of the extinction of the house. As he runs to the discovery space he locks the door of another, which is then broken open at the Viceroy's command. This suggests that at one set of performances at least the Court was aloft and sought to come down onto the stage by stairs within the tiring-house.

One problem remains: the reason for Hieronimo's declaration that he will be silent after he has in fact related the facts of the case. It may be that, as

Schücking and Edwards suggest,[38] the text prints alternative endings, one finishing with the long narrative followed by the murder of Castile and Hieronimo's suicide, the other omitting the narrative in order to shorten the play. Hieronimo's stubborn silence might then mark him as a vengeful villain – like Iago whose lines could be given to the earlier character:

Demand me nothing. What you know, you know.

From this time forth I never will speak word. (*Othello*, V.ii.306–7)

Alternatively, Hieronimo may wish to protect the memory of Bel-Imperia: the question he refuses to answer is Castile's 'But who were thy confederates in this?' (IV.iv.176). A common cause and shared love for Horatio unite Hieronimo and Bel-Imperia at their ends and presumably her suicide within the play took Hieronimo by surprise. It may even be that his refusal to speak is so that he can approach Castile himself who had been his confederate by throwing down the key to the gallery (IV.iii.13). Empson even suggests that 'the Duke of Castile had arranged to have [Andrea] killed in battle so that they could marry her to Balthazar . . . the audience has the interest of keeping half an eye on the Ghost, to see whether he has guessed the point yet.'[39] The state of the text at the end of the play, however, makes all this conjectural and a modern director must decide whether he wants a slow and precise set of executions or a confused image of murder and blood.

There is a double exit: the Court goes off to a dead march sounded on trumpets, and the Ghost and Revenge slowly make their way back down to hell. Their long speeches (in which we learn that the 'good' will be saved, the bad condemned to a kind of classical purgatory of 'unrest') would fit a stately descent of stairs if these were available on the stage or they could make their descent, as I have suggested, on a throne or platform lowered into the stage trapdoor.

Motive-hunting is in fact probably pointless: what an audience would be aware of is dissolution of order and the savage comedy at the end, so like that of *Titus Andronicus*, as the hero, alternating between rant and the precise action of mending his pen, a supreme act of dumb insolence, suddenly lunges out to exterminate Castile and himself. The sequence provides a moment of pleasure at seeing an enemy get his come-uppance but also of horror as this dumb gesture exposes the despair and impotence of those that do not have power.

What is remarkable about *The Spanish Tragedy* is the assured shape of its action, Kyd's skill in contriving a strong dramatic rhythm by his alternation of scenes of action and tableaux of lamentation, of intrigue in the real world and ceremony in the inserted shows. Its scenes are built around bold dramatic images, images of pathos and images of *virtù* incarnate in the characters. These scenes demand an intensive style of direction and acting; the images must possess what Puttenham called *energia* and *enargia*:[40] a sense of energetic action that is to be communicated to the audience but also a sense of clarity, hardness of outline, an assured conviction of the validity of the dramatic conventions employed. The repetition of image and situation is not merely mechanical but leads the audience to that 'feeling perception' Kyd describes in the play, turns theatrical convention into an image of life.

5 · *Mucedorus*: the exploitation of convention

Between 1598 and 1668 *Mucedorus* appeared in sixteen editions: in the same period *The Spanish Tragedy* was printed eleven times. There is of course no necessary correlation between the number of times a play was published and the number of times it was played, but there can be little doubt but that this, like Kyd's play, was one of the most performed plays of its age. However the authorship of *Mucedorus* and, unfortunately, its date and auspices, remain a matter for conjecture. Claims have been made that it was written by Peele, Greene, Lodge – and Shakespeare himself. C. F. Tucker Brooke, who edited the play for the *Shakespeare Apocrypha*, suggests that it was written by 'an obscure and only moderately gifted disciple' of the University wits.[1] The play probably dates from about 1590[2] and although the titlepage of the first Quarto states that it had been 'sundry times played in the honorable City of London' we do not know in what playhouse or by what company. It may have belonged to some company that became extinct, possibly the Queen's Men,[3] the company that included Richard Tarlton who may have been the first to play Mouse the Clown. Like *The Spanish Tragedy* it probably passed into the hands of strolling players, even of amateurs. Jones, the publisher, added a *dramatis personae* to the second edition which points out that the fourteen characters could be impersonated by only eight players. The Grocer's Wife in Beaumont's *The Knight of the Burning Pestle* refers to amateur revels when she says that her apprentice Ralph, who has ambitions to be an actor, 'hath played . . . Mucedorus before the wardens of our company' (Ind. 82–3), and it was 'surreptiously presented by strolling players while the theatres were closed during the Commonwealth, and was performed by village actors in the north of England as late as 1666.'[4] By 1610 the play had become the property of the King's Men. The third Quarto of that year advertises it as being 'Amplified with new additions, as it was acted before the King's Majesty at Whitehall on Shrove-Sunday night. By his Highness' Servants usually playing at the Globe'. This and all subsequent editions add to the text – a bad one, probably a faulty reconstruction from memory by the player who performed Mouse – a prologue and three new scenes.[5]

The corruption and curtailment of the text makes the large number of editions all the more remarkable. It suggests that if printed texts were used by players they provided only a scenario, a basis for verbal extemporization and a framework for knockabout clownage of the sort we know Tarlton to have performed – like the *lazzi* in *commedia dell'arte*. If the play was inspired by the routines of visiting continental troupes (see below), it is equally probable that it was toured in Europe by English comedians. It belongs to an international folk culture with characters that tend to the allegoric and sequences of self-delighting activities.

The history of this play therefore neatly illustrates the difficulty of making a separation between popular and courtly drama. The play must have enjoyed sufficient repute in the public playhouses for it to be commanded at Court, but it is also important to remember that the play and others of its kind may have derived their popular appeal from the fact that they gave the public playhouse audiences a taste of the dramatic fare offered before the monarch. In fact when James saw *Mucedorus* in 1610 he was witnessing a revival of tradition. Chivalric romances had been a staple of Shrove-tide entertainments at Court over thirty years before. In 1577 *The History of the Solitary Knight* had been performed by Lord Howard's company at Whitehall, the next year the Earl of Warwick's company had performed *The History of the Knight in the Burning Rock* on Shrove Tuesday while on Shrove Monday the Children of the Chapel played *The History of Loyalty and Beauty*.[6]

Like many of the romances of the period – Peele's *Old Wives Tale* and Greene's *James IV* are examples – *Mucedorus* begins with an Induction which establishes a code for the world of the play. Peele's Induction introduces three pages called Antic, Frolic, and Fantastic, whose names herald the blatant improbabilities, the spirit of revelry, and the deliberate use of the stereotyped characters and situations that are the marks of that play and so much popular drama. Here the characters are Comedy and Envy who engage in the folk-form of the *débat*, found throughout Europe,[7] a flyting match over the nature of the ensuing entertainment. Their costumes provide examples of what Henslowe called 'antik sutes'[8] – similar in kind to those worn by Revenge and the Ghost of Don Andrea. Comedy is described thus: '*Enter Comedy, joyful with a garland of bays on her head*', and Envy: '*Enter Envy, his arms naked, besmeared with blood.*'[9] An elaborate grotesque allegoric costume was obviously called for. Jonson introduced Envy to begin *The Poetaster* and had the character wreathed in snakes:

What's here? The arraignment! ay; this, this is it,
That our sunk eyes have waked for all this while:
Here will be subject for my snakes and me.

> Cling to my neck and wrists, my loving worms,
> And cast you round in soft and amorous folds,
> Till I do bid uncurl . . . (Ind. 3–8)

Possibly, if the company could afford the spectacle offered at Court, there was an elaborate headpiece as well: the Revels Office records payment in 1572 to the property-maker 'John Ogle for curling of hair made of black silk for Discord's head (being 40 ounces)'.[10] Perhaps, too, like Jonson's figure and Kyd's Revenge, Envy appeared through the stage-trap to enhance the demonic effect of her entrance. She promises a Marlovian banquet of blood:

> In this brave music Envy takes delight,
> Where I may see them wallow in their blood,
> To spurn at arms and legs quite shivered off,
> And hear the cries of many thousand slain. (ll. 30–3)

This suggests that Envy was associated in the author's mind with tragedy. In the Jacobean additions to the epilogue, vanquished by Romance, she promises at least a satirical comedy typical of those produced in the first decade of the seventeenth century.

The verbal contest is reinforced by a kind of musical battle: Comedy orders the playhouse musicians to 'Sound forth Bellona's silver tunèd strings'. The music is interrupted by Envy's entrance and by her counter-order:

> I'll thunder music shall appall the nymphs,
> And make them shiver their clattering strings,
> Flying for succour to their dankish caves.
> *Sound drums within and cry, 'Stab! Stab!'*
> Hearken, thou shalt hear a noise
> Shall fill the air with a shrilling sound,
> And thunder music to the gods above. (Ind. 20–6)

Like the cries of 'Revenge, revenge' that open *The Spanish Tragedy* these cries establish the home key, as it were, of the ensuing composition, announce its informing conventions. There is a song in III.i., music is used to ease the despair of Valencia in IV.i., and it is very likely that there was much more music, the evidence for which has disappeared from the text. (The interchange between the Clown and Mucedorus in III.i. might have consisted of two 'farewell songs' of the sort parodied by Beaumont in some of Merrythought's catches in *The Knight of the Burning Pestle*[11].) There is a similar musical induction to Greene's play *Alphonsus, King of Arragon*, a heroical romance of about 1587 that was performed at the Rose. There, after the third sounding of the trumpet, Venus was '*let down from the top of the stage*' to encounter the nine muses '*playing all upon sundry instruments*'.

Inductions like these remind us yet again of how the printed texts are records of only a part of Elizabethan plays. The effect of performances must have derived as much from music and spectacle as from the working out of

plot and the creation of character. A contemporary noted that a performance of *Mucedorus* (including intervals?) lasted three hours:[12] the extant
script would last perhaps an hour and a half. The effect of these romances is
cumulative as the dramatists and companies added episode to episode,
mode to mode, re-enacting and celebrating scenic patterns derived from
classical mythology, folk-tale, clownage, and the pageantry of Court and
City, as well as mystery and miracle (saints') plays. These performances are
not imitations of life but occasions for game and display by members of a
company, and their structure is that of a musical suite. Peele gives us the
principle of this kind of dramatic structure in his Old Wife's description of
the action. Events are strung together paratactically, connected simply by
'ands': the old woman's naïveté is a manifestation of Peele's careless
unconcern for the causal demands of classical plots:[13]

> There was a conjurer, and this conjurer could do anything, and he
> turned himself into a great dragon, and carried the king's daughter away
> in his mouth to a castle that he made of stone; and there he kept her I
> know not how long, till at last all the king's men went out so long that
> her two brothers went to seek her. O, I forget! she (he I would say,)
> turned a proper young man to a bear in the night, and a man in the day,
> and keeps by a cross that parts three several ways; and he made his lady
> run mad . . . (ll. 142ff.)

A play like *Mucedorus* appeals to an audience's delight in naïveté. Poetry
according to the Roman poets served to instruct and delight: Renaissance
theorists spent much time accounting for its capacity to instruct. Sir Philip
Sidney wrote very much in this tradition, but one of the best bits of his
Defence of Poesie comes when he forgets about classical didacticism, the
satire that breeds laughter, and distinguishes it from delight, that basic
constituent of popular literature:

> For delight we scarcely do but in things that have a conveniency to
> ourselves, or to the general nature; laughter almost ever cometh of
> things most disproportioned to ourselves and nature. Delight hath a joy
> in it either permanent or present; laughter hath only a scornful tickling.

He goes on to give an example of a painting of a subject very similar to those
that appear in romances:[14]

> Hercules, painted with his great beard and furious countenance, in
> woman's attire, spinning at Omphale's commandment, it breeds both
> delight and laughter; for the representing of so strange a power in love
> procureth delight; and the scornfulness of the action stirreth laughter.

A dramatist seeking to delight his audience must establish a fine balance
between their recognition of what is serious and permanent in the play and
their ability to retreat from seriousness by their enjoyment of the grotesque.

Popular art of this kind deliberately eschews complexity of characterization. Characters are functions of situations and generally conform to the

commonest of stereotypes: the King, the Princess, the Hero in his two most familiar aspects of shepherd and warrior, the Rejected Suitor, the Wild Man (here a villain), and the Clown. Motivation is provided by the emotion of the moment and the emotions the personages feel are the most generalized: love and hate, happiness and misery, bravery and fear. The dramatist moves from situation to situation deploying the common permutations of these figures. The play is like Elizabethan tapestry friezes and shares with them a naïve mixture of fantasy and realism. The dramatist can even dispense with reaction to event as we can see in V.i. where Mucedorus despatches Bremo in one blow and, after one perfunctory line, Amadine continues to narrate her tale which had been interrupted by Bremo's entrance:

BREMO: . . . take my staff and see how thou canst wield it.
MUCEDORUS: First teach me how to hold it in my hand.
BREMO: Thou holdest it well.
 Look how he doth; thou may'st the sooner learn.
MUCEDORUS: Next tell me how and when 'tis best to strike.
BREMO: Tis best to strike when time doth serve,
 Tis best to lose no time.
MUCEDORUS: Then now or never is my time to strike. *[Aside]*
BREMO: And when thou strikest, be sure thou hit the head.
MUCEDORUS: The head?
BREMO: The very head.
MUCEDORUS: Then have at thine!
  He strikes him down dead.
     So, lie there and die,
 A death no doubt according to desert,
 Or else a worse as thou deservest a worse.
AMADINE: It glads my heart this tyrant's death to see.
MUCEDORUS: Now, lady, it remains in you
 To end the tale you lately had begun . . . (V.i.57–74)

Delight comes not from recognition of reality but from the recognition of forms or conventions: here the figure of the self-possessed champion, the popular hero taking arms against the tyrant. The conventions are those of romance, but as there is no attempt to conceal these the tone is comic. This combination of romantic convention and comic tone forms a perennial recipe to please those who enjoy fictions for their own sake. Behind the façade there doubtless lurk disturbing myths or significant rituals, but there is no more need to make these explicit than there is when dealing with any play that is written for a group in a festive mood, whether an Elizabethan mummers play, a nineteenth-century melodrama, or a modern pantomime.

As we would expect of a play so readily adaptable for touring companies, the text demands no scenic devices. The stage with a throne serves for the court scenes in both Aragon and Valencia. Scenes when characters encounter one another, the scenes that nineteenth-century editors localized on 'A pathway through the forest', or, desperately, 'Another part of the forest', need no scenic devices – although property trees may have been used if the playhouse had them to hand.[15] Henslowe's inventory records 'ij mose banckes'[16] and conceivably devices like these might have been used in conjunction with a property representing the 'fair broad branched beech that overshadows a well' (III.i.106–7) where Mucedorus appoints to meet with Amadine. (Such a property was called for at the opening of a Court play, the broad oak that sets the scene at the opening of Lyly's *Gallathea*. It would, of course, be artificial: bringing a real beech bough on stage would destroy the convention.) The world of *Mucedorus* is timeless and needs no specific place: unlike *The Spanish Tragedy* it does not depict historical change. Aragon and Valencia are mere names, and the Alewife (like, say, the hedgepriest in *As You Like It*) comes from England and not Arcadia. In any case almost every scene in which the action is translated to the woods contains a reference in its first couple of lines to its setting. The reference to 'a noise of over-passing joy within the court' (V.ii.13–14) indicates that some sort of mansion, possibly in a *décor simultané*, may have been used, but that could have been a tent in an outdoor playing space, an anteroom to a hall, a room off the courtyard of an inn, or the tiring-house of a theatre. If the performance at Court demanded more spectacle, money might have been spent on an elaborate *décor simultané*: two states or thrones facing each other across the width of the hall and the tree-shaded well serving for all forest scenes at the end of the hall facing the throne of King James. (This would have provided an oblique compliment that would have opposed the wildness of the woods to the virtue and civilization of the monarch.) Alternatively one state could have been used for both Valencia and Aragon, with two forest pieces: the well and a cave for Bremo. Devices like these had been provided for performances of similar plays at Court shortly before *Mucedorus* was presumably written. In the Revels Accounts we find the following entry relating to the Queen's Men:[17]

An invention called *Five Plays in One* presented and enacted before her Majesty on Twelfth Day (1584–5) at night in the hall at Greenwich by her Highness' Servants wherein was employed a great cloth, and a battlement of canvas, and canvas for a well, and a mount, 15 ells of sarcenet, 9 yards of sullen cloth of gold purple.

The same Accounts give us some clues as to the appearance of Bremo, the Wild Man: they mention 'moss and young oaks for the Wild Men' and 'Ivy for the Wild Men and th'arbour' (1573).[18] The play can, however, be performed perfectly well without any scenery.

The success of a production of *Mucedorus* depends on its pace: a pace that was possible by virtue of the way in which popular stages could handle without pause a succession of scenes different in place and mode (I am not suggesting the play was garbled). Indeed the play resembles an old fashioned speeded-up film in which stock situations rapidly succeed one another. We know in advance what fare to expect and the author can therefore provide us with a procession of courses in a short time. To revert to Sidney, their strangeness breeds delight. The story succeeds by being little more than its own scenario, a frame for the added routines. After the induction Mucedorus appears to announce to Anselmo his intention of departing the court of Valencia to seek the love of Amadine. He dons shepherd's weeds, in fact a 'cassock' provided by his friend. A cassock was simply a loose coat or gown and the name was used for shepherd's clothing in the sixteenth century. It may have been made from lambskins as certain Court shepherds' costumes were[19] and worn over the white jerkin mentioned in the play (IV.ii.58), or it may have been simply a white coat like that worn in Lyly's *Gallathea* (III.i.46). Henslowe owned 'ij whitt sheperdes cottes'.[20] What is interesting is that Anselmo explains that he had worn the cassock at a dramatic entertainment, 'in Lord Julio's masque' (I.i.51), which reminds us of our artificial tree and that the play depends on dramatic shorthand, on the stylization of pastoral which makes no pretence at naturalism. We might infer therefore that in this respect at least the play as seen in the popular playhouses would have been little different from the play seen at Court. Mucedorus' donning of shepherd's weeds is the reverse of the transmutation in the second scene of *Tamburlaine* where Tamburlaine puts aside his shepherd's garb for the accoutrements of a warrior. It is thus another clear signal of the kind of play that is to follow. It is also conceivable that Mucedorus from this time on adopted the standard west country accent of a rustic like the shepherd Corin in a similar play, *Clyomon and Clamydes* of the late 1570s.[21]

The next scene opens dramatically with the entrance of Mouse the Clown carrying a bundle of hay. He is being pursued by a bear, an image that Shakespeare was to put to a sea-change in *The Winter's Tale*. His opening monologue aims some satirical barbs at puritans – lines that displeased a Commonwealth divine in 1653 when the play was performed surreptitiously in Witney, Oxfordshire.[22] His second appearance (I.iv.33) has him crying 'clubs', the cry used to summon the watch when brawls took place in London. The game has by then typically moved its setting to a more familiar world. Mouse in fact is a stock theatrical character to be known later in English jigs and already familiar on the continent. Baskerville notes he is 'the distinctly droll clown with a mixture of knavery and naïveté or of stupidity and blundering uncouthness'[23] and likens him to Derick in *The Famous Victories*, Adam in *A Looking Glass for London and England*, Strumbo in *Locrine*, and Shakespeare's Launce and Launcelot. The first two of these were Queen's Men plays, the second two unknown. Tarlton was the leading comedian of the Queen's Men until his death in 1588, so these parts and that of Mouse may have been created by him or played in his manner (see Chapter 3). Mouse ends his monologue by going out backwards and falls over the bear coming in behind him: it was a conventional *lazzo* for the clown to fall into the play on his first entrance. 'Politicke Persuasion, the Vice of *Patient and Meek Grissell* (1559) . . . tumbles into the action at the opening of the play, falling from the dwellings of the classical gods',[24] and the first entrance of Shift, the clown in *Clyomon and Clamydes* is described thus: '*Here let him slip on to the stage backwards, as though he had pulled his leg out of the mire, one boot off, and rise up to run in again*' (ll. 118–20).

As for the bear, Mouse's reference to her as 'she' (I.ii.12) might suggest that a real bear might have been borrowed from the Bankside bear-baitings. Later reference to the 'white bear' would indicate a polar bear. Polar bears are, however, apparently untameable so in all probability, although the part is missing from the *dramatis personae*, the part was taken by a man in a bearskin.[25] Henslowe owned 'j beares skyne'.[26] In the report of the perform-ance at Witney 'there was mention made of the Devil in a Bear's doublet, the Wild Man then acting the Bear's part'.[27] In mumming plays still played in a few English villages, plays that are the descendants of this kind of drama (scarcely the survivors of pre-Christian rituals), much of the fun comes from the use of hobby-horses, the deliberate childishness of the game. Real bear or man in bearskin, both kindle delight but both suggest the Elizabethan awareness of an ambivalent power in nature, at once ordering and unruly.

But there is little time for such conjectures for immediately Segasto, the unrequited lover, and Amadine rush in, also pursued by the bear. This is our first sight of the heroine and it is pure farce – few demands for psychological realism were made of the boy or young man who took the part. The cowardly Segasto has no concern for his love's safety and runs off to leave his lady to be comforted by the opportune entrance of Mucedorus who arrives carrying the bear's head. (In *Clyomon and Clamydes* it is a serpent's head that the hero brings in upon his sword [l. 636]). Again the tone is anti-heroic; after a few lines in the style of high romance a couplet deflates the moment:

> Stay, lady, stay, and be no more dismayed.
> That cruel beast, most merciless and fell,
> Which hath bereavèd thousands of their lives,
> Affrighted many with his hard pursues,
> Prying from place to place to find his prey,
> Prolonging this his life by others' death,
> His carcass now lies headless, void of breath. (I.iii.6–12)

Another example of a rhetorical convention drawing attention to the self-delighting artifice of the whole comes from the next sequence, Segasto's soliloquy. He returns to lament his cowardice:

A trusty friend is tried in time of need;
But I, when she in danger was of death
And needed me, and cried, 'Segasto, help!'
I turned my back and quickly ran away.
Unworthy I to bear this vital breath!
But what, what needs these plaints?
If Amadine do live, then happy I:
She will in time forgive and so forget.
Amadine is merciful, not Juno-like,
In harmful heart to harbour hatred long. (I.iv.23–32)

'What will she think of me?' – the simplicity of the situation contrasts with the attempts at high style, and brings the play back into the contemporary world. The rest of the scene, where Segasto takes Mouse into his service, is a further example of the way the author happily swings away from the demands of plot, illusion, or classical decorum. Instead he gives the two players a cross-talk routine full of amiable nonsense that delights in its own illogic:

CLOWN: I tell you what, sir, as I was going a-field to serve my father's great horse, and carried a bottle of hay upon my head – now do you see, sir – I, fast hoodwinked that I could see nothing, perceiving the bear coming, I threw my hay into the hedge and ran away.

SEGASTO: What, from nothing?

CLOWN: I warrant you, yes, I saw something, for there was two load of thorns besides my bottle of hay, and that made three.

SEGASTO: But tell me, sirrah, the bear that thou didst see,
    Did she not bear a bucket on her arm?

CLOWN: Ha, ha, ha! I never saw bear go a-milking in all my life . . .
    (I.iv.47–59)

'*Enter Bremo, a wild man*'. Wild men were popular figures in folklore and in Elizabethan pageantry and drama. In pageantry their function was to clear the way for royal or civic processions.[28] In Whetstone's *Promos and Cassandra*, a comedy of 1578, a stage direction stipulates the entry of '*two men apparelled like Green Men at the Mayor's feast, with clubs of fireworks*' (I.vi.). There is a reference (I.i.) in Dekker's *Old Fortunatus* to wild men who 'threw squibs among the commonalty'. A Sylvanus or Wild Man appeared in the entertainments offered to Queen Elizabeth at Kenilworth in 1575 and Bisham in 1592[29] – they are related to the evil Moors, the 'Blackmen' who captured maidens in certain jigs,[30] and to the 'wodemen' (wood- or mad-men) of Mummers' plays. 'Six wild men, clothed in leaves' (probably of oak or ivy) appear in the first dumb show of *Gorboduc*, in 1574 a Revels Account for the visit of Italian players at Windsor and Reading includes an item 'Horsetails for the Wild Man's garment', and Accounts for the revels of the Christmas before, which contained a masque of wild men, include payments for hair for their costumes and wigs and moss and young oaks for scenic properties.[31] In an engraving by Brueghel of a Flemish folk play (Plate 13) we find depicted a wild man with long hair, crowned and girt with ivy, bearing a spiked club, and wearing a costume covered with scales – he may be a folk prototype for Caliban in *The Tempest*. The figures were designed to arouse terror and amusement in those who saw them. Bremo's entrance, armed with a cudgel that he soon lays down, was presumably impressively frightening, but his soliloquy becomes comic as his ranting turns to lamentation that no one has come his way into his power.

The story moves quickly. Mucedorus is peremptorily sentenced to death for the murder of Tremelio (conveniently killed off almost immediately he appeared), which provokes a passage of gallows humour from the Clown. Amadine enters with the bear's head to plead for the life of her 'shepherd' and after a stichomythic quartet between Segasto, Amadine, the King, and the Clown the sentence is commuted to banishment. Mucedorus laments his lot, sings a farewell song with the Clown, and Amadine joins him to join in a spoken duet in which, like the unhappy lovers in Shakespeare's comedies, they resolve to meet in the woods. After repartee between Segasto and the Clown in which Mouse plays one of the oldest roles in comedy, that of the witty servant, Amadine appears to reflect upon her love and her lot. She is surprised by Bremo who finds his methodical sadism is defeated by her virtue. He is the pantomime villain defeated by the natural magic of the maiden:

BREMO: I'll crush thy bones betwixt two oaken trees.
AMADINE: Haste, shepherd, haste, or else thou com'st too late.
BREMO: I'll suck the sweetness from thy marrow-bones.
AMADINE: Ah spare, ah spare to shed my guiltless blood!
BREMO: With this my bat will I beat out thy brains.
  Down, down, I say, prostrate thyself upon the ground.
AMADINE: Then, Mucedorus, farewell; my hopèd joys, farewell.
  Yes, farewell life, and welcome present death!
      She kneels.
  To thee, O God, I yield my dying ghost.
BREMO: Now, Bremo, play thy part –
  How now, what sudden chance is this?
  My limbs do tremble and my sinews shake,
  My unweakened arms have lost their former force:
  Ah, Bremo, Bremo, what a foil hast thou
  That yet at no time ever wast afraid
  To dare the greatest gods to fight with thee,
      He strikes.
  And now want strength for one down-driving blow! (III.iii.28–44)

This is theatrical in two ways: it is dramatically gripping, which draws the audience towards the situation, but amusingly sterotyped ('now play thy part'), which encourages them to reject the illusion. Amadine is dragged off by Bremo, Mucedorus appears only to dodge off at the offstage cries of 'hold him, hold him' – the suspense is destroyed in another way by the entrance of Mouse running, this time not from a bear, but from an English alewife from whom he has stolen a beer-pot. She enters and they perform another stock comic routine which precedes another passage of cross-talk:

She searcheth him, and he drinketh over her head and casts down the pot; she stumbleth at it; then they fall together by the ears; she takes her pot and goes out. (III.v.37)

There is a very similar routine for Derick, certainly a Tarlton part, in scene x of *The Famous Victories*. Like the drunken Sly in *The Taming of the Shrew* we realise 'a comonty' is a 'Christmas gambold, or a tumbling-trick' (Ind. ii.134–5) as much as a narrative history.

After a musical interlude in which the melancholy strains that accompany Valencia's lament for the loss of his son change to notes of joy as news comes that Mucedorus yet lives, we encounter Mucedorus in the forest. To suit his melancholy he disguises himself as a hermit – 'in a white gown, and a white hat on his head, and a staff in his hand' (IV.iv.22–3). Mouse, who does not recognize him, brings news that Amadine is in the forest (after more cross-talk) and we encounter the heroine in the next scene. It is symmetrical with III.ii. in that she is still in the company of Bremo who, instead of attempting her virtue with force, woos her with fine words:

If thou wilt love me thou shalt be my queen:
I will crown thee with a chaplet made of ivy
And make the rose and lily wait on thee:
I'll rend the burly branches from the oak
To shadow thee from burning sun.
The trees shall spread themselves where thou doest go,
And as they spread I'll trace along with thee.

AMADINE (*aside*): You may, for who but you. (IV.iii.24–31)

The speech runs for some thirty lines, regularly interrupted by Amadine using the counterturn or some version of it, and so reminding us that yet again the play is using a variety of musical form. (It was at this point in the play, incidentally, that the floor collapsed of the inn at Witney, killing five people and injuring many others.[32]) Mucedorus enters in disguise and instead of using force he attempts to tame the Wild Man with a narration of how Orpheus arrived in a land where wrong and rudeness governed and, by calming men's passions, established a rule of reason which became a golden age. Perhaps there was a musical accompaniment to this set piece as, strangely, Mucedorus does not mention Orpheus' music. But Bremo is unmoved, threatens Mucedorus with death which is averted only by Amadine's pleas and Mucedorus' agreement to become his servant. The scene may lack action, but like so many other scenes in the play it is based on an emblematic pattern, and depicts a significant metamorphosis as the prince turned hermit now turns servant.

After a glimpse of Segasto and his servants seeking the vanished Mucedorus, Bremo discovers the Prince still in disguise and the Princess alone. A comic fight ensues in which Mucedorus pretends to be quite ignorant of the martial skills and promptly slays his master. Mouse enters, repeats his tumbling-trick with the bear as he falls over the body of the Wild Man – the dramatist has made a virtue of necessity as Mouse is then used to get the body off the stage. Segasto enters, and Amadine is invited to choose her husband. She chooses the virtuous shepherd and not the rich and noble Segasto. Mucedorus reveals that he is Prince of Valencia and Segasto surrenders his claim, converted from his ambition by this emblem of love and virtue. They return to court to convert sorrow to joy by a double reunion of Amadine with her father, Mucedorus with his. The story ends with the pealing of bells, the sounding of trumpets and drums.

All that remains is for Comedy and Envy to return and resolve their contest. Comedy boasts of her triumph in the story, Envy vows revenge by threatening to conjure a poet who will write a comedy of a different sort, dark and satirical:

> This scrambling raven with his needy beard,
> Will I whet on to write a comedy
> Wherein shall be composed dark sentences
> Pleasing to factious brains,
> And every otherwhere place me a jest,
> Whose high abuse shall more torment than blows. (Ep. 40–5)

These lines were added in the 1610 Quarto after satirical comedy had entered the repertory of the private theatres to complement the romantic comedy of the sort we have witnessed. In any case Comedy prevails, and the two kneel to beg applause from the court.

No one could claim that *Mucedorus* has much in the way of literary or even dramatic merit. It is a gallimaufry, a pleasant pastime – reassuring in its romantic view of the world, amusing in its exposure of those very conventions of romance. We can see why Shakespeare called his pastoral romance *As You Like It*.

6 · *Edward II*: dramatic documentary

In a long speech at the beginning of Act V, King Edward II reflects:[1]

> But what are kings, when regiment is gone,
> But perfect shadows in a sunshine day? (V.i.25–6)

The lines are often quoted as a political maxim, but the second contains a familiar Elizabethan playhouse pun. 'Shadows' are actors: Marlowe, therefore, as Shakespeare often did, is presenting us with an emblem of the player king on an open stage, a mere 'shadow' of the real monarch who, conversely, on the stage of the world, might be only as powerful as an actor. Such a king's strength would derive merely from the shows he could muster, and he might well, despite the finery of his appearance, be reduced to directing four or five vile and ragged foils in brawl ridiculous. In *Tamburlaine* Marlowe had shown a dream of power, how a great and violent man might become his own myth, draw to himself a regiment of glamour, so long as his physical mastery remained to him. Edward II, however, is not a powerful figure and does not surpass his adversaries in cunning or might. He may have affected the gawdy brilliance of Tamburlaine in his campaigns at Court and in the battlefield:

> thy soldiers marched like players,
> With garish robes, not armour; and thyself,
> Bedaubed with gold, rode laughing at the rest,
> Nodding and shaking of thy spangled crest,
> Where women's favours hung like labels down . . . (II.ii.182–6)

but we may presume that his antagonists wore drab and workaday costumes to show up the vanity of this show and thereby point to the insubstantiality of his power. *Edward II* in other words is a demythologizing work, uncompromisingly realist. It is therefore not surprising that this play calls for the use of only one stage level: no ghost need appear from below, no character, devil or god, appears above to submit the actions the political antagonists to moral scrutiny.

In contrast, moreover, with *The Spanish Tragedy* (and *Richard II*), *Edward II* uses the lavishness of costumes and the lavishness of stage decoration² to point up opportunism and the improvisatory quality of the action. Marlowe himself had probably moved nearer the Court than any other of the Elizabethan dramatists. As a habitué of the Walsingham circle, a member of the Elizabethan secret service, he knew when the emperor, his acolytes and catamites, wore no clothes. In this play he uses the non-illusionistic stage to uncover 'theatocracy', the illusion of power. Costumes and regalia are donned before the audience to show that all power is merely borrowed, that politics is play. Characters put on their robes of office, but unlike our reaction to Tamburlaine whose shedding of shepherd's weeds signifies his translation to a kind of fearful demi-god, we feel here that these robes signify only a desperate attempt at self-assurance, are the transactions Edward embarks on in his desire to be loved, or are emblems of the vanity of inherited power. Marlowe's verse, more subtly than Kyd's, is almost constantly ironic, drawing attention to the ways in which men create roles for themselves by their styles of speech. Like Kyd, Marlowe imported court shows into the play, but the audience is never invited to revel in their spectacle but rather to ponder the political statements they make. Ceremonies are interrupted, portraying the collapse of political ideals, and fights are no ritual conflicts between good and evil as they are in *Mucedorus* but compulsive animalistic struggles for physical domination. The play has a populist point of view, without bringing on the people as Shakespeare does: cynicism for metropolitan politicians competes with sympathy for the suffering individual.

In Chapter 3 we saw how Shakespeare in *Hamlet* analysed the iconic style of Marlowe's dramaturgy. Players in this work are called upon to move deftly from poise to poise, gest to gest, like a film projected slowly frame by frame. And yet the realism of the play demands that the shape of the scenes be not too polished, the blocking of the action not built about the architectural patterns we saw in *The Spanish Tragedy* but on the interrupted trajectories and impulsive spurts of movement traced by those seeking power. The play is full of short speeches, commands obeyed or flouted, spasms of energy that reveal personality. Individual scenes, unlike those in *Richard II*, are not shaped into universal patterns, but compose a sequence of bleak documentary reports of the skirmishes that drive Edward around his kingdom and eventually into a castle's sewer to die a horrific death. Grandiloquence and bravura comic playing of the sort that occurs in *The Jew of Malta* or in the Pedringano scenes of *The Spanish Tragedy* are quite out of place in this play. Instead players are called upon to get ordinary actions right: putting on costumes, capturing and tying up a man, or, most horrible, making certain that the most grotesque but ingenious of executions should be seen to work with the maximum of pain. The play does not address itself to the question of why the king should be killed but how the king should be killed.

Marlowe dramatizes events. Later, Shakespeare shaped his scenes into entities partaking of ritual, with beginnings, middles, and ends. We feel that all his history plays are built in some way about an idea of England, whether it be described in John of Gaunt's dying speech or be implicit in our awareness that Falstaff and Bolingbroke are both children of commodity or, to put it another way, that just as peoples get the rulers they deserve, so monarchs get the subjects they deserve. But Marlowe's historiography, like his dramaturgy, is demystificatory: there are few references to God and no sense that the monarch rules by divine right. Instead we witness a play that is wholly concerned with the Court, with the political basis of power. When Edward said, 'Two kings in England cannot reign at once' (V.i.58), he presumably reminded the audience of the awful pragmatism that had led to the execution of Mary Queen of Scots only a few years before the play. Edward can rule only when he has the support of the Queen and the barons. This he throws away by flaunting his homosexuality and by elevating his base minions to positions of command over the *noblesse de race*. Apart from his minions, only his brother, Edmund Earl of Kent, feels any sort of loyalty for him, but he can wield no power. His chief rival, Mortimer Junior, reflects when his own power is at its height: 'Feared am I more than loved: then let me be feared' (V.iv.52). Edward, however, does not have the power to be feared, only an ability to be hated. He childishly believes that respect is automatically due to him by virtue of his office and does not realize that he must win power by his actions as a man. His enemies are able to order his death by instructing the executioners that with the stripping away of Edward's regiment there is nothing to fear.

This view of politics is obviously Machiavelli's – the lines I quoted refer back to the famous chapter (xvii) in *The Prince* on whether it is better for a prince to be loved or feared. (Machiavelli in fact gives us another analysis of the player king.) Marlowe had brought Machiavelli on to the stage as Prologue to his *Jew of Malta*, but the earlier play is still basically Christian. The villain there is a form of vice, manipulating those who have espoused the evil of this world, and he, like all scourges of God, receives condign punishment. He perishes in a boiling cauldron, a stage tableau that recalls medieval visions of the punishment of the greedy. Barabas and Ithamore are dramatizations of the popular Machiavelli, the bogyman created in Catholic Europe who played the role of devil in newly protestant England. Barabas may die only by accident, but we do feel that Malta has purged itself of one moral cancer. Marlowe uses all the spectacular effects of the popular theatre and Barabas' energy, his ferocious assaults against hypocritical authority, make him an attractive stage figure. His fall, as we saw in Chapter 2, is a spectacular stage fall. In *Edward II* there is no symbol of a new order, only a boy king, a notorious sign of an unstable kingdom (witness the procession of weak boy kings in France at the time) who orders the death of Mortimer as an act of private revenge. As we noted, the play takes place on one level, suggesting a lack of moral dimension in its politics. It does not, in other words, contain any trace of the *psychomachia*, the battle between good and evil. Like *Richard II* it is truly Machiavellian in that it is a neutral record of what men do that does not assert what they ought to do. (Although *Richard III* has a 'Machiavellian' hero, he is a bogyman, opposed by Henry Tudor who fights to all intents as God's champion.)

The predominant impression that a performances gives, then, is of people being busy – the action is seldom interspersed, as it is in *Richard II*, by allegorical scenes although individual characters may deliver brief choric commentary. Marlowe has condensed Holinshed's Chronicle of the twenty-three years of Edward's reign to about a year. The text is itself brief: the recording of the Prospect production which contains few cuts and ample music lasts only 2½ hours.[3] Characters often remark on the haste of others as they enter: everyone is obsessed with securing power. Our study of *Mucedorus* revealed the pace possible on Elizabethan popular stages: Marlowe too leaps deftly from place to place, jumping over months and years, but his intention is more serious – not just to tell a story quickly and get the audience to delight in its conventions, but to show the race of history. It is arguable in fact that whereas Kyd was seeking to turn history to tragedy, Marlowe in this play sought to turn tragedy back towards history. For at the end the king dies powerless, almost naked, but, unlike Lear, little more self-aware than he was at the start. Power, as Machiavelli realized, derives not from integrity but from seeming, and the play is a bitter comedy as well as a tragedy, as the characters allow their humours or infatuations to dictate their actions, thus fatally revealing the realities that lie beneath the shows of their power. Brecht realized this, for he entitled one of the scenes from his version of the play: 'The Queen laughs at the emptiness of the world'.[4]

According to the titlepage of its first edition (1594), the play was 'publicly acted . . . by the right honourable the Earl of Pembroke his servants'. Pembroke's company seems to have been a group of players drawn from the amalgamation of Strange's and the Admiral's company that, according to Chambers,[5] was formed for provincial touring during the plague-years 1592–3. From II.v.98ff. 'Matrevis' occurs in stage directions and speech prefixes for Arundel. This probably indicates that these two parts were doubled: Fleay calculated that the whole play could be performed by thirteen players.[6] There is no record of London performances except for two appearances at Court in those early years. The fact that the play seems to have appeared first on provincial stages rather than in the professional playhouses may account for its use of only one stage level, even its politics. Pembroke's Men may well have been taken into Worcester's company, a group which in turn passed under the patronage of Queen Anne. The title-page of a 1622 Quarto of the play records that the play was performed by 'the late Queen's Majesty's Servants at the Red Bull'.

In a play so centred on the acquisition of power, it is likely that the stage was adorned only with the 'state' or throne. It must have been large enough for Edward and Gaveston to sit side by side, a symbol of the King's violation of law and custom, and consequently, when empty, a looming image at the centre of the stage of the power vacuum created by the King's abdication. It is likely that Gaveston, who opens the play with a soliloquy, used it as a focus for his movements and gestures. Like Richard Gloucester in *Richard III* Gaveston is planning to work his way to power. Richard's physical appearance is villainous, but his skill in feigning enables him to achieve two acting coups, the incarceration of his brother Clarence and the winning of the Lady Anne for his bride. Carried on by the momentum of his success, he resolves to 'entertain a score or two of tailors, To study fashions to adorn my body' (I.ii.256–7). His visual transformation marks the psychological transformation that makes him so fascinating to audiences. Gaveston, however, 'a goodly gentleman and a stout' (bold) according to Holinshed,[7] probably appeared richly dressed from the first, so appearing to the audience as a figure of vanity (I.iv.406–14) whose reign cannot be long. Gaveston's flamboyant demeanour must have been fairly shocking. Like Faustus, moreover, Edward and Gaveston were guilty not only of crimes against the state but of sins against God. Homosexuality was savagely condemned in the Bible. Leviticus 18 and 20 catalogue what the Elizabethan translators termed abominable acts, and prescribe death for 'the man . . . that lieth with the male, as one lieth with a woman' (Lev. 20:13, Geneva Version). This law of Moses against sodomy was encoded into English law. As the Attorney General remarked in the notorious Castlehaven trial of 1631: 'sodomites are to be buried alive in the earth . . . The statute of 25. Henry 8 Cap. 6. made it felony without clergy, which though repealed by I. Mar., yet it was revived by the 5. El. Cap. 17 and is still in force'.[8] The vice seems, however, to have been more tolerated at court. In his first Satire, written within a couple of years of *Edward II*, Donne castigates those who

> not only approve,
> But in rank itchy lust, desire, and love
> The nakedness and barrenness to enjoy,
> Of thy plump muddy whore, or prostitute boy,
> Hate virtue, though she be naked and bare. (ll. 37–41)

But although homosexual acts were abominated, modern homosexual types emerged only in the nineteenth century – there is no reason to believe that Gaveston was effeminate.[9]

His fine disdainful aristocratic conceits are interrupted by a show of three poor men. It is a truly Brechtian montage that juxtaposes luxury with poverty and brings us back to reality after the seductions of Gaveston's rhetoric. The poor men alienate us from Gaveston: they must be as grotesquely poor as Gaveston is suavely extravagant. They might stand in line in distorted poses, a parade of grotesques like the beggars in *The Threepenny Opera*. He dismisses them with false promises in order to 'make them live in hope' and continues with his sensual reverie. His verse depicts a world of art and the imagination, attractive in its way, but as the audience now knows, only because the ugly reality of poverty has been banished from it. It may also sound a note of wistfulness for the great allegorical entertainments like those offered the Queen at Kenilworth in 1575 or at Elvetham in 1591.[10] The story of Actaeon was customarily moralized into an allegory of man destroyed by his passions[11] and prefigures the deaths of Gaveston and Edward – the technique we saw Marlowe using in his description of Hero's costume. What is important, however, is that we do not *see* these shows. All we see is one man jetting it alone on an empty stage, possibly embarrassing the audience by direct address, turning the soliloquy into a shared intimacy. The contrast between Gaveston's imagined world and his real world is ironic and bitterly comic. None of the characters in fact will be able to enter their imagined worlds of power or sensual delight; each can only strut on the stage where their fellows will claw their gawdy robes from off their backs, a point made almost every time a new character appears.

The court enters, presumably its first assembly since the coronation – the Bishop of Coventry announces (I.i.175) that he is on the way to the funeral rites of Edward I. But instead of a scene of celebration as Edward mounts the throne we witness disorderly dissension. Gaveston stands aside to watch the unseemly squabble between king and lords, probably standing behind one of the stage pillars or, if as on its provincial tour the play was performed simply in an open space, sitting or squatting at the edge of the playing space. From there he appears to the audience as a kind of presenter of a comedy, like Hieronimo a truchman to this political masque, in Brechtian terms a demonstrator, pricking the bubbles of the nobles' vanity. His presence 'makes strange' the world of the nobles, demonstrates its absurdity. Mortimer blusters:

> And know, my lord, ere I will break my oath,
> This sword of mine that should offend your foes
> Shall sleep within the scabbard at thy need,
> And underneath thy banners march who will,
> For Mortimer will hang his armour up.

GAVESTON: *Mort Dieu!* (I.i.84–9)

Gaveston's punning interjections ('Mortimer' and '*Mort Dieu*') act as a kind of frame, creating a tableau which demonstrates that power derives not from words but from the real forces the opposed factions might muster. Indeed the players within the pageant realise this too: when Edmund Earl of Kent comes to the aid of his brother with what Mycetes had requested from Cosroe in the first scene of *Tamburlaine*, 'a great and thundering speech', he is cynically mocked by the man he threatens:

> Yet dare you brave the King unto his face.
> Brother, revenge it; and let these their heads
> Preach upon poles for trespass of their tongues.
> WARWICK: O our heads! (I.i.116–19)

These interjections are like the 'gag' of an inferior clown whose abilities only enable him to spoil scenes played by his betters. What is important about this scene is that nowhere do the nobles reveal a disinterested concern for England, a concern that is revealed in Holinshed's account of this part of Edward's reign.[12] Later (II.ii.156ff.) they accuse the King of draining his treasury as he showers gifts on Gaveston, threatening the security of the realm and of the English territories in France and Ireland. Our first impression in the play, however, is that they are incensed because their own proximity to the throne, the source of power, is threatened and, conceivably, because they feel their own masculinity threatened by the overt homosexuality of the King. As Judith Weil writes, 'Edward's enemies use the condition of England as the pretext for a revolt on which they have already determined'.[13]

The nobles storm out and Gaveston comes forward to take his part in the play for power. He kneels at his lover's feet and possibly stays kneeling, mutely begging his reward, until Edward compulsively decks him with the insignia of Lord High Chamberlain, Secretary, Earl of Cornwall, and, to climax with a sly pun, 'King and Lord of Man'. He and Edward probably mount the throne together as Gaveston, after this tawdry piece of emotional blackmail, muses on the great image of power that thrilled the audiences at *Tamburlaine*:

> It shall suffice me to enjoy your love,
> Which whiles I have, I think myself as great
> As Caesar riding in the Roman street
> With captive kings at his triumphant car. (I.i.170–3)

Having outraged the lords temporal, the two minions alienate the spiritual power of the realm. From the throne they witness the first disinvestiture of the play, the savage baiting of the Bishop of Coventry. Like Kyd, Marlowe was undoubtedly counting on anti-Romish feeling in the audience – anti-Papal arguments appear in the text at I.iv.96ff. – to balance the scene, but the wanton savagery of Gaveston's pronouncement: 'He shall to prison, and there die in bolts' (I.i.196) is disturbing and ends the scene on an ominously prophetic note.

We have examined so far only the first 206 lines of the play. It is extraordinarily economical: Marlowe has created the world of the Court and established a double perspective on it. Gaveston who has himself been 'placed' by the pageant of the three poor men, presents to us the comedy of politics, then coolly moves into the pageant to grab from it what he can. Marlowe deliberately establishes a comic distance on a set of situations sketched out in caricature in the manner of old comedy, in order to isolate those moments that reveal to the audience the inner emotions and sufferings of his leading characters.

The first of these poignant moments occurs in the next scene, where we encounter the rejected Queen. She appears in an action of gathering pace, but is unable to joint the conspiracy, being paralysed by self-pity. In a later sequence Marlowe assigns what we might take to be an extremely formal manner for her, suited to the particular talents of a boy player dressed in a rich iconic costume:

Look where the sister of the King of France

Sits wringing of her hands and beats her breast. (I.iv.187–8)

In fact he has made a virtue of necessity: the Queen in this play is a passive creature, taken up by Mortimer only when he needs her to consolidate his position. Here he ignores her muted appeal for his affection: 'Farewell, Sweet Mortimer; and for my sake Forbear to levy arms against the king', responding only with an obscene pun, as he and his conspirators seek out a *casus belli*. 'Ay, if words will serve; if not, I must.'

Scene iv chronicles the seesawing between sexual infatuation and political contrivance that characterizes the play's action; after the establishing of individual characters we see in it the real sexual and political allegiances between the King and Gaveston and the Queen and Mortimer Junior, while at the end the King plans a marriage of convenience between Gaveston and his niece. It begins with Edward daring to seat Gaveston at his side in full view of the barons, an action which whips them into fury and leads to Gaveston (and Kent to boot) being hauled ignominiously off stage. Edward's want of prudence may have cost him authority in the audience's eyes; he may regain their sympathy as the Archbishop of Canterbury threatens to discharge the allegiance the lords owe the King, and when, asked bluntly by Mortimer, 'Why should you love him whom the world hates so?', he cries out, 'Because he loves me more than all the world' (I.iv.76–7). It is a simple cry, a commonplace sentiment perhaps (it may well be an echo of Don Andrea's profession of love for Bel-Imperia[14] and even of Chiron's passion for Lavinia[15]) but none the less moving for that. When Gaveston returns, before he departs into exile, he and the King exchange pictures. The gest is a moving dramatization of their love: these miniatures hung about the neck might be useful later, for the actor playing Gaveston to gaze upon when he is taken prisoner and perhaps for Edward in his prison. In the exchange of pictures Edward as it were confides his 'self' to his friend, all too aware that his divorce from Gaveston marks a divorce between his role and his sense of his own identity.[16] So when his weeping Queen appears, Edward treats her with unaccustomed brutality, possibly descending from the state where Gaveston sits in her place, and possibly throwing her to the ground, and banishing her from his sight until she has secured the repeal of Gaveston's banishment. 'A French strumpet', he labels her: ironically Gaveston too was French. When the lords return she draws Mortimer aside and seemingly wins him over to her cause. The audience does not hear her arguments, but the tableau they make together, commented on by the lords, is crucial to the development of their relationship. The technique is like that in *The Winter's Tale* where Hermione urges Polixenes to prolong his stay at Leontes' court. There we may presume the two were innocent: here Marlowe uses the ambiguities of dumb show to reveal the subtle transformation of sympathetic association into an adulterous passion. At this point neither presumably acknowledges even inwardly their growing attraction to one another. These two sequences, the exchange of pictures and the Queen's pleading – which could be played in the same stage space to great effect – undermine the celebrations that follow Edward's return '*mourning*' and reception of the news of his minion's recall.

Act I chronicled the rise of Gaveston; Act II depicts the consolidation of Mortimer's power and the appearance in Edward's circle of two new minions, Baldock and Spenser. The first scene is built around two gests. In the first Spenser urges Baldock to cast off the garb and manner of the puritan scholar for the flamboyant mien of the man of action:

> You must be proud, bold, pleasant, resolute –
> And now and then, stab as occasion serves. (II.i.42–3)

The second line undoubtedly contains a sexual pun. In the second gest Gaveston's betrothed Margaret appears. Her first entrance 'quotes' the first entrance of her betrothed in that both bear letters from their lovers. She will also be associated in the audience's consciousness with Isabella in that each will be ignored by her frolicking spouse. When Edward appears he restlessly attends the return of Gaveston while almost oblivious to groundswell of the revolt of the barons. In a scene reminiscent of the masque of the scutcheons in *The Spanish Tragedy* (I.iv.), Mortimer and Lancaster prepare an allegorical show, a ceremonial tilt that forecasts the ruin of Gaveston and Kent.[17] What is significant is that the shields with their *imprese* need not be shown on stage, since they are fully described by Mortimer and Lancaster. Perhaps this was an economy for the touring company; perhaps Marlowe was simply refusing to glamorize the court of Edward. The shows of *Tamburlaine* may anaesthetize us to the brutality and violence that they accompany. Here Marlowe is insisting on the isolation of his characters. Gaveston returns presumably in full splendour and presumably again mounts the throne to Edward. The lords wheel across the stage with sarcastic greetings and Gaveston from his eminence taunts them politically and sexually:

> Base leaden earls that glory in your birth,
> Go sit at home and eat your tenants' beef,
> And come not here to scoff at Gaveston,
> Whose mounting thoughts did never creep so low
> As to bestow a look on such as you. (II.ii.74–8)

The covert threat breaks out into overt rebellion as Mortimer wounds Gaveston, perhaps sexually. The King exits with his wife and brother, only to return thirty-six lines later during which time there comes news of the capture of Mortimer Senior. With his brother, the King faces a barrage of threats: again the sequence begins with Mortimer drawing his sword. Threat follows threat as the King is subjected to the kind of verbal battery familiar to modern audiences from interrogation sequences. He is probably driven down-stage so that he can turn to address the audience directly on the nobles' departure: 'My swelling heart for very anger breaks' (II.ii.199). His only ally Kent admonishes him for his impolitic love. Impetuously Edward dismisses him and is left quite alone for a moment before the Act rushes to its close in a montage of scenes of league-making and threat.

Marlowe seems to end the Act with a quoted gesture reminiscent of Kyd's figural construction and anticipating Brecht (see Chapter 2). The original stage directions are puzzling and this is only one way of recreating their sense. After Pembroke has left the stage, Gaveston is addressed in one line by a 'Horse-boy': 'My lord, we'll quickly be at Cobham' (II.v.111). The character is unidentified – he may be a servant of 'James' (see below). But could he approach Gaveston mutely suggesting sexual favours in return for advancement just as Baldock and Spenser had approached Edward? He is introduced without explanation and without comment – rather like Mortimer Senior who appeared earlier to make a plea to the King for toleration. These figures have so few lines that their 'characters' cannot be established by their verbal styles but by the appearances of the players taking the parts: we might compare the eloquence of faces in documentary films like Eisenstein's *Battleship Potemkin*.

In Act III we witness a movement that leads Edward to the height of his fortunes in the play, his victory over the rebels. Yet this is brought about not by a desire to assert political supremacy or protect the integrity of the realm but only as his emotions are goaded into a great passion of revenge. We know his supremacy is precarious because regularly throughout the Act we catch glimpses of other more politic creatures methodically working their own ends.

The Act begins with the eclipse of Gaveston. His end is muted and inglorious. He comes back '*mourning*', probably with folded arms, the conventional pose, at last perhaps conscious of the love rather than the power he has lost and reminding us of the moment in I.iv. when Edward had appeared mourning for him. The forlorn procession is rudely ambushed by

Warwick and his party and Gaveston is bundled off to execution, without being given the chance to vindicate himself or even express his farewell to the earth. All that we hear is a typically Marlovian sardonic exchange:

GAVESTON: Treacherous earl, shall I not see the King?

WARWICK: The king of heaven perhaps, no other king.

　Away! (III.i.15–17)

There is no preacher, no parting bell, just a glimpse of a life about to be efficiently extinguished. Another character who appears nowhere else in the play, called simply 'James', remonstrates perfunctorily with Warwick, but concludes 'it booted not for us to strive' (III.i.18) and resigns himself to going to break the news to Edward. Gaveston's is a lonely death as is going to be that of his lover.

Ironically the next scene shows Edward armed and accoutred for war. The man who had shunned the regiment of the court for his private infatuation appears '*with Drums and Fifes*' at the very moment of Gaveston's execution. He is still self-absorbed, however, and instead of the usual rolling and thundering Marlovian rhythms that accompany great shows of strength we have rhythmic irregularity and a plaint which is saved from petulance by its matter-of-fact report:

Warwick I know is rough; and Lancaster

Inexorable; and I shall never see

My lovely Piers, my Gaveston, again.

The barons overbear me with their pride. (III.ii.6–9)

Spenser and Baldock attempt to stiffen up his sinews and the rest of the scene quickens as different groups enter Edward's presence in a rhythmic montage of characters bearing token properties. First comes '*Hugh Spenser, an old man, father to the young Spenser with his truncheon and soldiers*' (III.ii.30). This little pageant seems like a popular rising for the King – it is, apart from the pageant of the three poor men at the beginning of the play, the only glimpse of the common life we have. But it turns out there is no sense of altruism or duty to the country here. The truncheon is a false symbol of command and order, for this regiment is only a faction.

Bound to your highness everlastingly

For favours done in him unto us all. (III.ii.41–2)

Edward presumably embarrasses them both with his arch quip at the lack of style that this sincerity shows (or does it contain a bawdy pun?):

Thy father, Spencer?

To which Spencer replies with an unfortunate attempt at courtly compliment:

True, and it like your grace,

That pours in lieu of all your goodness shown,

His life, my lord, before your princely feet. (III.ii.44–6)

It is enough, however, for Edward yet again to shower his friend with offices.

There is an ominous reversal when Isabella enters with news that Normandy has been lost to France. She presumably wears her crown, a mute comment on the usurped truncheon of Spenser. Edward again seems not to take the point: his joy at this show of loyalty makes him confident that the crisis can be solved simply by sending off an embassy of his wife and son. The joy is shattered when Arundel comes to tell him bluntly that Gaveston is dead. The original speech prefixes assign his lines here to 'Lord Matre' – an indication that the two parts were taken by the same player. Marlowe might have made this doubling intentional – Matrevis will be the agent of Edward's death. He artfully gives Arundel a long and plain narrative that tells us what we have already been shown (in the manner of Kyd) so that we can attend to Edward's reaction to the news. For once we feel that he will compose himself for action, and so it seems he does when he kneels and works himself up to fury:

> Treacherous Warwick! Traitorous Mortimer!
> If I be England's king, in lakes of gore
> Your headless trunks, your bodies will I trail,
> That you may drink your fill, and quaff in blood,
> And stain my royal standard with the same;
> That so my bloody colours may suggest
> Remembrance of revenge immortally
> On your accursed traitorous progeny,
> You villains that have slain my Gaveston. (III.ii.134–42)

But the vision is childishly ingenious and suggests martial impotence rather than strength. Ian McKellen, who took the lead in the celebrated Prospect production of 1969, having thrown himself indulgently to the ground at this point, rose slowly during these threats. But then his sword dropped ineffectually as his thoughts returned to the slaying of Gaveston. Instead of making preparations for battle, Edward upon compulsion begs in his usual manner for affection:

> Spencer, sweet Spencer, I adopt thee here,
> And merely of our love we do create thee
> Earl of Gloucester and Lord Chamberlain,
> Despite of times, despite of enemies. (III.ii.143–6)

Indeed the Barons seem to have sensed that Edward will form another homosexual alliance and, as if to flaunt their power, send a herald wearing Edward's own bearings to offer peace on condition he renounce this faction. The courtly prurience of the speech

> from your princely person you remove
> This Spencer, as a putrefying branch
> That deads the royal vine, whose golden leaves

Empale your princely head, your diadem,
Whose brightness such pernicious upstarts dim . . . (III.ii.161–5)
merely goads Edward into embracing his new minion – and battle commences.

Like so many battles on the Elizabethan stage, this is a musical battle with alarums of drum and trumpet and 'excursions': sallies of two or three soldiers across the stage. In the midst of the brawl Spencer is heard crying 'Right will prevail' (III.iii.5), and yet of course Marlowe has turned his scanty resources to dramatic effect in that this battle should not be a formal exchange of challenges and taunts: instead these occur in the middle of the fray as if to emphasize this disorder. Not that Edward would recognize this; when he has the barons captive he vaunts:

Now, lusty lords, now, not by chance of war,
But justice of the quarrel and the cause,
Vailed is your pride. (III.iii.36–8)

But justice does not appear in the action of this play. Might and the chance of war are the sole arbiters. Edward sends Warwick and Lancaster to instant execution in revenge for the execution of Gaveston: Warwick's final words, 'Farewell, vain world' (III.iii.64), and the blocking of his exit might well recall the end of Gaveston. Edward shouts in triumph:

Sound drums and trumpets! March with me, my friends;
Edward this day hath crowned him king anew. (III.iii.75–6)

(Here the Prospect production effectively added a song from the *Carmina Burana*, '*O Fortuna, velut luna!*') Shakespeare might have ended the scene there: Marlowe, typically, instantly deflates the moment by showing the caterpillars of Edward's commonwealth, Spencer and Baldock, plotting to frustrate the embassy of the Queen. They have no care for the realm but only for the frustration of the enemy faction.

Act IV opens with another montage, a series of short scenes that here constitute a kind of dramatic shorthand – under them, the Prospect players sounded a racing piano tune suggestive of the action's gathering pace. Each scene is a little gest in which a character moves on to the stage to state his case: Kent, the 'conscience' of the play, faithful to the body politic although he finds the King's private conduct repugnant; Mortimer, freshly escaped from prison, resolute and ambitious; the Queen, again alone and bereft until the appearance of Mortimer gives her new confidence. In this scene and in the next but one there is no evidence elsewhere in the text that 'Mortimer and Isabel do kiss while they conspire' (IV.i.21), as Kent claims, so it may be better to stage their allegiance with dignity and circumspection, in contrast to the frolics of Edward and his minions. The only action or change of Fortune begins in IV.iii. when Edward appears triumphant to announce 'great execution Done through the realm' (IV.iii.6–7), a line that might well draw a guffaw from the crowd of sadistic toadies that surrounds him. The note containing the names is missing from the text: reading aloud a catalogue compiled from Holinshed might restore decorum (or more guffaws?) to the scene. It would work like the catalogue of the Agincourt dead in *Henry V* (IV.viii.78ff.). Another letter arrives which casually announces the escape of Mortimer. Edward proclaims his confidence and, growing in kingliness, musters his forces, interrupting his proclamation with an aside(?) to himself:

> Ah, nothing grieves me but my little boy
> Is thus misled to countenance their ills. (IV.iii.47–8)

At this moment Edward is impressive, a contrast with Richard II who greets adversity with self-indulgent poesy and maudlin repentance – and with his wife who has now turned hysterical. But he will shortly lapse into childish impotency.

Marlowe feels no need to portray the battle that follows; another battle here would distort the balance of the play. Instead we hear the sound of trumpets and zoom in on its latter stages as the hunted Edward '*flies about the stage*'. The playwright then internalizes the conflict between, to use the categories of Marvell's 'Horatian Ode', the 'industrious valour' of Mortimer and the 'ancient rights' of Edward by bringing on Kent, who had been impulsively banished the King's person for speaking against Gaveston. His agonized debate in the soliloquy in the middle of the battle prepares us for the return of a natural if not a just order at the end of the play. Edward has just, after all, urged his minions into battle with an intoxicated cry for death in love:

> Give me my horse, and let's reinforce our troops,
> And in this bed of honour die with fame. (IV.v.6–7)

The Queen's faction is victorious: when she appears, however, she disconcertingly chooses as her first action to invest her son impulsively with the title of Lord Warden of the Realm – exactly in the manner of her husband. Mortimer smothers Kent's enquiries about the future of the King and ruthlessly dispatches the dignified figure of Spencer Senior to execution. He has been brought in by another 'documentary' character, Rice ap Howell, who will also figure in the capture of Edward. It might be that Marlowe is simply following his chronicle sources, although the device is effective: Edward will die among strangers.

After this scene of movement, we turn to one of the few emblematic scenes of the play, built about a Latin motto, here quoted by Leicester from Seneca's *Thyestes*:

> quem dies vidit veniens superbum,
> Hunc dies vidit fugiens iacentem. (ll. 613–14)

Jonson translated the lines at the end of his *Sejanus*:

> For whom the morning saw so great and high,
> Thus low and little 'fore the even doth lie.

By such a device Marlowe like Kyd tilts his documentary a little towards ritual for this part of the play. (There is also an analogy with the similarly placed 'Beggar and King' scene in *Richard II* that we examined in Chapter 2.) The scene was prepared for by Mortimer's masque of *imprese*: it is all the more effective as this is a *living* emblem of grief – we may not have seen but only heard about the earlier emblems. To mark the change in Edward's fortunes, Marlowe has him disguised in monkish weeds; he enters to sit and philosophize at the feet of the Abbot and monks of Neath, perhaps before the empty stage throne, now a mute symbol of his former estate. Translated to a life of contemplation, he is a pitiful figure, fearful lest the monks might betray him for gold, hugging his minions to him, and like a tired child, casting his head into the lap of the Abbot when he hears Baldock mention the name of Mortimer. Rice ap Howell enters with Leicester and 'a Mower'. This is presumably the traditional figure of Time and Death, carrying a scythe, even perhaps an hourglass.[18] Edward bids a fearful farewell of his friends, but suddenly collects himself and, in a dramatic gesture reminiscent of Tamburlaine, divests himself of his disguise to appear at last as the natural person of the King:

> Hence feigned weeds, unfeignèd are my woes. (IV.vi.96)

He has snatched the advantage of the scene by destroying its mode, interrupting the ritual, and boldly and alone goes to confront his fate in contrast to his minions who mouth vain professions of love and conventional pieties:

> O is he gone! Is noble Edward gone,
> Parted from hence, never to see us more?
> Rent, sphere of heaven, and, fire, forsake thy orb,
> Earth, melt to air; gone is my sovereign,
> Gone, gone, alas, never to make return. (IV.vi.99–103)

The scene moves back to documentary with Rice ap Howell's matter-of-fact instructions in prose, although we note a haunting pun as the Mower begs his reward with 'Remember me' – the words used later by *Hamlet*'s Ghost who, like him, brought death to the realm.

Act V portrays the protracted agony of Edward's captivity and death. His friends have fallen away; only his brother Kent makes an abortive attempt to succour him and is quickly beheaded by Mortimer. Between the abdication scene and the scene of Edward's death, we witness the rapidly ascending power of Mortimer and his consort, Edward's Queen. Just as quickly as Mortimer's light shines in the kingdom is it extinguished by a sudden flaring of power by the boy king. The cheerless comedy of the opening of the play has gone, but it is not necessarily sympathy for the King that has taken its place. It is arguable in fact that in this play Marlowe deliberately chooses not to have the hero achieve tragic recognition. Whereas Richard II or Richard III come to understand something of the universal condition of man or some understanding of the roles they had created for themselves, Edward is now displayed almost entirely from without, with the emphasis on his physical suffering and endurance. Marlowe traces the particular pathology of a mind moving towards the brink of madness. Edward's mordant wit may be impressive as he confronts his tattered robes and excrement-covered body:

> Tell Isabel the Queen, I looked not thus
> When for her sake I ran at tilt in France,
> And there unhorsed the duke of Cleremont. (V.v.67–9)

A few lines later, in very unimpressive lines, he shows that he realises what his state is without suggesting that he recognizes why he should be brought thus low:

> Know that I am a king – O, at that name
> I feel a hell of grief! Where is my crown?
> Gone, gone; and do I remain alive? (V.v.88–90)

The play, in other words, reverts to documentary at the last.

The Act opens with the King confronting Leicester and the Bishop of Winchester who have come to Killingworth to fetch the crown from the King. Most of the dialogue is Edward's as he muses on the cares of kingship, the wrongs done him by Mortimer and Isabel, and the appearance of the crown itself. He signally fails to reflect upon the importance of this event, his giving up of the crown, perhaps because this scene is not a ceremony but a formality. Power was transferred earlier, on the field of battle. When Richard II comes down from the walls of Flint Castle and then later uncrowns himself we feel that we are watching not only a man realise his role but the ritualised end of an old order. As Briggs remarked, 'Richard is intellectually master of the situation';[19] Edward's grief, as he confesses himself, makes him lunatic (V.i.114). Accordingly Mortimer's emissaries should not arrange themselves in formal positions: perhaps just wait casually as the King 'rages' and stand patiently while he offers them the bauble and snatches it back. Edward has no conception of the shape of the scene: the blocking of his moves should therefore be unsymmetrical, un-geometrical. Having lost the crown he might be expected to win some sympathy for his personal grief, but his impotent gesture of sending the Queen a tear-stained handkerchief with the command that, if she be not moved by it, should be returned to dip in his blood is too self-pitying and childishly self-dramatizing – Marlowe might be remembering Hieronimo's handkerchief – to be impressive. Edward is not even permitted to continue to dwell alone in peace, establish a setting for his woes, for Berkeley arrives to move him across the land to another place of sorrows. Again the king is given a melodramatic gesture as he offers his naked breast as if to Berkeley's sword.

Just as we had to look behind the shadows of the action in V.i. for the political substance of the scene, so in V.ii. we must look beyond the forms of Mortimer's court. Although it is in this scene that Mortimer is brought the crown and privy seal, we witness how the Queen, despite the bold confidence of her lover, fears for her life and in fact is the first to overtly but obliquely suggest that her husband should die:

But Mortimer, as long as he survives
What safety rest for us, or for my son. (V.ii.42–3)

She too sends her spouse some token: what it is is not specified, but a handkerchief would echo the last scene and signal the complete extinction of the love that used to bind her to Edward.

For scene iii Marlowe departed from Holinshed, his principal source, and went to an episode narrated in Stow's *Annals* (1592), which recounts how the King was shaved of his hair and beard to disguise him as he was moved about from one stronghold to another. Edward has moved from one kind of masculine society, the homosexual glamour of the Court, to another. He has been disinvested of his robes of office, and the brutal shaving with puddle-water, performed by Matrevis and Gurney who are to be accomplices in his murder, is, like an army or public school initiation ceremony, compounded of sadistic violence and sexual humiliation. They bring torches, the customary playhouse signification for night, here emblematic of the darkness that will now invade the stage. The scene is made more pathetic as the King has a last glimpse of his brother Edmund whom he had previously ignored and whose agonized loyalty will cost him his life at Mortimer's hands. The scene is both naturalistic (perhaps the stage trap was used) and ritualistic as Edward is prepared for extinction. The quenching of the torches (V.iii.47) reminds us of the masque at the end of Act III of *The Spanish Tragedy* and, like that, occurs immediately before the industrious scenes of death.

Mortimer has now become a stage villain, confiding his ambitions and fears to the audience, a game played earlier by Gaveston. Kent's prophecy (IV.v.24) of 'that love that hatcheth death and hate' is being realised. It is the facelessness of his ambition, his refusal to express emotion either here or earlier in the play, that makes him such a frightening figure.[20] He plans the death of the King by a riddlingly worded order, and like Faustus, conjures a diabolic agent to effect his plans. This agent, Lightborn, bears Lucifer's name. He is Marlowe's invention although he may have borrowed the name from one of the devils in the Chester cycle. It is possible that he made his entrance at Mortimer's command – 'Lightborn, come forth' – (V.iv.20) from the cellarage through a trap in the stage. So he appeared in Toby Robertson's Prospect production, as a suave and glistening creature from the homosexual underworld. Like Ithamore he boasts of his quaint and brave 'tricks' of murder. When Lightborn is dismissed, Mortimer boasts that he is at the height of his powers:

And, to conclude, I am Protector now.
Now all is sure: the Queen and Mortimer
Shall rule the realm, the King and none rule us.

> Mine enemies will I plague, my friends advance,
> And what I list command, who dare control? (V.iv.65–9)

Yet his power seems less certain as we watch the traditional ceremonies of the coronation scene to which this sequence acts as grotesque prologue. It would be possible to play the Archbishop of Canterbury as a mere puppet of Mortimer, theatrically investing a child with vain emblems of power – as Robertson did – but the toasting of the King's Champion in a gold goblet gives us an image of righteous aspiration to set against the stage images of sewer and vulpine intrigue we have just witnessed. In any case the coronation seems to have given Edward III a real strength for, although he cannot save Edmund who is carried out to be beheaded, he is able to resist his mother's advances and stand out against Mortimer.

The murder of Edward is one of the most horrific scenes in all drama, more horrible in that Edward dies in a manner that befits his private vice. Richard II at least died for crimes committed in the public world, having hammered out in his mind his thoughts about his life to come. He is also able to rise to unexpected feats of strength as he kills two or three of the executioners sent to dispatch him. Edward is cruelly and systematically extinguished in a little room without achieving peace of mind or even making a manful end. Lightborn enters with a torch – the image of the extinguished torches of Matrevis and Gurney lies still in our minds, although it may have been necessary to illuminate the end of the play (see Chapter 2) and conceal the stage contrivance. When the actual deed is committed we hear mention of a table and a feather bed to smother the King. Previously, however, Lightborn had ordered a red-hot spit, and Matrevis' line, 'I fear that this cry will raise the town' (V.v.113), makes it apparent that Marlowe intended the murder to be performed as Holinshed had described:[21]

> they came suddenly one night into the chamber where he lay in bed fast asleep, and with heavy featherbeds or a table (as some write) being cast upon him, they kept him down and withal put into his fundament an horn, and through the same they thrust up into his body an hot spit, or (as other have) through the pipe of a trumpet a plumber's instrument of iron made very hot, the which passing up into his entrails, and being rolled to and fro, burnt the same, so as no appearance of any wound or hurt outwardly might be at once perceived. His cry did move many within the castle and town of Berkeley to compassion, plainly hearing him utter a wailful noise, as the tormentors were about to murder him, so that divers being awakened therewith (as they themselves confessed) prayed heartily to God to receive his soul, when they understood by his cry what the matter meant.

The moment is scarcely tolerable: some may shield themselves from full horror by speculating that Edward's death is a parody of his sodomy, or even by feeling that in his last moments he has come to be a martyr. (He is so depicted in a roof boss at Bristol cathedral.) Marlowe makes nothing sensational, neither does he offer any comfort, either by humour as at the end of *The Jew of Malta* or by allowing his hero to carry some victory out of defeat. He gives merely a dramatic report of the events.

The scene opens with Lightborn, Matrevis, and Gurney making preparations for their awful labour. The order attached to the original warrant, '*pereat iste*', prepares us for the stabbing of Lightborn immediately after Edward's death, and perhaps prefigures the action in the final scene where Mortimer must pay the price for his ambition. Edward is discovered, perhaps in a discovery place, perhaps emerging almost naked from the stage trap, the sewer where he had been kept. He can be only an object of pity here as he encounters the smooth hypocrisy of Lightborn and narrates the manner of his life (V.v.51–66). During this speech the bed may have been thrust out. Lightborn prevails upon him to lie down, probably with his head towards the audience, so that the table placed on top of the body can shield the audience from Lightborn's fatal act.[22] Robertson made the execution an act of love – the same actor could possibly play Gaveston and Lightborn – and had Lightborn fall across Edward's body as he too died, stabbed by Gurney.

All that is left is to watch the reversal of fortune for Mortimer and the Queen. Acts IV and V chronicled Mortimer's relentless rise: his fall is sudden and complete. Just as Marlowe allowed Edward to play his final part with dignity and without self-dramatization, so Mortimer and the Queen face death with stoical firmness. He might remove his own coronet as he speaks his final lines:

Farewell, fair Queen, weep not for Mortimer,

That scorns the world, and as a traveller

Goes to discover countries yet unknown. (V.vi.64–6)

Quem dies vidit veniens superbum . . . There is a simple tragic response engendered when his head is brought in thirty lines later, the response that comes, as with the bringing on of Hastings' head in *Richard III*, from realizing simply that he who was living is now dead. So too the Queen's life has run its course. She, who had been neglected by her husband, had gratefully accepted the attentions of Mortimer, is now reduced to grief again as her son orders her to the Tower. Unlike Shakespeare, Marlowe does not end his tragedy with reflections on the quality of his hero's life and if he does suggest that the land has been cauterized of a cancerous evil, 'hatched' by Mortimer, the sense of justice is mitigated as we watch the boy king in a gruesome act of private revenge place the traitor's head on the funeral hearse of his father. With the hearse are brought on funeral robes. Throughout the play we have witnessed scenes of lavish investiture: the action ends in stark contrast with the King donning the sombre black robes of mourning and leaving the stage to the accompaniment, probably, of a funeral march.

7 · *Doctor Faustus*: **ritual shows**

There could not be a greater contrast between the dramaturgy of *Edward II* and that of *Doctor Faustus*. In the former play Marlowe eschewed both the devices for dramatic spectacle provided by the popular playhouses and symmetrically shaped scenes of the sort we found in *The Spanish Tragedy*. In effect, if *Edward II* is like street theatre *Doctor Faustus* is like grand opera. In this play instead of documentary we find ritual, a play in which the magical practices are patterned on religious ceremonies, in which the life of the hero is defined not in historical and political terms but as he experiences the rites of passage from one mental state to another. (The play, like *The Spanish Tragedy*, might be topical, exploiting for the popular theatre the reports of the activities and tribulations of Dee and Kelly, two London magicians of the 1580s.) By depicting the practices of ceremonial magic – the magic of witches who employed demonic agents – Marlowe revealed the creative powers of ritual through all the spectacular devices the playhouses had to offer. The play is a great phantasmagoria of scenic properties, ceremonial and emblematic costumes, battle-games between powers of good and evil, action portrayed on the three levels of the stage, dances, music, Latin declamations, mirror scenes in which the portentous actions of the hero are travestied in the cross-talk and knockabout games of the playhouse clowns. The unlocalized and empty stage of the popular play-houses was as suited to the procession of shows as it was to narrative. The play moves from the sardonic to the sublime, taps an important vein of folk culture as well as drawing on the high culture of theology. Faustus is a juggler in its etymological sense of 'joker' (*joculator*), and as a conjurer of spirits he is like a modern conjurer or trickster. In this respect the play, like *The Spanish Tragedy*, aims satirical barbs at privilege and authority (especially papal authority). But it is also a tragedy: whereas in *Edward II* we noted that the play moved away from tragedy towards history as the hero was denied recognition, here the shows staged by and for the devil serve not only to delight the minds of Faustus and the audience but to instil into the hero the most intense kind of experiential knowledge, the kind of tragic recognition Kyd described as 'feeling perception'.

Uncertainties, however, over the text, the date, and even the authorship of parts of *Doctor Faustus* make it very difficult to reach firm conclusions about the author's intentions or the response engendered by early performances. The play was first printed in 1604, eleven years after Marlowe's death. Of that Quarto (A), Sir Walter Greg writes:[1]

> The text printed in 1604 I believe to represent a reconstruction from memory of the piece as originally performed, but shortened for provincial acting, occasionally interpolated, and progressively adapted to the capacities of a declining company and the taste of a vulgar audience. It preserves, however, almost all Marlowe's share in the composition, and presents it with substantial fidelity though far from verbal accuracy.

On 22 November 1602 Henslowe had paid £4 to William Birde and Samuel Rowley 'for ther adicyones in doctor fostes',[2] and then in 1616 there appeared another Quarto (B), 2,121 lines in length as opposed to the 1,517 lines of the 1604 text, which presumably includes these or other additions, and which Greg believes to have been 'prepared for publication by an editor on the basis of a manuscript containing the author's drafts from which the prompt-book had in the first instance been transcribed'.[3] The new material is largely comic – it contains notably the Pope-baiting sequence – and it is difficult to decide whether it was included simply to please further Greg's 'vulgar audience' or whether these scenes conform to Marlowe's original design for the play. They may well do, for most of the added scenes come from the same source that Marlowe used. Like the additions to *The Spanish Tragedy* they represent the response of a near contemporary to the play, perhaps a response to its possibilities in the popular playhouses of London. Certainly the A text could like *Edward II* be performed on the simple stages available outside London: it does not stipulate an upper level from which the devils might preside over the conjuring of Mephostophilis and over Faustus' leave-taking of the Scholars, does not require a 'window' for the horned knight Benvolio, and omits the final scene in which the Scholars enter to find Faustus' scattered limbs[4] – property limbs which a touring company may not have wanted to transport about.

The source of the play is the English translation that appeared in 1592 – the translator is known only by his initials, P.F. – of a German chapbook, *The Historie of the damnable life, and deserved death of Doctor Iohn Faustus*. Verbal parallels between Marlowe's play and certain plays of the late 1580s have, however, led some scholars to conjecture an earlier date for the play, and so displaced it from the regard in which it was once held as the culmination of Marlowe's career – he was stabbed in 1593. If though the play dates from 1592, it was probably first performed by Pembroke's Men, possibly at Court in the winter of 1592–3, more probably at the Theatre during the brief abatement of the plague in 1593, and then in the provinces

as mentioned above. The book of the play was probably then sold to
Henslowe and the Admiral's (or Strange's) Men so that from late 1594 the
play was available for performance at the Rose.[5] It may have opened on 30
September 1594 when Henslowe took £3.12.0, a large amount, and it was
played regularly thereafter.[6] One further piece of evidence (difficult to
interpret though it is) for the contemporary staging of the play is worth
reproducing here. It comes from *The Second Report of Doctor John Faustus,
containing his Appearance, and the Deeds of Wagner*, an anonymous work of
1594 which, 'although based upon a German original, is largely an independent work by an author who shows . . . familiarity with the English
theatre.'[7] In Chapter 7 we find a description of a vision seen outside
Wittenberg that gives all the signs of being based on memories of performances of the play either in a London playhouse or more probably at
Court:[8]

> they might distinctly perceive a goodly stage to be reared (shining to
> sight like the bright burnished gold) upon many a fair pillar of clearest
> crystal, whose feet rested upon the arch of the broad rainbow; therein
> was the high throne wherein the king should sit, and that proudly
> placed with two and twenty degrees to the top, and round about curious
> wrought chairs for divers other potentates; there might you see the
> groundwork [foundation] at the one end of the stage, where out the
> personated devils should enter into their fiery ornaments, made like the
> broad wide mouth of a huge dragon, which with continual armies of
> smoke and flame breathed forth his angry stomach's rage; round about
> the eyes grew hairs, not so horrible as men call bristles, but more
> horrible, as long as stiff spears; the teeth of this hell's-mouth far
> out-stretching, and such as a man might well call monstrous and more
> than a man can by words signify; to be short, his hue of that colour
> which to himself means sorrow . . . a thick lamp black . . . At the other
> end in opposition was seen the place wherein the bloodless skirmishes
> are so often performed on the stage, the walls . . . of . . . iron,
> attempered with the most firm steel, which being brightly filed, shone
> as beautifully over the whole place as pale shining Cynthia, environed
> with high and stately turrets of the same metal and beauty, and hereat
> many in-gates and out-gates out of each side lay the bended ordnance
> showing at their wide hollows the cruelty of death; out of sundry loops
> many large banners and streamers were pendant; briefly nothing was there
> wanting that might make it a fair castle. There might you see to be short
> the gibbet, the posts, the ladders, the attiring-house, there everything
> which in the like houses either use or necessity makes common. Now
> above all was there the gay clouds *Usquequaque*, adorned with the heavenly
> firmament . . . There was lively portrayed the whole imperial army of the
> fair heavenly inhabitants, the bright angels . . . They were so naturally

done, that you would have sworn it had been heaven itself or the epitome of it, or some second heaven.

. . . now this excellent fair theatre erected, immediately after the third sound of the trumpets, there entered the Prologue attired in a black vesture, and making his three obeisances, began to show the argument of that scenical tragedy, but because it was so far off they could not understand the words, and having thrice bowed himself to the high throne, presently vanished. Then out of this representation of hell's mouth, issued out whole armies of fiery flames, and most thick foggy smokes, after which entered in a great battle of footmen devils, all armed after the best fashion with pike, etc. marching after the stroke of the courageous drum, who, girded about, laid siege to this fair castle, on whose walls after the summons, Faustus presented himself upon the battlements, armed with a great number of crosses, pen and ink-horns, charms, characters, seals, periapts [amulets], etc., who after sharp words defied the whole assembly, seeming to speak earnestly in his own defence, and as they were ready to rear the ladders, and Faustus had begun to prepare for the counterbattery, determining to throw down upon the assemblies heads so many heavy charms and conjurations that they should fall down half way from the ascendant: whilst these things began to wax hot, from the aforesaid heaven there descended a legion of bright angels riding upon milk white chariots, drawn with the like white steeds, who with celestial divine melody came into the tower, to the intent to fight for the doctor against his furious enemies, but he wanting pay-money and void indeed of all good thoughts . . . sent them away . . . At length the alarm was given, and the ladders cleaved to the walls, up the assailants climbed, up they lifted their fearful weapons. Faustus not able (destitute of help) to withstand them was taken prisoner, and his tower down rased to the earth . . . whom when they had fettered they left there, they marching out and the forenamed chairs were presently occupied with all the imperial rulers of hell, who clothed in their holiday apparel, sat there to give judgment upon this wilfull Faustus, whom two hangmen of hell unloosed, and there in presence of them all, the great devil afore his chief peers, first stamping with his angry foot, and then shaking his great bush of hair, that therewith he made the near places and the most proud devils' courages to tremble, and with his fire-burnt scepter, and his like coloured crown all of gold setting one hand by his side, and the other upon the pummel of a chair, shook a pretty space with such angry fury, that the flames which proceeded from his frightful eyes did dim the sight of the Wittenbergers below . . . [Faustus] began to speak, and yet not long, then he began to walk up and down, and to show strange gestures, when suddenly for some bug words escaped by Faustus, all the devils there rose up, and with their swords drawn threatened with them the poor Doctor, turning all their bodies and directing their faces to the king, who with a stern countenance commanded silence. When Faustus having long raged, of a sudden howling loud and tearing his hair, laid both his arms upon his neck and leaped down headlong off the stage, the whole company vanishing, but the stage with a most monstrous thundering crack followed Faustus hastily . . .

I have quoted this at length, for, although it does not describe a sequence from the play as we have it, certain of the events in the action here related are close to incidents in the play, and may therefore give us hints for reconstructing the style of the costumes and scenic properties used. To pick out some of the significant details: the first 'stage' was built to bear the throne of a monarch spectator which suggests that the performance remembered was one of those at Court rather than in a playhouse. An intriguing implication is that the devils may in Act V have left the stage used by players and sat in judgment around the monarch's throne. The description suggests two mansions, one a hell-mouth, the other a castle. These could have been erected on a playhouse stage, although the stage directions indicate that hell-mouth was 'discovered'. Alternatively these could indicate that the two sides of the concave tiring-house were given false fronts in the manner indicated. The description of the heavens may derive from the paintings on the underside of the playhouse canopy (see Ch. 1). The account of the battle, however, probably describes the action in V.i.120ff., where the Old Man leaves Faustus to his fate. The only stage direction extant is *'Enter the Devils'*; if this report is to be believed this scene was one of the most spectacular in the play. As in *A Looking Glass for London and England*, flying apparatus was used to lower players to an upper stage level. Finally the passage may describe the final scene of the play: Faustus' 'bug words' being his heretical call for his soul to be changed into little water drops (V.ii.179). Perhaps Alleyn ended his performance by leaping into the trap. The passage of course proves nothing, but it is suggestive, confirms my inclination to see the play as a spectacular pageant, in contrast to the austerities of *Edward II*, an opportunity to exploit all the resources of the popular playhouses.

Given this fundamental incertainty over the status of the text and the method of its staging it is not surprising that there has been radical disagreement over the nature of the play. To simplify the debate very sharply, there have been two critical traditions. The first dates from the seventeenth century. It begins in the moralistic tone of Marlowe's source and is encapsulated in accounts of the story like that of Thomas Beard (he was Oliver Cromwell's schoolmaster) who included an account of 'John Faustus, a filthy beast, and a sink of many devils'[9] in a book that also contained a severely disapproving life of Marlowe himself. Beard's account indicates that some contemporaries at least would have regarded the play as an uncompromising moral fable. Other evidence comes from a theatrical tradition: the nature of the additions to the text, and the fortunes of the play on popular stages in the seventeenth and early eighteenth centuries. The original additions found in the 1616 text tend to present the hero not only as a great speculator but also as a juggler, a theatre clown, content to waste the diabolic powers he had achieved by his pact on petty acts of revenge and the sort of conjuring tricks one would expect to encounter at a country fair. Certainly the emphasis is likely to have been on knockabout games in those Faust plays, probably derived from Marlowe's original, that were performed by English comedians in Europe from 1608 onwards.[10] This aspect of the play was still further developed in further additions that were inserted in the text when it was printed in 1663,[11] and this tradition culminates in William Mountfort's *The Life and Death of Doctor Faustus, made into a Farce, with the Humours of Harlequin and Scaramouche* (1686) and finally, two pantomimes, John Thurmond's *Harlequin Doctor Faustus: with the Masque of the Deities*, first performed at Drury Lane on 26 November 1723, and its rival, John Rich's *The Necromancer: or Harlequin Doctor Faustus*, performed a month later at Lincoln's Inn Fields.[12] Mountford's version ends thus:

Scene discovers Faustus's limbs.

SCHOLAR: O help us, Heav'n; for here are Faustus's limbs
All torn asunder by the Hand of Hell.

OLD MAN: May this a fair Example be to all,
To avoid such Ways which brought poor Faustus' fall.
And whatsoever Pleasure does invite,
Sell not your souls to purchase vain Delight.

Scene changes to Hell. Faustus's Limbs come together. Exeunt. A dance, and a song.

These entertainments, however debased, serve as a corrective to portentous romantic interpretations of the play. The original performances also, after all, may well have ended with a jig, and certainly contained dances and spectacles which were as memorable as the play's mightiest lines. The tone of their moralism, at once serious and perfunctory – it hardly exhorts the audience to go forth and mend their ways although it may put a check on their daydreams of the power that comes from acquisitiveness – is closer to the original than the interpretations of some modern scholars who have forgotten that the play was a spectacular entertainment as they have exhumed moral treatises and used these to 'prove' that Marlowe's play was based on a high moral seriousness.

These versions of the work define a critical and theatrical tradition that could be described as 'Icararian' in that it presents the hero as an over-reacher brought low as a punishment for his pride. The second, the

Promethean, presenting the hero as a noble and lonely searcher for new truths, is inspired by cultural events even further removed from Marlowe's late sixteenth-century play. Apart from those pantomime versions of the play, *Doctor Faustus*, unlike most of the plays of Shakespeare, was unperformed and virtually unknown throughout the eighteenth century. Attention started to be paid again after the publication of Goethe's *Faust* (Part I, 1790) and after the series of romantic dramas depicting brooding titanic heroes (*Manfred* in particular) that Byron wrote shortly after. The emphasis turns to the psychological intensity of the hero, and the accounts of the play (like Hazlitt's[13]) are fuelled by knowledge of Marlowe's own atheistical positions. There are obvious dangers in interpreting the play through these romantic refractions that are oblivious to Marlowe's moral exhortations.

More accurate indications of the tone of early performances may well come from the various anecdotes that accumulated about the play. In his *Black Book* (1604), Middleton says of someone: 'He had a head of hair like one of my Devil's in *Dr. Faustus* when the old Theatre cracked and frighted the audience'[14] (The *Second Report* notes Lucifer's 'bush of hair' as well as a 'crack'.) That was probably in 1593 as argued above. Second, there is an account published in 1620:[15]

Another will foretell of lightning and thunder that shall happen such a day when there are no inflamations seen, except men go to the Fortune in Golding Lane to see the tragedy of *Doctor Faustus*. There indeed a man may behold shag-haired Devils run roaring over the stage with squibs in their mouths, while drummers make thunder in the tiring-house, and the twelve-penny hirelings make artificial lightning in their heavens.

Third is an account from a famous puritan tract, Prynne's *Histrio-Mastix* of 1633, of 'the visible apparition of the Devil on the stage at the Belsavage Play-house, in Queen Elizabeth's days (to the great amazement both of the actors and spectators) while they were there profanely playing the History of Faustus (the truth of which I have heard from many now alive, who well remember it) there being some distracted with that fearful sight.'[16] Finally an undated account by 'J.G.R.', which the seventeenth-century antiquary Aubrey associates with Alleyn:[17]

Certain players at Exeter acting upon the stage the tragical story of Dr. Faustus the conjurer; as a certain number of Devils kept every one his circle there, and as Faustus was busy in his magical invocations, on a sudden they were all dashed, every one harkening other in the ear, for they were all persuaded, there was one devil too many amongst them; and so after a little pause desired the people to pardon them, they could go no further with this matter; the people also understanding the thing as it was, every man hastened to be first out of doors. The players (as I heard it) contrary to their custom spending the night in reading and in prayer got them out of the town the next morning.

What these anecdotes indicate is that the Elizabethans found the play *frightening*, an occasion for collective exotic *frissons*. For them it was the spectacle of the devils and not the mind of the hero that was at the centre of the play. This response allows for both the piety of the moralists and the admiration of the romantics: the impression given by Faustus' grand temerity is not forgotten when he is cruelly rent apart. Indeed it seems to me the final Chorus subsumes both of these attitudes.

If we align ourselves simply with the moralists, we are not going to appreciate Faustus' great rashness. His perverse resolution would have been thoroughly familiar to the Elizabethans – from Seneca's Medea, whose *video meliora proboque, deteriora sequor* ('I see the better and approve of it, although I follow the worse' – VII.20–1) is in turn the epitome of the tragic recognition of St Paul as he expressed it in the Epistle to the Romans. That rashness will take Faustus to hell despite the promptings of the Good Angel, his own experience, and the advice of Mephostophilis himself. If we side with the Romantics, Faustus will be found lacking in a Byronic grandeur of soul, and the comic scenes will be mere bathos, unfortunate slapstick interludes inserted for 'comic relief' or at best to satisfy the prejudices of a chauvinist or anti-Catholic audience. So we find J.S.F. writing with surprise in the *Dublin Evening Herald* of Gareth Morgan's 1970 Royal Shakespeare production: 'There is in the Vatican scene a pie-throwning episode reminiscent of an early Chaplin or Keystone cops film'. Whereas Ronald Bryden writing in *The Observer* on 30 June 1968 of Clifford Williams's Stratford production noted that 'the scene in which Faustus and Mephostophilis break up the Pope's banquet is played, like the similar ones in *The Jew*, as broad anti-clerical farce, and clearly executes Marlowe's intention'. No reconciliation between the moral and romantic approaches seems possible. If, however, we put aside anachronistic views of tragedy and range the play among the moralities and popular narratives of the time, attend to the subtle alterations of dramatic tone Marlowe contrives, take a hint from that phrase 'scenical tragedy' used in *The Second Report*, we may understand the play better. With its apparatus of good and bad angels, a central character choosing between Hell and Elysium, and pious speeches from the Old Man, the play has been often seen as the descendant of 'the medieval morality'. But too often these moral plays are seen through the eyes of an almost Victorian rectitude – the available editions are often from that period and are even bowdlerized – and critics are loth to admit that the knockabout humour, ghoulishness, lacings of obscenities, and sardonic pleasure from common folk as great men get their come-uppance, are part of a coherent view of life that is in fact religious. To blaspheme (as Marlowe himself did), one must be disturbed by one's faith, and the humour here is the cockiness of the condemned criminal, laughing that he might not weep. It is aptly illustrated in a tympanum at Bamberg Cathedral in Bavaria where the faces of the damned being led away to hell are fixed in a weird *rictus*, the expression of a grinning corpse. In our own time Grotowski has written:[18]

> The theatre, when it was still part of religion, was already theatre: it liberated the spiritual energy of the congregation or tribe by incorporating myth and prophaning or rather transcending it. The spectator thus had a renewed awareness of his personal truth in the truth of the myth, and through fright and a sense of the sacred he came to catharsis. It was not by chance that the Middle Ages produced the idea of 'sacral parody'.

In regard to its structure *Faustus* is perhaps more related to pageant or montage than tragedy;[19] it bears a close resemblance in this respect (and in theme) to Dekker's *Old Fortunatus* played at the Rose in 1596 and, in the form we now have it, at Court in 1600. Marlowe did, after all, have to attend to the life of his hero over twenty-four years, so that the scenes are a kind of sampling of that chronicle. The play is a kind of bricolage held together by the Chorus who, unlike Machiavel in *The Jew of Malta*, enters regularly throughout the action, and by the presence of Faustus and Mephostophilis. The subsidiary characters have no relationships with one another and are related according to the demands of the source, the *Faustbook*, which is, as Harry Levin says, 'at once a cautionary tale and a book of marvels, a jest-book and a theological tract'.[20] It may well be that the pageant of the seven deadly sins was placed centrally in the play as a reminder that the hero is successively tasting of each.[21] In the playhouse, the Aristotelian 'recognition' or discovery of the hero is affected by having Mephostophilis, acting as a kind of dramatic presenter, discover or reveal to Faustus these scenes of delight, so that these theatrical discoveries are counterpointed against Faustus' moral discoveries – a 'scenical tragedy' indeed:[22]

> as [Faustus] moves deeper into damnation the more aware he becomes of his danger, so that, paradoxically, the ultimate discovery – that he *is* damned – comes when he is most aware of what he has lost. This point is dramatized by another theatrical discovery: the Good Angel 'discovers' Hell, and Faustus is confronted with the physical evidence of his flight from salvation.

The Chorus, dressed in the customary black velvet cloak and crown of bays, discovers Faustus in his study, the first great gest or show. Taking a hint from the woodcut to the 1616 edition (Plate 14) we may presume that it was furnished with a few books and a celestial globe to fix Faustus' profession as a scholar and astrologer. At the Globe Volpone's gold was to be similarly displayed, and in *The Devil's Charter* in one discovery the audience saw '*Books, coffers, [a] triple crown upon a cushion*'.[23] It is unlikely, however, that

Faustus remained in the 'study' throughout the whole of his first long speech. He may well have come out on to the stage and rushed feverishly back to pick up a new book each time he turns to a new branch of learning. Similarly Barabas, who is likewise discovered at the opening of *The Jew of Malta*, must have come downstage before the entrance of the First Merchant. The 1616 woodcut shows a magic circle described on the floor and at II.iii.11 Robin warns Dick: 'Keep out of the circle.' This suggests that the circle was painted on a cloth laid on the stage proper instead of the usual rushes: Faustus presumably gravitated towards it, a centre of his temptation, as he made his way through the speech. The *Faustbook* notes: 'sometime he would throw the scriptures from him as though he had no care of his former profession . . . in so much that he could not abide to be called Doctor of Divinity':[24] casting the Bible to the floor as he moved toward the magic circle would be a shocking demonstration of Faustus' depravity.

As has often been pointed out, Faustus' aphorisms reveal the imperfections rather than the proficiency of his studies. His definition of logic comes from Ramus, the master of the short-cut, whose attempts to reform and simplify Aristotelian logic were angrily dismissed by many scholars of Marlowe's Cambridge, and his rational proof of the necessity of damnation rests on the notorious devil's syllogism, exposed by Luther and incorporated into the homilies, those officially sanctioned sermons which had to be read every week in Elizabethan church services.[25] Faustus' lines, therefore, scarcely made him a Titanic figure in the eyes of the audience. The 1616 woodcut shows him wearing a cassock with the fur trimmed gown of a Doctor of Divinity over it, and in a satirical poem a contemporary wrote:[26]

> The gull gets on a surplice,
> With a cross upon his breast,
> Like Alleyn playing Faustus,
> In that manner he was dressed.

He bears a magic wand – there is reference to Faustus' conjuring stick in Act IV of Jonson's *Tale of a Tub*. This suggests that it was used for memorable business, perhaps to 'scourge the air cross-wise within the circle'.[27] He may also have worn spectacles – this is Greg's interpretation of the Horse Courser's threat to 'break his glass-windows about his ears' (A.1194). His appearance makes him a divine, but a divine wracked with banal fantasies of wealth and power:

> I'll have them fly to India for gold,
> Ransack the ocean for orient pearl,
> And search all corners of the new-found world
> For pleasant fruits and princely delicates. (I.i.80–3)

He is a man alone, obsessive, afflicted perhaps with scholar's melancholy, and, like the figure described by Donne at the opening of his first satire, restless to escape from his 'standing wooden chest' to the giddy world of princes and the court. He talks almost incessantly for the first 120 lines of the play, interrupted only by the first and perfunctory appearance of the Good and Bad Angels. They may have appeared from opposite side doors (they enter '*at several doors*' at V.ii.91), possibly on opposite sides of the gallery. Their lines are flat and perfunctory so it is almost certain that their entrance must have been enhanced by spectacle or music. Faustus in his restlessness does not respond to them, which may indicate that he did not see them, that they represented inner voices. In his 1974 production John Barton made the Good and Bad Angels puppets held in each hand by Faustus as if to suggest this.

On impulse he calls his associate Wagner to summon Valdes and Cornelius, two infamous magicians who do not appear in the *Faustbook*. Their entrance marks the culmination of what is for Faustus his first tragic recognition. He has come to realize his own nature as that of fallen man and there may be as much feverish melancholy as fervent excitement in this opening scene. By summoning Valdes and Cornelius he has acknowledged his temptation to evil although he will proceed to damnation alone. Greg argues that 'the precious pair are no deeply versed magicians welcoming a promising beginner, but merely the devil's decoys luring Faustus along the road to destruction'.[28] Accordingly they should be showily dressed, an advertisement for the specious glamour they have acquired. If we do not think of them as diabolic agents they might, alternatively, be shabby: they have explored the tawdry world of the black magician and are eager to find a new recruit for their cult. They know how empty it all is, but like all adherents of counter-cultures seek to sustain their own faith by feeding on the eagerness of neophytes, here with their images of remote exoticism.

There is no doubt in my mind that the Wagner scenes are authentic.[29] They constitute a series of mirror scenes – like the Portuguese sequences in *The Spanish Tragedy*. The first, the encounter between Wagner and the two scholars, is a figure for the recklessness of Faustus' household. The chop logic of the apprentice is as patently fallacious as the deductions of the master in the previous scene, but then the automatic and pious responses of the scholars are merely comic – their status is like that of the nuns in *The Jew of Malta*.

Understanding the ritual conjuring scene is crucial to the understanding of the play. The stage direction for the 1604 text reads '*Enter Faustus to coniure*', that for the 1616 text, '*Thunder: Enter Lucifer, Belzebub, and Mephostophilis.*' Lucifer's opening line then suggests that they view Faustus' final agony from the gallery: 'Thus from infernal Dis do we ascend'. Alternatively they may, as was customary with devils, have ascended from the stage trap. I think that use of the gallery is appropriate here: the effect of the devils, coolly watching Faustus' actions, possibly from the oriel-like structure at the Rose, would be to diminish his stature. He steps into the magic circle, possibly surrounding himself with lighted candles. The players may well have worn animal headpieces like the procession of Devils that is described in the *Faustbook*:[30]

> Lucifer himself sat in manner of a man, all hairy, but of a brown colour like a squirrel, curled, and his tail turning upwards on his back as the squirrels use; I think he could crack nuts too like a squirrel. After him came Beelzebub in curled hair of horse-flesh colour, his head like the head of a bull, with a mighty pair of horns, and two long ears down to the ground, with two wings on his back, with pricking stings like thorns; out of his wings issued flames of fire, his tail was like a cow. Then came Astaroth in form of a worm, going upright on his tail; he had no feet but a tail like a slow-worm; under his chaps grew two short hands, and his back was coal-black, his belly thick in the middle and yellow like gold, having many bristles on his back like a hedgehog.

Henslowe's inventory of properties includes a selection of animals heads.[31] And yet, of course, Faustus' great and thundering speech and the hocus-pocus of his spell, performed to an inverted parody of the ritual actions of the priest at mass, are, as Mephostophilis points out, without any power to raise spirits. Lucifer and his attendants arrived simply because:

> when we hear one rack the name of God,
> Abjure the scriptures and his saviour Christ,
> We fly in hope to get his glorious soul. (I.iii.47–9)

Half-way through Faustus' Latin invocation in the 1616 text there occurs the English word '*Dragon*'. This is probably a stage direction deriving from the manuscript which the compositor mistook for part of the spell. The English *Faustbook* records that 'suddenly over his head hanged hovering in the air a might Dragon' followed by 'a monstrous cry . . . as if hell had been open, and all the tormented souls crying to God for mercy'.[32] We know that the Admiral's Men, according to their 1598 inventory, had 'j dragon in fostes'[33] and it may have been equipped with squibs: 'a Dragon with the fireworks' is mentioned in a Court account of 1581.[34] In *Friar Bacon and Friar Bungay* when Bungay conjures (III.ii.), a tree appears '*with the dragon shooting fire*'. This too was a Henslowe play and the same machine may have been used. The effect is spectacular but also ironic, even comic: Faustus does not see the dragon which serves to warn the audience of the powers which he has unleashed but which he cannot properly control. It may be, however, that the figure rising through the floor in the 1616 woodcut is the dragon rather than the devil although it does look more like one of the animal devils described above. If Faustus sees and is undaunted by the dragon the effect is to magnify his boldness – or his temerity. It might also be the case that the 'dragon' refers to the ugly devil that appears briefly but without speaking before he returns as Mephostophilis. Alternatively the stage direction and the property dragon could refer to the hell-mouth which might have been briefly discovered, again behind Faustus.

If the scene continued this way, however, with Faustus as mere dupe of the devils and a pantomine dragon, we could not have much interest in the hero. With an inspired stroke Marlowe has Faustus, like Edward with the Monks of Neath, snatch back the advantage of the scene, interrupt his own ceremony, by having him dismiss Mephostophilis as soon as he appears, taunting his ugliness, and charging him 'return an old Franciscan friar, that holy shape becomes a devil best' (I.iii.25–6). (The stage direction reads '*Enter a Devil*', presumably a player other than the one acting Mephostophilis who would not have had time to change in the seven lines between entrances.) Faustus has re-established himself as an interesting individual, but the sardonic and conventional anti-clerical satire has the effect of taking Faustus out of his role, giving us some assurance that the whole performance is but play. Presumably during this speech Faustus stepped out of the circle, boldly eschewing the protection it afforded even to the extent of sharing his taunting game with the audience. We cannot know whether Mephostophilis in fact did return as a friar – the unction of this first line, 'Now Faustus, what wouldst thou have me do' (I.iii.35), suggests that he might have, and would add to the impact the scene has as a black mass – or whether he remained in that costume throughout the play. A friar's costume would have been a convenient substitute for his presumed goat's feet and may well, in the tradition of anti-Romish satire, have been lavish. Revels Accounts indicate that the costumes for clerics were commonly very rich in Court plays.[35]

After such spectacle the dialogue that follows between Faustus and Mephostophilis has another ritual effect but of a different, quieter kind. In a parody of the catechism Faustus questions Mephostophilis (as a friar?):

> Tell me, what is that Lucifer, thy Lord?
> MEPHOSTOPHILIS: Arch-regent and commander of all spirits.
> FAUSTUS: Was not that Lucifer an angel once?
> MEPHOSTOPHILIS: Yes Faustus, and most dearly loved of God.
> FAUSTUS: How comes it then that he is prince of devils?
> MEPHOSTOPHILIS: O, by aspiring pride and insolence,
> For which God threw him from the face of heaven.
> FAUSTUS: And what are you that live with Lucifer?
> MEPHOSTOPHILIS: Unhappy spirits that fell with Lucifer,
> Conspired against our God with Lucifer,
> And are for ever damned with Lucifer. (I.iii.62–72)

By breaking the stichomythic pattern Mephostophilis too is disrupting the ceremony, and it might be appropriate for him to direct these last two lines to the audience. The mute and horrific pageant of devils behind Faustus (or to one side unseen if a stage with no gallery was being used[36]) is testimony to the immutability of God's will. Such advice, even such direct advice, however can have no effect on Faustus delighted with his new power. The devils remain there impassively, overlooking Faustus' soliloquy when he dreams of marvels, confident he has obtained what he desired.

Like the first, the second Wagner scene provides an instant perspective on what we have just watched. Wagner now plays a cat-and-mouse game with the Clown, promising him rich apparel and then raising two familiar devils, Banio and Belcher, to make him '*run up and down crying*'. Presumably these would be ugly, hairy, pantomine devils. The farce parodies Faustus' conjuring and indeed the banality of all conjuring; and, with its indirect jibes at Faustus' dreams of wealth and prefigurations of his dismembering, it insists on the frightening obtuseness of the hero. The differences between the two texts, in particular the insertion of the actor's 'gag',[37] indicate how two comics forged their direct relationship with the audience by throwing each other lines in a conventional cross-talk game:

WAGNER: Sirrah, has thou no comings in?
CLOWN: Yes, and goings out too, you may see, sir.
WAGNER: Alas, poor slave, see how poverty jests in his nakedness. I know the villain's out of service, and so hungry that I know he would give his soul to the devil for a shoulder of mutton, though it were blood raw.
CLOWN: Not so neither; I had need to have it well roasted and good sauce to it, if I pay so dear, I can tell you.

WAGNER: Tell me, sirrah, has thou any comings in?
CLOWN: Ay, and goings out too, you may see else.
WAGNER: Alas, poor slave, see how poverty jesteth in his nakedness. The villain is bare and out of service, and so hungry that I know he would give his soul to the devil for a shoulder of mutton, though it were blood raw.
CLOWN: How, my soul to the devil for a shoulder of mutton, though it were blood raw? Not so, good friend – by'r Lady I had need have it well roasted and good sauce to it, if I pay so dear.

(Modernized from Greg's text, B.344–53 and A.364–73)

Now Faustus seems hypnotized by his success, is resolute to be as wicked as he can conceive:

The God thou serv'st is thine own appetite,
Wherein is fixed the love of Belzebub.
To him, I'll build an altar and a church,
And offer lukewarm blood of new-born babes. (II.i.10–13)

It might be effective, therefore, if Faustus was now well distanced downstage from the Good and Bad Angels who enter again from their opposing doors, so suggesting the way in which Faustus has suppressed his own conscience and moved into a private fantasy of evil. The ensuing great ritual scene, the signing of the deed of gift – 'the necromantic equivalent of a christening' it has been called[38] – is, at the moment when Faustus' blood will not run, the emblem of a man who has driven himself into an impasse by pursuing his perversion. The saucer of blood mentioned in the *Faustbook* and now placed on the top of the chafer of fire brought by Mephostophilis may have looked like a travesty of a font, and may have been full of squibs to bang or aqua-vitae to flare up alarmingly. Such clownage does not preclude seriousness for Faustus' flippant blasphemy, '*cosummatum est*' (II.i.73), the last words of Christ on the cross (John, 19:30), precedes a sudden fall into despair as he finds a warning, '*Homo Fuge!*', appear on his arm. His certain awareness of the destruction he is wreaking on himself can be averted only by the spectacle Mephostophilis arranges for him: '*Enter Devils, giving crowns and rich apparel to Faustus; they dance and then depart*' (II.i.81). It may be that the giving of apparel represents a dramatic enactment of the widespread belief that witches gave garments to the devil who enchanted them and returned them to cement the bond more fully.[39] Faustus has not given them garments, of course, but the lines that follow the dance

FAUSTUS: What means this show? Speak, Mephostophilis.

MEPHOSTOPHILIS: Nothing, Faustus, but to delight thy mind.

(II.i.83–4)

suggest that the dance may be a dance of triumph, the import of which Mephostophilis sardonically denies.[40] The scene, therefore, is another of Marlowe's important investiture scenes, like that at the opening of *Tamburlaine* and those throughout *Edward II*; unlike them, however, it is ironic in that Faustus' donning of rich apparel in fact takes away from his power to control his fate.

It may well seem that the next sequence in the play completes the process of Faustus's enslavement in that Faustus in signing the diabolic deed of gift swears to 'be a spirit in form and substance' (II.i.96). It has been claimed that throughout the play 'spirit' and 'devil' are used almost interchangeably, so that Faustus has in fact ceased to be a man and is therefore beyond salvation.[41] It is doubtful, however, whether a playhouse audience would be able to distinguish an actor playing a man from an actor playing a spirit, and to seal Faustus' doom at this stage in the play would destroy the suspense over his possible repentance later. Faustus' spiritual nature may therefore simply establish a stage convention whereby he may be deemed to be invisible in the scenes at the papal court. Nor, in fact, would orthodox authorities on witchcraft allow that a diabolic pact could be binding.[42]

Faustus' first act after he has achieved his desires is to sit and dispute with Mephostophilis concerning hell. Mephostophilis propounds the familiar protestant doctrine that hell is a state of mind, not a place, a realization that is dramatically enacted when Mephostophilis brings Faustus a wife who appears to him as '*a Devil, dressed like a woman, with fireworks*' (II.i.144).

She is a 'hot whore', a clown wife, burning with venereal disease, with the fireworks probably hung about her hips. The pattern of perverted Christian ritual (here the catechism again) followed by ribald spectacle mirrors that of the previous sequence where the dance followed the baptism. In resignation, therefore, Faustus turns from pleasures of the flesh to pleasures of the mind, asking for and being given books for conjuring and containing the names and characters of the stars and of all plants, herbs, and trees. The A text contains two stage directions, '*There turn to them*' and '*Turn to them*', which may indicate that Mephostophilis demonstrates that all these things are contained in the one book. On the other hand it may indicate that Mephostophilis went back to whatever was used as a study – this text derived from provincial performances – so that Faustus is being fobbed off with books he already possessed.

The scene must have been followed by a comic scene now lost, perhaps one in which the Clown steals one of the conjuring books,[43] for Faustus and Mephostophilis re-enter immediately – or conceivably there was an interval. Faustus announces that he will repent, which brings the Good and Bad Angels immediately back to the stage. Their precipitate entrance may be comic, but Faustus' dialogue indicates that the Bad Angel brings with him 'Poison, guns, halters and envenom'd steel', the traditional properties brought on to tempt a man to suicide. Suicide, the manifestation of despair in the saving hope of Christ, was regarded by some sixteenth-century theologians as the sin of sins. Redcrosse is tempted to despair in *The Faerie Queene* (I.ix.28ff.), so is the Usurer in V.ii. of Greene and Lodge's *A Looking Glass for London and England*, and the dagger in *Macbeth* (II.i.) is a symbol of the despair into which Macbeth will fall after his murder of Duncan. No actual dagger, of course, should be brought on stage in *Macbeth*: it is a vision 'proceeding from the heat-oppressed brain' (II.i.39). But it might be effective for the Bad Angel to repeatedly offer Faustus the instruments of his own destruction: later Mephostophilis too will offer him a dagger just before the apparition of Helen (V.i.57). Faustus' steadfast refusal to take it would be an emblem of his resolution: a resolution however, that emerges from dogged anticipation of pleasures to ensue and not from faith.

As a prelude to the spectacle of the Seven Deadly Sins, Faustus disputes again with Mephostophilis, this time about astronomy. Mephostophilis' answers disappoint Faustus: it would have been against the spirit of the play if Mephostophilis had brought news of a Copernican 'revolution'. The devil's knowledge is drab and Faustus realizes that he must while away his years having cut himself off from the sources of Christian humanism and make himself a social and intellectual outcast. All he draws from Mephostophilis is a denial of the crystalline sphere introduced to explain the phenomenon of planetary trepidation. Marlowe may have been indebted to

Augustinus Ricius for this modification of orthodox Ptolemaic cosmography, but the dramatic point is that this sphere is invisible and that Faustus is unable to entertain any knowledge that is not empirical. Accordingly his intellectual disappointment is alleviated by yet another playhouse spectacle, the pageant of the Seven Deadly Sins. But before they appear, Faustus is visited by Lucifer for the first time in the play, although in the 1616 text he had appeared aloft to look down silently on Faustus' conjuring. He appears on cue immediately Faustus calls on Christ to save his soul. With Beelzebub and Mephostophilis (still as Friar?) the diabolic trinity should present a terrifying spectacle: it may have been at this moment that the extra devil appeared at Exeter. But characteristically terror is juxtaposed against a kind of grim humour with the subsequent appearance of the Seven Deadly Sins. Faustus seats himself, perhaps at Lucifer's feet, as they are led in by a piper (II.ii.154). Although there is keen social satire here on the conspicuous consumption of the time, the tone of their speeches is comic, especially of the last two, Sloth and Gluttony. I cannot agree with Greg that 'the purpose of the show is to terrify rather than to entertain'.⁴⁴ Terror could have no more effect on a man in Faustus' state of mind, and there is a dramatic irony, a greater terror perhaps, in our knowledge that Faustus is watching mere shows, playhouse shadows of the real experiences that are denied him by virtue of his social and spiritual isolation. In 1968 at Stratford Farrah found a most successful solution for a modern designer by making them grotesque caricatures, intriguing rather than real. For an Elizabethan or modern audience, making them horrific would be risking laughs that would betoken a disbelief in the devil and his power. Rather they were a familiar spectacle: Tarlton the clown may have been the author of the two-part play of *The Seven Deadly Sins* of which only the 'plot' survives. Horror, or perhaps a sense of mysterious power, returns at the end of the scene when Lucifer gives Faustus a book instructing him how to change his shape, after which, according to the 1616 text, '*Exeunt omnes, several ways*' (III.iii.163): the devils could melt away through the three or five doors that led from the Rose stage. And this movement of the play is completed as we witness Robin the Clown and Dick the ostler preparing to conjure, but wisely changing their minds and deciding to melt away themselves to the sinful delights of the neighbouring tavern. The scenic montage shows that, for all his evil, Faustus has achieved no more than they.

If a modern director chooses to include the almost certainly unauthentic comic scenes in his production, he might begin by asking his chief actor whether he feels that Faustus enjoys the practical jokes that fill Acts III and IV as we have them, or whether he might maintain a melancholy distance from the sports and pranks – like that some Prince Hals maintain between themselves and the companions of the tavern. J. C. Trewin reported in the *Illustrated London News* of 6 July 1968 his pleasure

to see how Clifford Williams [at Stratford] has treated the valley
between the crests. How Faustus, for once, seemed to enjoy his tricks as
a mischievous Antichrist – the grave papal procession capers, the grave
singers hiccough – and how the spirits move with a dark silvery grace,
and even the episode of the pregnant duchess and the grapes has its
strange overtones . . .

Act III in fact begins with a somewhat overlong travelogue from the Chorus
paraphrased from the *Faustbook* and perhaps necessary to allow the players
who had appeared as deadly sins to change into costumes for the papal
court, perhaps also to allow Henslowe's 'sittie of Rome'[45] to be prepared for
the stage. There is no way of telling whether this was a three-dimensional
house, thrust out perhaps from the discovery space, or a painted cloth hung
against the tiring-house façade and behind the papal throne, or even a
structure that had stood on stage from the beginning of the play. The
dialogue from ll. 51ff. indicates that Faustus wants to leave the stage to
explore 'Rome' but that Mephostophilis entices him to watch the papal
triumph, perhaps from the gallery. (Did they fly on to the stage together at
the conclusion of the Chorus' speech?) The next scene allows the author to
indulge popular suspicion of papal rites with farcical entertainment. The
procession could well be a travesty, exemplifying Roman decadence, and
comes to a climax when the Pope uses the Emperor as a footstool by which to
ascend his throne. This was a familiar icon: the dramatist may have used
Foxe's account in his *Acts and Monuments* (1563) as his source.[46] Marlowe
had also used the device in *Tamburlaine* where Tamburlaine mounts his
throne from Bajazeth's back (IV.ii.) and there was an engraving in Foxe of
Henry VIII climbing on the Pope's back. This scene, then, is a kind of
comic revenge for the Pope on protestant iconography: the Pope's triumph
is short-lived, however, perhaps signifying the vanity of pride, as Faustus
and Mephostophilis, disguised as cardinals, interrupt yet another ceremony, rescue the Emperor, and send him speeding back to Germany. Their
behaviour becomes even more outrageous when they re-enter: Mephostophilis speaks a charm and gives Faustus a girdle to make him invisible ('a
robe for to goo invisibell' is listed among Henslowe's costumes[47]), and they
disrupt the banquet, snatching dishes from the Pope's hand, and speaking
curses in his ear that seem to come from the cardinals present. The scene
ends with a travesty of the curse by bell, book, and candle, interrupted by
the two 'invisible' fiends who beat the friars and throw more fireworks
about. Admittedly there is no evidence that any of this is by Marlowe, but
the sequence is in accord with the spirit of the play. The audience would be
grimly aware that this slapstick comedy, very like the knockabout of silent
films, is the diversion of a man whose time is running out and who avoids
facing his situation by desperately moving about the world seeking novelty
at everyone's expense including his own. The A text adds a scene (III.iii.) in

which Mephostophilis appears with yet more fireworks to frighten Robin and Rafe who have stolen Faustus' book and are attempting to conjure: the 'quoted gesture' thus incorporated into the familiar tale of the sorcerer's apprentice (of which there is a version in Foxe[48]) economically displays the remorseless nature of the devil although the 'gag' that fills the text that survives suggests that the moment was never taken very seriously.

Act IV is a mish-mash of comic scenes that are almost certainly un-Marlovian and a modern director would probably want to construct his own text from the fragments that the two early texts provide. The clownage dramatises the failure of Faustus' achievements to match his aspirations, but a production that included all the material available would risk being tedious and its audience might find this interlude a cancer on the design of the play. The pattern throughout is a juxtaposition of high Renaissance art and second-rate farce. Alexander and his paramour appear in dumb show to the Emperor, who leaves his 'state' and joins the spectacle. This is the reverse of the order of Court masques, where the masquers 'took out' the spectators in the concluding dance. So, too, the references to Actaeon that precede the dumb show have a moral significance: Benvolio gapes upon Faustus' mystery as Actaeon had gaped upon Diana and is fittingly rewarded with stag's horns.[49] It is also an act of petty revenge in that Benvolio had earlier mocked Faustus' power and is horned to teach him to 'speak well of scholars' (IV.i.153–4). In turn Benvolio prepares his act of revenge and with his soldiers ambushes Faustus who enters wearing the company's false head. He allows it to be cut off and restores himself by magic, presumably by pulling the neck of an oversized costume down over his real head which had been concealed. This episode and the later incident with the horse-courser who finds Faustus sitting asleep, perhaps a personification of Sloth,[50] and, furious at having been sold a horse that turned into a bottle of hay, inadvertently pulls off his leg,[51] belong to a long tradition of revelry. They remind us of the circus, of the moment in *Sir Gawayn* when the Green Knight picks up his head after Sir Gawayn has chopped it off. Such moments combine farce with awesomeness. They have been described as 'kitchen humour' by E. R. Curtius, as belonging to the 'eldritch' tradition by M. C. Bradbrook:[52]

> Eldritch diabolism, while both comic and horrific, is amoral and does not involve personal choice or the notion of personal responsibility. The cackle of ghoulish laughter is essential to winter's tales of sprites and goblins, phantoms and illusions.

And yet, of course, these scenes do prefigure the final tableau of the play where Faustus' body is discovered rent asunder by the devils. The audience is being merely lulled into forgetting the consequence of Faustus' choice and is horribly awakened by that final vision. There is the possibility of great spectacle where Mephostophilis, Asteroth, and Belimoth hoist Benvolio,

Martino, and Frederick on their shoulders and carry them off to be dragged by the heels through a 'lake of mud and dirt' (IV.ii.85) to have horns fixed on their heads again. It seems that more devils or attendants were hidden behind property trees which probably concealed the stage doors. At Faustus' command they emerged to defeat further soldiers who had come to ambush Faustus, thus revealing the doors which opened for a procession of armed devils led by a drummer. But the Clown's narration of Faustus' further acts of cozening is lame stuff, as is the episode when Faustus fetches grapes for the Duke of Vanholt and his pregnant Duchess, a scene which quotes the gestures of Gluttony and which prefigures Faustus' final banquet, served by devils at the beginning of the next Act. The sequence ends with a very satisfactory gest as Faustus charms dumb each of his dupes to silence their wailing.

There was little sense of an informing design during Act IV, probably due to major adaptations to the text. But Act V is different: Henry Crabb Robinson reports that Goethe in conversation 'burst out into an exclamation of praise. "How greatly is it all planned":[53] this Act vindicates his enthusiasm. After Faustus' fitful attempts to win wisdom through sorcery and his restless roamings through Europe, he settles himself to a resolute feast of sensuality. Scenes of sensual indulgence alternate with scenes of spiritual agony and work towards the final climax in spectacle, where all the playhouses's resources are employed to stage Faustus' hellish doom. The play moves very quickly towards its end: Marlowe is able to do this because in this Act, as Kyd had done, he re-introduces many of the visual devices he had used earlier. The opening stage directions:

> *Thunder and lightning. Enter Devils with covered dishes. Mephostophilis*
> *leads them into Faustus study*

indicate a dumb show of a banquet of sense[54] where Faustus and the scholars eat, drink, and are merry and may use the same properties as the Pope's banquet, so foreshadowing interruption and catastrophe. Mephostophilis offers Faustus a dagger that the scholar might kill himself as he had in Act II, devils ascend to the gallery as they had during the conjuring scene, and Faustus is visited by the scholars as he had been at the opening of the play. Marlowe is therefore able to create a quickening dramatic rhythm and review the ages of Faustus' life. As a result we approach Faustus' death with the feeling that it could not have been otherwise, that his character dictated his destiny. In *Macbeth*, by contrast, we witness the working out of one dramatic action in which the catastrophe depends not only on the hero's nature but on his fortune, his reaction to prophecy and his failure to match the forces raised against him. Shakespeare is dramatising a life whereas Marlowe is dramatizing a condition.

After the adventures of the court scenes, Wagner's opening lines create a chill perspective on Faustus' last plunge into evil:

I think my master means to die shortly.
He hath made his will, and given me his wealth,
His house, his goods, and store of golden plate,
Besides two thousand ducats ready coined.
And yet methinks, if that death were near,
He would not banquet and carouse and swill
Amongst the students, as even now he doth,
Who are at supper with such belly-cheer
As Wagner ne'er beheld in all his life. (V.i.1–9)

The lines indicate that Wagner may be here a kind of presenter of a speaking
picture in the discovery space. After the audience have been caught up in
Faustus' energetic cozening in the preceeding scenes, they find themselves
witnesses of a moral demonstration. Wagner's neutral tone, the sense of
speculation without wonder, the complete lack of affection, the sense of a
man whose relationship with Faustus is only that of servant and betokens no
personal bond, make us aware how alone Faustus is even as he sits carousing
with the scholars. At their request he conjures the spirit of Helen, who
arrives to the sound of music. For them she is simply the final rarebit in an
evening of feasting, for Faustus a glimpse of love and beauty that his life of
conjuring and attempts to achieve fame had completely lacked. For the
audience who may have seen her first as she entered the yard before 'passing
over the stage' between them and the discovery space, the fact that she is
accompanied by Mephostophilis is a reminder of her infernal origins. Her
appearance provokes the appearance of a new character, the Old Man who
enters as the scholars leave, and whose urging of Faustus to repentance is far
more passionate and human than anything we have heard from the Good
Angel.

O gentle Faustus, leave this damnèd art,
This magic, that will charm thy soul to hell,
And quite bereave thee of salvation.
Though thou hast now offended like a man,
Do not persever in it like a devil.
Yet, yet, thou hast an amiable soul,
If sin by custom grow not into nature:
Then Faustus, will repentance come too late,
Then thou are banished from the sight of heaven;
No mortal can express the pains of hell. (V.i.36–45)

This character plays a role like that of Time the Mower in *Edward II*. He is
both of the society of the play – if it has been decided to use make-up to show
Faustus ageing during the production it might be effective to have him and
the Old Man look alike – and the incarnation of allegorical values: 'He is a
harbinger of Death; he represents Wisdom, Time, Faith'.[55] But Faustus'

vision has narrowed to an infatuation that does not permit him to examine
the state of his mind or soul. His lines:

Hell claims his right, and with a roaring voice,

Says 'Faustus, come, thine hour is almost come' (V.i.55–6)

suggest that Marlowe might have indicated his mental frenzy with a
drum-roll, and the Old Man's line, 'O stay, good Faustus, stay thy
desperate step', suggests that Faustus is rushing off the stage with the
dagger that Mephostophilis coolly but silently gives him. Faustus is
floundering: the Old Man leaves him (there is little understanding or
compassion here) and he rapidly reconfirms his allegiance to Mephostophilis. The devil realizes, however, that he has not quite reduced Faustus to the
emotional and psychological state when he will make his final renunciation
of salvation and is only too willing to humour Faustus' wish for more
distraction, making Helen his paramour.

There has been much written about the appearance of Helen and the
speech with which Faustus greets her and which rapidly became one of the
most famous speeches in English drama. For the Elizabethans, as for the
Greeks, Helen was an ambiguous figure, the paragon of beauty, but also the
cause of the destruction of Troy. She is an unattractive person in
Shakespeare's *Troilus and Cressida* and there are numerous moral poems of
the period that inveigh against her character. Yet it would be a mistake to
present her merely as an object of carnality – some modern directors have
chosen to have the part played by a man to suggest that Faustus has been
duped by the devil. Her appearance in this entrance between two cupids
establishes her as a Venus figure, an apotheosis of earthly love, although in
announcing his intention to sleep with her Faustus is announcing his
descent to demoniality, sexual intercourse with a *succuba*, the sin which
according to the Old Man excludes the grace of heaven from Faustus' soul
(V.i.118). It may also be the case that Faustus' famous line, 'Her lips suck
forth my soul, see where it flies' (V.i.100), would remind the audience of the
Ars Moriendi tradition, 'with its pictures of a devil dragging the naked soul
out of the mouth of a dying man'.[56] It may equally, on the other hand, be the
distillation of the neo-Platonic celebration of the kiss as an occasion when
the souls of two lovers unite in ecstasy. So Cardinal Bembo argued in
Castiglione's *Book of the Courtier*.[57] This double perspective on the stage
image and the whole tenor of Faustus' speech are at odds with any sort of
simple moralizing. Faustus, after all, must be allowed one moment of joy to
make his story credible. The audience's awareness that they are at a play,
that Helen is a spirit or shadow conjured by art, is sufficient for them to be
aware of the ephemerality of Faustus' joys and there is no need to make a
heavy insistence on this.

During Faustus' speech the Old Man re-enters. I have already quoted his
dictum that by following his senses Faustus has damned himself. The text

also indicates that after Faustus has gone out with Helen there occurs the spectacular stage battle between him and the devils described in *The Second Report*:

> Satan begins to sift me with his pride,
> As in this furnace God shall try my faith.
> My faith, vile hell, shall triumph over thee!
> Ambitious fiends, see how the heavens smiles
> At your repulse, and laughs your state to scorn.
> Hence, hell, for hence I fly unto my God. (V.i.120–5)

The last line might indicate that the Old Man is 'flown' to the stage heavens in a throne, but there is no telling from the text whether he has to make his escape thus or whether he ascends in triumph, perhaps having routed the devils by charming them to stillness with the sign of the Cross. It may be that the ambiguity of this scene is intentional, a sign that Faustus' doom is not, as some critics have argued, sealed at this point in the play.

We must return a moment to the Helen scene. W. Bridges-Adams reports that in a celebrated production early this century, William Poel chose for Helen 'the shapeliest model in London and put her in a damped dress that clung to her. She entered downstage and moved slowly upstage; we never saw the face that launched a thousand ships, save through the eyes of Faustus'.[58] The effect would be that the audience would concentrate entirely on Faustus, witnessing his submission to his sensual appetite. This interpretation, however, assumes that Faustus will be damned by his works, visible to the audience. In the last scenes, as we shall see, Marlowe addresses himself to the problem of dramatizing Faustus' failure to perform the necessary and saving act of faith.

The devils enter, perhaps through the stage trap, perhaps, as *The Second Report* suggests, through a hell-mouth in the form of the mouth of a dragon. The opening lines of the scene in the B Text

> Thus from infernal Dis do we ascend
> To view the subjects of our monarchy (V.ii.1–2)

suggest that they were spoken either as the trio emerged from the trap or as they ascended to the gallery. Many scholars have conjectured that they viewed the last scene from there. It is impossible to prove that they are there rather than on one side of the stage. Placing them aloft makes the scene pleasingly symmetrical with that way of staging the conjuring scene. With an inspired touch, Marlowe cast in prose the opening of the scene in which Faustus confesses the story of his life to the scholars. Confession here is tragic recognition, and the simplicity of the lines draws both pity and admiration, inverts the playhouse icon, giving us an awareness that Faustus' moral stature exceeds that of the diabolic spectators above:

FAUSTUS: . . . Ah gentlemen, I gave them my soul for my cunning.

ALL: God forbid.

FAUSTUS: God forbade it indeed, but Faustus hath done it. For the vain
pleasure of four-and-twenty years hath Faustus lost eternal joy and
felicity. I writ them a bill with mine own blood; the date is expired;
this is the time, and he will fetch me. (V.ii.56–62)

Certainly there is something repulsive in the way Mephostophilis taunts
Faustus by claiming that he had led Faustus' eyes to the biblical passages
that had led him to deduce that all men are condemned to everlasting death.
Mephostophilis' tone is that of a child bully – he actually reduces Faustus to
tears before he exits. There follows the dual pageant of heaven and hell,
staged by the Good and Bad Angels who speak antiphonally from '*several
doors*', presumably on either side of the stage. Heaven is symbolized by a
throne that descends to music from the canopy above: perhaps it held boys
to sing a hymn. Hell is discovered, presumably a dragon's mouth in the
discovery space which, having being revealed for the devils' entrance, now
is uncurtained for Faustus' vision of damnation. Its presence on the stage
does not of course signal to the audience that Faustus is doomed: a player is
always free to move to another part of the stage, a character in a play free to
fall. It seems that in a recent production Clifford Williams delayed the
discovery until near the end of Faustus' final speech – where the stage
directions read '*Thunder and lightning*' (V.ii.178):[59]

Eric Porter plays the last scene unforgettably, matching the mental
torment with a physical struggle as he combats the inevitable summons
to damnation, until, with a stunning theatrical coup, the looming black
wall at the back falls down to reveal the flames of Hell, and the devils
swarm out to claim their prey.

The playhouse bell begins to toll the chimes of midnight, moving the play
towards its consummation but increasing the audience's hope against hope
that Faustus will yet repent. No theologian would allow that a diabolic pact
was binding nor that the Devil could conquer a resolute soul by force. But
Faustus does not have that strength for the saving act of will, that act of
faith. No play of the period dramatizes more forcibly what is meant by that
phrase. For only at the end of the play is Satan's power fully experienced.
The long speech is symmetrical with the opening soliloquy of the play, and
although the devils are now present, impassive spectators, it is for the actor
playing Faustus to conjure up their power here. No speech like this had
been written before in England: no one had managed its distinctive mixture
of inward terror and rhetorical argument, of exclamation and definition.
Like Kyd, Marlowe realized that the obvious rhetorical progression of the
speech might help the player built up to peaks of passion and also convey, by
its numbed repetition, the sterility of a wasted mind:

Fair Nature's eye, rise, rise again, and make
Perpetual day; or let this hour be but
A year, a month, a week, a natural day . . .

One drop would save my soul, half a drop. (V.ii.131–40)

Marlowe has gone beyond the hypnotic regularity of Kyd's rhythms to something much more expressive, using rubato and syncopation, and in its contrast with the formality of the Good and Bad Angels' speech, creating a sense of an individual consciousness.

Faustus seems to glimpse the saving blood of Christ, but repeatedly throughout the speech as throughout the play he thinks of his body and not his soul – 'O spare me, Lucifer' (V.ii.142), rather than 'O save me, Christ.' He thinks of physical escape, perhaps tugging in vain at the stage trap:

Then will I headlong run into the earth.

Earth, gape! O no, it will not harbour me. (V.ii.148–9)

Even after the clock has struck twelve and the thunder has sounded for the first time, Faustus could have repented. The stage directions then of the 1604 text are perhaps more accurate. They indicate that the devils appear only after Faustus has been unable to repent before the glimpse of an angry god ('My God, my God! Look not so fierce on me'), whereas the 1616 text has them coming in before that line, thus suggesting that their presence finally swayed Faustus into damnation. Empson has argued that the metre of Faustus' final lines minimises the stress on the negatives:

Adders and serpents, let me breathe awhile,

Ugly hell, gape not! Come not, Lucifer!

I'll burn my books. Ah Mephistophilis. (V.ii.182–4)

'. . . behind this there is also a demand for the final intellectual curiosity, at whatever cost, to be satisfied:

Let Ugly Hell gape, show me Lucifer.'[60]

That may be: it could be realized by showing Faustus walking resolutely towards the back of the stage. His damnation would then be a voluntary act, and the sight of his retreating back could provide the audience with a heroic image to set against the diabolic clownage. Empson, however, concludes that 'it is evident that with the last two words he has abandoned the effort to organize his preferences, and is falling to the devil like a tired child'. Alternatively his cry, 'I'll burn my books', could be a cue for the player to rush impulsively towards the discovery space that had been his study, only to be surprised by the advancing devils and hauled ignominiously off to hell. Perhaps, as in A Looking Glass for London and England, III.ii., 'a flame of fire' could appear from the trap to cover their exit.

Again the curtains close while the hell-mouth is moved from the space and property limbs quickly substituted to signify Faustus' dismembered body while the scholars talk. As these are so obviously property limbs the sight of these relics rouses neither of the Aristotelian emotions of horror and pity: rather it reinforces the sense of the quickness of Faustus' end, the sudden extinction of life. The second scholar attempts no moralizing or explanation for Marlowe is again employing the basic technique of the play:

the presented show. Moral comment is left to the Chorus and it is possible that that final discovered spectacle will make the audience think that these last lines represent Marlowe speaking not what he feels but what he ought to say. So it may be tempting to a modern director to conclude the play with the curt Latin motto, possibly like the gnomic end of *Love's Labour's Lost*: 'The words of Mercury are harsh after the songs of Apollo', possibly added by the owner of the manuscript or by the printer: *Terminat hora diem, terminat Author opus*. The hour concludes the day, the author concludes his work. It suggests a retreat by Marlowe towards impersonality, an awareness that the play's ending might have been dictated by convention and expectation, or perhaps a confession that, once the author has finished, it is for players to bring the text to life.

8 · *Titus Andronicus*: strange images of death

It is impossible yet again to fix the date of first performance or the theatrical provenance of this play with any certainty. The most informed opinion places it in 1589–90,[1] that is within a year or so of the probable composition of *The Spanish Tragedy*,[2] and many passages of the verse are infused by Marlowe's potent rhythms.[3] It was a popular play, performed successively by Pembroke's, Strange's, Sussex's, and the Chamberlain's Men. It may have been performed at the playhouse at Newington Butts and then been moved to join *Doctor Faustus* in repertory at the Rose in 1594, when the companies could return to London after the ferocious plague of 1593.[4] It is the only Elizabethan play of which we have definite record of a private performance: a company from London presented it as the culmination of the Christmas Revels of 1595–6 offered by Sir John Harrington to his two hundred guests at Burley-on-the-Hill in Rutland. Of the performance Anthony Bacon's French secretary, Jacques Petit, opined that 'la monstre a plus valeu q̄ le suiect'[5] – the worth of the spectacle exceeded that of the text. It was revived in Jacobean times. Just as Hamlet admitted that the old-fashioned style of Marlowe was nevertheless 'as wholesome as sweet', so Ben Jonson, drawing up articles of attention for his audience at the Hope, had to conceed that the method of *Titus Andronicus*, by 1614 even more out of date, could not be dismissed:

> He that will swear *Jeronimo* or *Andronicus* are the best plays yet, shall pass unexpected at, here, as a man whose judgement shows it is constant, and hath stood still these five and twenty years, or thirty years. Though it be an ignorance, it is a virtuous and staid ignorance – and next to truth, a confirm'd error does well – such a one the author knows where to find him. (*Bartholomew Fair*, Ind., 107ff.)

In modern times reluctant acceptance has turned to embarrassment. Shakespeare's authorship has been denied, and it has seemed a chore for editors and sometimes a temptation for sensation-mongering directors. Critics who have entered the play armed only with the literary probes of genre, plot, and character have been led into *impasses* or premature

186

inferences of lack of substance or quality. The play could be labelled melodrama in that its resolution is imposed on rather than developed from the action although there is little of the conflict between good and evil found in that genre. If narrated baldly, the plot contains little obvious significance: it is merely complicated and gathers to almost ungraspable swiftness towards the end. Reading the text alone would indicate that Titus achieves none of the final recognition that seems to me to be the prime attribute of a tragic hero – his impulsive actions at the end of the play are no different from those at the beginning, and the one scene that seems to bring him to a kind of awareness, III.i., does not really focus on his consciousness as do the recognition scenes of the great tragedies, but is presented merely as the most savage of a set of savage spectacles. Recognition may subsume despair, but not rest upon only that.

This play, however, more than any of the others we have examined, must be considered not simply in dramatic terms but as an artefact for the theatre. Its structure, as Jacques Petit noted without appreciating, is visual rather than literary, and although it may have the relentless consistency of a dream or nightmare, it is not just a bloodbath of classical horrors but does make a political statement – as a pageant, however, and not in conventional literary-dramatic terms. It is very different, therefore, from the other plays Shakespeare was writing at this time. In the early histories Shakespeare was fostering his skills in dramatic narrative and developing concepts of monarchy and state. In *Romeo and Juliet* he went to a tragic narrative of a simple kind and developed the psychological dimensions of the central characters to make it significant. In *Titus Andronicus*, however, he seems to have turned his attention to the creation of dramatic images, explored kinds of spectacle that produce a compulsive response from the audience, and, like Kyd, tried to work towards a dramatic rhythm based on word, gesture, and music in which concord is invaded by discord. The effect is to lay bare the piece of work that is man and, specifically, to remind the audience of the irrational and violent elements in classical culture. Perhaps the play's popularity was due to the strident claims it makes against the elitist Apollonian plays of the court, 'English Seneca read by candlelight', as Nashe archly described them. It hints also that the neo-classical ideal of consistency of character is not true to experience as it traces the awesome metamorphosis of a choleric soldier into a crazed revenger – like Kyd, Shakespeare knew the dramatic power of a figure seized by monomania. It portrays Goths on stage and arguably is the first 'Gothic' work in the language. In this respect it is shocking because it violates not social norms but the sense of self (the rape scene is accordingly central); it tears aside not Burckhardt's veil of faith but Dostoevsky's veil of familiarity. It is a reminder to popular audiences of what they already know of the precarious foundations of society where hatred is as common as love, faction as familiar as league, quaintness

as widespread as normality. It resembles the underworld literature
of the period where reality and fancy are indistinguishable, where
characters 'from life' people a looking-glass world where morality and
order are strangely displaced. Those who were familiar with the pictur-
esque roles attributed to rogues in, say, Harman's *Caveat for Common
Cursetors* (1567) would have no trouble in seeing Tamora play her part as
Revenge.

   The overall pattern is simple: the play begins and ends with the election of
a Roman Emperor: the middle is occupied by a grim vision of the wild
justice of revenge. Within that pattern Shakespeare worked in an ex-
perimental but methodical and schematic way to explore the theatrical
effects at his disposal. He tried out, for example, using the gallery aloft,
putting characters above others and also by using a pit on the stage – in a
'Roman' play from which the traditional Christian associations of the gallery
with grace or moral superiority and the pit with evil and hell have been
conspicuously banished. His characters, like those of Marlowe, are icons,
realist in the sense that they are created with some degree of individuality
and that they violate the moral ideals of world modelled on law or restraint,
but unreal in the sense that they are, as Roy Strong wrote of the portraits of
the time, 'isolated, strange, and exotic'.[6] There is no sense of families in this
play, only of powers – Tamora's pleading for her sons, Aaron's defence of
his child, the gathering of family remnants at Marcus' banquet are political
rather than domestic affairs. And Shakespeare was seeing what happens
when a thing, a human hand, for example, is thrust repeatedly before the
audience's consciousness. The word occurs forty-six times in the play, and
as if that were not enough, a hand, Titus' severed hand, is carried off by the
handless Lavinia who holds it between her teeth. Shakespeare is deliberately getting us to look at it purely as an object, quite displaced from its usual
position in the world and therefore strange and frightening. In the next
scene when Marcus remonstrates with his brother not to teach his daughter
to 'lay such violent hands upon her tender life', Titus rejoins in manic
compulsion:

> How now! has sorrow made thee dote already?
> Why, Marcus, no man should be mad but I.
> What violent hands can she lay on her life?
> Ah, therefore dost thou urge the name of hands,
> To bid Aeneas tell the tale twice o'er,
> How Troy was burnt and he made miserable?
> O, handle not the theme, to talk of hands,
> Lest we remember still that we have none.
> Fie, fie, how franticly I square my talk,
> As if we should forget we had no hands,
> If Marcus did not name the word of hands! (III.ii.23–33)

In fact severed hands were a common motif in Renaissance emblems of justice,[7] but that haunting phrase, 'name the word of hands', suggests that Shakespeare was displacing the figure from the moral to the psychological domain, exploring a world so terrifying that all action is meaningless because the words used to describe it have been raped of their metaphorical significance. We may compare the repetition of words like 'shadow' and 'face' in *Richard II*, but whereas in the latter play these words become symbols in that they accrete meanings that can be arranged into statements about the action of the play, the hands of Titus and Lavinia remain remorselessly hands. The word designates only its accustomed object and moves towards neither metaphor nor metonym, the thing moves no distance towards emblem. We have therefore an index of the play's peculiar kind of realism. It is not based on exactness to life but on the creation of a series of images, academic 'figures' and popular fancies, that by iteration etch themselves on our imagination.

Tragedy at this time was modelled on Seneca, and Senecan tragedies had strong stories and were built about a fairly consistent moral philosophy, although they did present in narrative, if not in spectacle, scenes of horrific violence. *Titus Andronicus*, however, is as Ovidian as it is Senecan.[8] Shakespeare's theatrical imagination has been siezed by the images of the poet.

Overall the play creates dramatic images out of Ovid's vision (*Metamorphoses*, trs. Golding, I. 154–70) of an Iron Age – ironically the home of *Titus Andronicus* under Saturninus is shown during its most un-Saturnine reign. Saturn had presided over the Gold Age of plenty and justice. Aaron, whose malignity lies at the centre of the play, is specifically identified as Saturnine in temperament (II.iii.31), and his blackness is the appropriate colour for that humour; the passionate Tamora is governed by Venus, whose colour was yellow, appropriate for a fair-haired Goth. Titus is obviously Martian and choleric – a red costume could have suited his temper late in the play. Motivation therefore is created by their generic and psychological characteristics not by singular traits of personality. These mythic resonances as well as the play's mode of characterization are what prevents the work being merely sensational, a parade of obscene violence.

Although Shakespeare may have felt that tragedy, until then mainly academic tragedy, had excluded direct experience of horror and suffering, he was as concerned to demonstrate how we perceive violence as well as the violence itself. Marcus, confronted with the mutilated figure of his niece, anaesthetizes himself by attempting to see her as an emblem:

> Fair Philomel, why, she but lost her tongue,
> And in a tedious sample sewed her mind:
> But, lovely niece, that mean is cut from thee;
> A craftier Tereus, cousin, hast thou met,

And he hath cut those pretty fingers off,

That could have better sewed than Philomel. (II.iv.38–43)

Because of the play's concern with perception, naturalism of presentation is quite inappropriate: members of the audience fainted at Peter Brook's 1955 production at Stratford not because Lavinia was really bleeding but because of the suggestiveness of the image. Richard David describes it thus:[9]

> Who could forget the return of the ravishers with Lavinia? They bring her through the leafy arch that was the central pillar and leave her standing there, right arm outstretched and head drooping away from it, left arm crooked with the wrist at the mouth. Her hair falls in disorder over face and shoulders, and from wrist and wrist-and-mouth trail scarlet streamers, symbols of her mutilation. The two assassins retreat from her, step by step, looking back at her, on either side of the stage. Their taunts fall softly, lingeringly, as if they themselves were in a daze of horror of their deed; and the air tingles and reverberates with the slow plucking of harp strings.

Seventeen years later Trevor Nunn presented this scene in another way:

> Where Brook presented the violence symbolically, Mr. Nunn gives it rapid materialistic weight and stress: the raped, tongueless Lavinia, for instance here becomes a pitiable, hunched grotesque, crawling out of the darkness like a wounded animal and even moments like Titus' severance of his own hand are deprived of their crude sensationalism by the stress on the sheer physical difficulty of the action. (*Guardian*, 13 October 1972)

These then are the principles of the dramaturgy of *Titus Andronicus*. The play accordingly is related to the last plays in which Shakespeare was also working by juxtaposing great images or ceremonies and fusing them into a whole that cannot be explained from the shape of the narrative or by development of character. Significantly the play focuses narrowly on an oligarchy – the populace do not appear here as they do in *Coriolanus* and the spectacles of violence are images of corruption in this decadent class. No dialectic is possible. As Gareth Lloyd Evans wrote: 'Like Seneca, the play is concerned exclusively with the affairs of the highborn in which political and social life is conditioned entirely by lust, greed, cruelty, ambition, and revenge.'[10] Fantastic though the verse may be, like *Edward II* the play has a documentary quality to it and sometimes demands the kind of naturalistic playing the *Guardian* reviewer described where players are, as it were, called upon to work on the stage.

Like *Coriolanus*, on the other hand, and so many popular plays, *Titus Andronicus* demands more than the usual amount of music. Shakespeare's frequent calls for flourishes and trumpets are not a tacit admission that non-verbal devices are required to flesh out the text nor do they serve merely to create a martial atmosphere. Rather, as we have seen, music serves for perspective, for symbols of concord and discord, political league and political chaos, the harmony of love and the broken chords of passion. A musical metaphor is used in connection with the state in II.i. where Aaron quiets the 'braving' of Tamora's sons Chiron and Demetrius who are rivals for the possession of Lavinia:

> What, is Lavinia then become so loose,
> Or Bassianus so degenerate,
> That for her love such quarrels may be broached
> Without controlment, justice, or revenge?
> Young lords, beware; and should the empress know
> This discord's ground, the music would not please. (II.i.65–70)

Two scenes later Tamora woos Aaron using commonplace conceits of the hunt where the harmony of echoes, hounds, and horns ironically symbolises a legitimate and decorous love. The sexual images (snake, horns, etc.) lead towards images not only of storm and disruption but of children and generation (babbling, and the nurse's song):

> My lovely Aaron, wherefore look'st thou sad
> When everything doth make a gleeful boast?
> The birds chant melody on every bush,
> The snake lies rollèd in the cheerful sun,
> The green leaves quiver with the cooling wind,
> And make a chequered shadow on the ground;
> Under their sweet shade, Aaron, let us sit,
> And, whilst the babbling echo mocks the hounds,
> Replying shrilly to the well-tuned horns,
> As if a double hunt were heard at once,
> Let us sit down and mark their yellowing noise;
> And – after conflict, such as was supposed
> The wandering prince and Dido once enjoyed,
> When with a happy storm they were surprised,
> And curtained with a counsel-keeping cave –
> We may, each wreathèd in the other's arms,
> Our pastimes done, possess a golden slumber,
> Whiles hounds and horns and sweet melodious birds
> Be unto us as is a nurse's song
> Of lullaby to bring her babe asleep. (II.iii.10–29)

The verse is of notable complexity, again a pointer to how far the play is from Kyd or from naturalism, yet able as well to suggest not only a moral frame for this tableau and to forecast its outcome – the conception of the bastard child – but also Tamora's wistfulness and capacity for self-deception. The association of hounds with the passions derives from moralizations of the Actaeon myth – Chapman's *The Shadow of Night* (1594) provides an example. In *Twelfth Night* Orsino laments that the sight of Olivia made him an Actaeon:

> O, when mine eyes did see Olivia first,
> Methought she purged the air of pestilence;
> The instant was I turned into a hart,
> And my desires, like fell and cruel hounds,
> E'er since pursue me. (I.i.18–22)

Shakespeare developed the conceit in the hunting scene of *A Midsummer Night's Dream* where he combined images of the hunt with the Ovidian paradox of the *discors concordia*, that discordant harmony that from the fusion of opposites creates generation (*discors concordia fetibus apta est* – *Metamorphoses*, I.433). In that play, after the trials of the night, the lovers are prepared for marriage and Theseus has learnt that the state cannot be ruled simply by applying the strictness of the recorded law. In *Titus Andronicus*, however, the play is resolved only by deaths, and there is no sense that the state has been renewed or that the characters have attained maturity through adversity. It is therefore significant that the final lines of the play, Lucius' instructions for the disposing of the bodies of the Emperor and Tamora, explicitly forbid the sounding of ritual funeral music:

> Some loving friends convey the Emperor hence,
> And give him burial in his father's grave.
> My father and Lavinia shall forthwith
> Be closèd in our household's monument.
> As for that ravenous tiger, Tamora,
> No funeral rite, nor man in mourning weed,
> No mournful bell shall ring her burial;
> But throw her forth to beasts and birds to prey.
> Her life was beastly and devoid of pity;
> And being dead, let birds on her take pity. (V.iii.191–200)

Modern productions have been notable for their use of music. Richard David describes how Peter Brook matched spectacle to sound:[11]

> The compulsive and incantatory nature of the production (which sent some spectators off into faints before ever a throat was cut) was reinforced by the musical effects, all of a marvelous directness. The overture was a roll of drum and cymbal, the dirge for the slain Andronici, so strange and powerful, no more than the first two bars of *Three Blind Mice*, in the minor and endlessly repeated. A slow seesaw of two bass notes, a semitone apart, wrought the tension of the final scene to an unbearable pitch, and ceased abruptly, with breath-taking effect, as the first morsel of son-pie passed Tamora's lips.

Later Trevor Nunn began his production with groans that turned to exclamations, while in the first scene dirges alternated with shouts of agony. As B. A. Young reported, his Titus (Colin Blakely) delivers his lines in a kind of Schoenbergian speech-song, prolonged vowels as if to music; his gestures, mostly made with both arms together as long as both his arms are complete to make them with, are bold and artificial but expressive. (*Financial Times*, 13 October 1972)

The play opens with a flourish and a stately entrance of tribunes and senators on the gallery above the black-draped stage. They represent justice and the constituted power of Rome and have gathered to hear pleas for the crown from Bassianus and Saturninus, sons of the late Emperor and rivals for power. The latter enter from opposite doors with their own drums and trumpets: perhaps their music was a challenge to the established order like the musical battle at the opening to *Mucedorus*, anticipating the anarchy that is to prevail throughout the play. There is a preliminary touch of comedy as Marcus reveals in a formal speech that both their pleas are vain as the crown will be awarded out of the family, to Titus Andronicus who has recently saved Rome from the Goths.[12] He is successful, but Saturninus' suave Marlovian rejoinder, 'How fair the tribune speaks to calm my thoughts' and Bassianus' immediate proclamation of love for Titus' daughter Lavinia suggest they both have an eye for the main chance. It is like the political scenes of *The Jew of Malta*: the cynicism of the potentates adds a dimension of savage farce, feeds the fancies of the audience concerning the realities of power at court. Saturninus formally dismisses his followers and then bluntly demands, 'Open the gates and let me in' (I.i.62), as he turns to the stage doors to mount with his brother to the gallery, the fountainhead of power. From there they witness the next procession, the arrival of Titus with Tamora captive. The stage direction is probably authorial:

> *Sound drums and trumpets, and then enter two of Titus' sons, and then two men bearing a coffin covered with black; then two other sons; then Titus Andronicus; and then Tamora, the Queen of Goths, and her sons Alarbus, Chiron, and Demetrius, with Aaron the Moor, and others as many as can be; then set down the coffin, and Titus speaks.*

The establishing of powers above witnessing a procession of powers below resembles the opening gest of *The Spanish Tragedy*. The succession of 'thens' suggests a prolonged entrance to music through one of the doors or, effectively, as with the procession of captives early in *The Spanish Tragedy*, through one of the yard entrances. The two parties, captors and captives, take up positions on opposite sides of the stage. For once we have a drawing that may depict an early staging of part of this scene. It comes from a manuscript attributed to Henry Peacham but it is impossible to tell whether it was sketched at a performance or done afterwards from memory. Some of the lines accompanying the sketch begin at line 105. It is interesting that Titus wears something approaching Roman costume – a toga-like garment, sandals, and a crown of oak-leaves – while his attendants are obviously

Elizabethans with halberds although one carries an exotic-looking sword.[13] Aaron is black, has negroid hair and features, and may be helpfully pointing out which of the hand-bound sons is Alarbus doomed to sacrifice. (The third son, other characters, and the coffin do not appear in the drawing.) There is no indication in the text that he does this, but it may be in character for this humorous opportunist villain, even if he is later to become Tamora's lover. The fact that he bears a sword suggests that Shakespeare may not have thought of him as a Roman captive as the stage directions imply. The conventions of the costuming remind us of the play as myth, the double awareness of the audience that what they are watching is of the past and of the present. (See Plate 10.)

Another gest is created as the coffin of one of Titus' sons is laid to rest in the tomb. Lucius' demand that the son of Tamora be sacrificed 'Before this earthly prison of their bones' (I.i.99, reading *F*'s 'earthly' rather than *Q*'s 'earthy') suggests that the discovery space would have been used rather than the stage trap. So the first procession and action created an emblem of vaulting ambition, the second a figure of death – the architecture of the tiring-house was such that these images of senate house and tomb were placed, significantly, one below the other – and the two leading ideas of the play have been thus economically established. This double visual image resembles the structuring of emblems on the arches erected for civic shows and royal progresses. It creates a significant frame for the ensuing action when the funerary ceremonies are interrupted by the savage spectacle of Alarbus being led off to vengeful execution.

It is significant that the Tribunes, joined by Saturninus and Bassianus, re-enter aloft. This is indicated by *F*'s later stage direction after line 233, '*A long flourish till they come down.*' The effect is to leave the Andronici vulnerable on the stage below. There they stay during the manoeuvring that leads to Saturninus' acceptance of the crown from Titus. Like the Ghost and Revenge in *The Spanish Tragedy*, their presence creates a speaking picture, or visual irony: Titus' gift of the crown takes place under their shadow, or as if, like the planets, their 'virtue' influences those below. It is also notable that Aaron has remained on stage (with Tamora?) during this sequence. He remains silent throughout the Act, a black and ominous presence.

The interest now moves from politics to passion. Saturninus, having like Tamburlaine invested himself with the costume of office (here the white toga of the candidate), comes down to announce his betrothal to Lavinia, even as he hints broadly to the Venerian Tamora that she can expect 'princely usage'. The white robe scarce conceals his 'black' nature. Formalities are yet again invaded when Bassianus with the apparent connivance of Titus' brother and two sons, seizes Lavinia. Titus impetuously slays Martius, his son, and during the fray Saturninus and Tamora ascend to the gallery together. These two supremes and stars of love have played their coup. They vaunt their passion and leave Titus to a debate that is obviously now irrelevant to the realities of power: whether or not his son should be buried in the family tomb. The Act ends with a return to a kind of equilibrium as the Emperor and Tamora, Bassianus and Lavinia enter symmetrically at opposite doors to stage a reconciliation and plan 'to hunt the panther and the hart' (I.i.493) – by now the symbolism is all too obvious.

The Act has been like a dance in which partners and patterns have been changed in marching and counter-marching, ascents and descents. Titus has been elbowed aside and his personality has been established by his extremes of stoic resignation and fits of fury. The use of stage levels and the emblematic rhythm and its consequent ironies enable us to feel that the scene is firmly planned and give us a weapon with which to meet Kenneth Muir's blunt challenge: 'in the early part of the play . . . characters portrayed with little skill orate at considerable length in undifferentiated verse.'[14] Certainly the characterization is schematic. To my description of Titus we can add Irving Wardle's account of the 1972 Saturninus:

John Wood's marvellous performance of the Emperor Saturninus.
From his murderously hysterical first speech, Mr. Wood presents a man governed by whims; and it is characteristic of him to drop Lavinia because she is momentarily unavailable and marry the Queen of the Goths instead.

His performance is spell-binding to watch: endlessly mobile and unpredictable as it drops into the chatty cadences of modern English or rises into spitty fury: linking blood-drenched inhumanity with domestic realism. Mr. Wood arrives for the morning hunt bleary-eyed after his first night with Tamora; and at the news of the Goths' invasion, he raises a finger to his lips warning the messenger not to wake the baby.
The performance is a wonderful blend of deadly vigilance, petty rancour, and buffoonery. (*The Times*, 13 October 1972)

Likewise, we shall see the player of Tamora called upon to swing from pained impotence to cool calculating triumph.

Act I established the patterns of politics in Rome. Act II will reveal the natures, the characters in action, of those we have been introduced to in the exposition of the play. After his political manoeuvring and spurts of action, Titus has, it seems in this Act, settled into acceptance of the new political order. When he appears at the opening of scene ii there is no indication that he resents the settlement, although the opening words may well be ironical:

The hunt is up, the morn is bright and grey,
The fields are fragrant and the woods are green.
Uncouple here and let us make a bay,
And wake the Emperor and his lovely bride,
And rouse the Prince, and ring a hunter's peal,
That all the court may echo with the noise. (II.ii.1–6)

The revenge of the Goths and the Moor therefore is the more outrageous in that it befalls him suddenly and is revealed as being personal and not political in motivation.

The act is symmetrical in that it begins and ends with soliloquies: Aaron's plans to vault to power with his mistress and Marcus' lament for the violation of his niece. Between these we have a pattern in which the Goths appear, and in their dialogues or soliloquies unfold the chaos and violence which they then proceed to wreak when the innocent appear. The effect is of a cancer working fearful change on the body politic. Evil has moved inside the city and innocent and active alike succumb. This movement from public to private action is symbolized by Aaron's appearance in this scene on the level of the main stage, the world of political action. His presence below counterpoints the metaphors he uses to describe Tamora's rise: his power is such that it need not be impressed on others from above:

> Now climbeth Tamora Olympus' top,
> Safe out of Fortune's shot, and sits aloft,
> Secure of thunder's crack or lightning flash,
> Advanced above pale envy's threat'ning reach.
> As when the golden sun salutes the morn,
> And, having gilt the ocean with his beams,
> Gallops the zodiac in his glistering coach,
> And overlooks the highest-peering hills;
> So Tamora. (II.i.1–9)

The speech is obviously Marlovian, and in ll. 16–17:

> Away with slavish weeds and servile thoughts!
> I will be bright, and shine in pearl and gold

Shakespeare quotes the famous moments in which Tamburlaine divests himself of shepherd's weeds and dons the armour of a warrior. There is no indication in the text, however, that Aaron should actually change his costume on the stage at this moment. His power comes from his personality and his sexual vitality; with Tamburlaine there is little sense of sexual vigour (although we note his power of words over Zenocrate) and we feel that his power derives from his success-breeding success, his robes of office. The difference between them is like the difference between the heroic figures of Verrochio and Bernini: Marlowe's hero gains his effect by filling the stage space others create for him, Shakespeare's player must be fuelled by energy within. Aaron, like Gaveston having announced his intentions, demonstrates his sway immediately when Chiron and Demetrius enter 'braving'. He converts their rival lusts for Lavinia to a plan to rape her together in the forest while she is hunting. They had insulted each other by mocking each other's potency:

> Why, boy, although our mother, unadvised,
> Gave you a dancing-rapier by your side,

Are you so desperate grown to threat your friends?
Go to; have you lath glued within your sheath
Till you know better how to handle it. (II.i.38–42)

Aaron controls them cunningly by inviting them to join him in an exchange of bawdy:

AARON: Why, then, it seems some certain snatch or so
   Would serve your turns.
CHIRON: Ay, so the turn were served.
DEMETRIUS: Aaron, thou hast hit it.
AARON: Would you had hit it too!
   Then should not we be tired with this ado. (II.i.95–8)

The scene ends with two great verse emblems. First we hear described the forest, a fine Arcadian place until it is invaded by Aaron's naming of 'rape and villainy':

My lords, a solemn hunting is in hand;
There will the lovely Roman ladies troop:
The forest walks are wide and spacious,
And many unfrequented plots there are
Fitted by kind for rape and villainy.
Single you thither then this dainty doe,
And strike her home by force, if not by words. (II.i.112–18)

Second, a vision of the House of Fame, drawn either from Chaucer's poem or Ovid (*Metamorphoses*, XII.42ff. in the Golding version):

The emperor's court is like a house of Fame,
The palace full of tongues, of eyes, and ears:
The woods are ruthless, dreadful, deaf and dull:
There speak, and strike, brave boys, and take your turns;
There serve your lust, shadowed from heaven's eye,
And revel in Lavinia's treasury. (II.i.126–31)

Such a dramatic technique, of course, is completely unsuited to any illusionistic stage. Here it serves to remind us that in Elizabethan playhouses the concept of place existed only so far as it was perceived by the characters or, to put it more briefly, place is a stage of mind (remember Mephostophilis' 'Why this is hell, nor am I out of it'). Palace and wood are imposed on one another: the Court may seem a moral wilderness, nature may be corrupted by the ubiquity of man's evil. The juxtaposition of these two images is an emblem of the metamorphosis of the characters in the play, a change that is imposed by the pattern of the action as much as it originates from their personalities. This is demonstrated in another way when Demetrius concludes the scene with some words in Latin:

Sit fas aut nefas, till I find the stream
To cool this heat, a charm to calm these fits,
Per Stygia, per manes vehor. (II.i.133–5)

Some editors have translated the last line as 'I am ready for anything' (it derives from Seneca's *Phaedra*, 1180, where Phaedra proclaims she will follow Hippolytus over Styx and the fiery rivers) but it makes more sense to interpret it as 'I am carried through the Stygian regions of the underworld, i.e. I am in hell. The Latin quotation, like those used in *The Spanish Tragedy*, turns the scene to emblem, transforms the character from individual to archetype. Personality dissolves and hence the possibility of audience 'identification' with a particular character. Rather the play assumes the quality of a phantasmagoria where legitimacy is challenged by evil in a realm that is nowhere and everywhere.

The same technique is repeated in the next two sequences. Titus greets the newly married Emperor and Empress with a cry of hounds and a peal of hounds, a musical confusion of ceremonial love and anarchic passion like that we saw in our examination of analogous emblems in *A Midsummer Night's Dream*. The musical emblem is accompanied by a pastoral description of the woods. This composite emblem serves as an ironic accompaniment to the adulterous love-making of Aaron and Tamora – the familiar device of thrusting Elysium into hell that Nashe saw in *The Spanish Tragedy*.

The rest of the Act contains one of the principal sequences of violence in the play. In it we witness the death of Bassianus, see Lavinia led off to rape and mutilation, the fall into Bassianus' grave of Quintus and Martius and their false accusation of the murder of the Emperor's brother, and finally Marcus' discovery of the ravaged Lavinia. The whole sequence has been master-minded by Aaron. It seems that Shakespeare has gone again to Marlowe for the mode of this part of the play, to the quaint devices of Barabas. He indulges popular fancies of destruction – Hamlet's *Mousetrap* provides another example. Like Barabas, Aaron displays a grim humour (that provokes audience laughter in modern productions) as he cynically plants the gold and then leads Titus' son to fall into the stage trapdoor, 'A very excellent piece of villainy' (II.iii.7). But this sequence is far more disturbing than analogous scenes in *The Jew of Malta*. Marlowe's characters remain consistent, mere silhouettes in a sort of shadow play. The audience's lack of involvement with the savage farce is a corollary of their awareness that the subject of that play is not the fates of those individuals but the degenerate natures of all the inhabitants of Malta – Christians, Jews, and infidels. But there never was a God for pagan Rome, and there is no comforting moral generality to shield us from the violence of the action. It is not even a morality play or a melodrama that has run out of control, for Lavinia is no helpless piece of fair virtue set against the swart villainy of the Moor. Instead we hear her vilely taunting Tamora with what Nicholas Brooke calls 'the beastliness of conscious virtue':[15]

Under your patience, gentle Emperess,

'Tis thought you have a goodly gift in horning,
And to be doubted that your Moor and you
Are singled forth to try thy experiments.
Jove shield your husband from his hounds today!
'Tis pity they should take him for a stag. (II.iii.66–71)

This makes her later prolonged plea for mercy to Tamora the more disturbing: she has our sympathies for her general predicament, but we are equally aware that she has precipitated her catastrophe.

Shakespeare refuses to let the comedy he had established inform the next episode of the scene, that in which Martius and Quintus successively fall into the pit. (It is significant that the Arden editor, J. C. Maxwell, does not even supply the necessary stage directions for this sequence.) The tone at first seems to be that of farce.

QUINTUS: . . . I have no strength to pluck thee to the brink.
MARTIUS: Nor I no strength to climb without thy help.
QUINTUS: Thy hand once more; I will not loose again,
  Till thou are here aloft, or I below.
  Thou canst not come to me – I come to thee. *Falls in*. (II.iii.241–5)

But in the pit they find the body of Bassianus, 'a fearful sight of blood and death' (II.iii.216). The savage spectacle is described with a mixture of imaginative realism:

Lord Bassianus lies berayed in blood,
All on a heap, like to a slaughtered lamb,
In this detested, dark, blood-drinking pit (II.iii.222–4)

and baroque formality in which the perceived reality is turned into something akin to a sculptured funerary icon:

Upon his bloody finger he doth wear
A precious ring, that lightens all this hole,
Which, like a taper in some monument,
Doth shine upon the dead man's earthy cheeks,
And shows the ragged entrails of this pit. (II.iii.226–30)

Like the fancy of destruction this is the fancy of the graveyard: the images are like those in modern fairground ghost trains or the chamber of horrors at Madame Tussaud's. But Shakespeare extends the conceit to the utmost – and to horrific seriousness in the famous speech in which Marcus describes the violated Lavinia who is standing before him:

Speak, gentle niece, what stern ungentle hands
Hath lopped and hewed and made thy body bare
Of her two branches, those sweet ornaments,
Whose circling shadows kings have sought to sleep in,
And might not gain so great a happiness
As half thy love? Why dost not speak to me?
Alas, a crimson river of warm blood,

> Like to a bubbling fountain stirred with wind,
> Doth rise and fall between thy rosed lips,
> Coming and going with thy honey breath.
> But, sure, some Tereus hath deflowered thee,
> And, lest thou should'st detect him, cut thy tongue.
> Ah, now thou turn'st away thy face for shame!
> And, notwithstanding all this loss of blood –
> As from a conduit with three issuing spouts –
> Yet do thy cheeks look red as Titan's face
> Blushing to be encountered with a cloud. (II.iv.16–32)

Dover Wilson thought that this was a burlesque of similar moments in the works of Shakespeare's lesser contemporaries,[16] but I think that Shakespeare's mind was captured by the idea of translating to the playhouse images of violence he had found in the prototype of this story, Ovid's telling of the rape of Philomel in *Metamorphoses*, VI.702–15:

> . . . drawing out his naked sword that at his girdle hung,
> He took her rudely by the hair, and wrung her hands behind her,
> Compelling her to hold them there while he himself did bind her.
> When Philomela saw the sword, she hoped she should have died,
> And for the same her naked throat she gladly did provide.
> But as she yearned and callèd aye upon her father's name,
> And strivèd to have spoken still, the cruel tyrant came
> And with pair of pinsons fast did catch her by the tongue,
> And with his sword did cut it off. The stump whereon it hung
> Did patter still. The tip fell down and quivering on the ground
> As though that it had murmured it made a certain sound.
> And as an adder's tail cut off doth skip a while: even so
> The tip of Philomela's tongue did wriggle to and fro,
> And nearer to her mistress-ward in dying still did go.

The rape and the wriggling tongue could not be portrayed on the stage, but Shakespeare seems insistent on exposing to the audience what Marlowe had flinched from. Its necessary stylization may serve in fact a kind of psychological realism: as H. T. Price pointed out, Marcus enters 'in that mood of hearty cheerfulness which is always produced by a day's hunting in the forest' to find Lavinia in her sorry plight. His attempt to emblematize the sight, turn her into a kind of Marlovian figure not unlike the portrait of Hero we have already examined, is a kind of shield from the awfulness of the sight, an imposition of fancy on reality. Yet again, Shakespeare is concentrating on violence not for itself but as it is perceived. It is an experiment, not wholly successful, as the playwright relentlessly uncovers what emblems conceal, reveals the savagery that underlines comedy.[17]

In Act III Shakespeare returns to the city. Grotesqueries and violence continue and for the first time Titus becomes an object of pity as he enters

before the Tribunes' procession and, presumably walking backwards until
he prostrates himself before them, begs in vain for the life of his son. They
pass by, and like Richard II on his return from Ireland, Titus grovels on the
ground in childlike petulance:

> . . . I tell my sorrows to the stones,
> Who, though they cannot answer my distress,
> Yet in some sort they are better than the Tribunes,
> For that they will not intercept my tale.
> When I do weep, they humbly at my feet
> Receive my tears, and seem to weep with me;
> And were they but attirèd in grave weeds,
> Rome could afford no tribunes like to these. (III.i.37–44)

(Does 'stones', however, mean 'statues' here?) Here is incipient madness,
but Titus' anguish is cauterized by the appearance of Lavinia. From the
strong simplicity of

> MARCUS: This was thy daughter.
> TITUS: Why, Marcus, so she is. (III.i.63)

he embarks on one of the play's most memorable speeches:

> For now I stand as one upon a rock,
> Environed with a wilderness of sea,
> Who marks the waxing tide grow wave by wave,
> Expecting ever when some envious surge
> Will in his brinish bowels swallow him.
> This way to death my wretched sons are gone;
> Here stands my other son, a banished man,
> And here my brother, weeping at my woes;
> But that which gives my soul the greatest spurn
> Is dear Lavinia, dearer than my soul. (III.i.93–102)

The lines remind us of some of the final gnomic utterances of Timon of
Athens, but whereas Timon was attempting to draw his life to a significant
close, Titus is, like Marcus, protecting himself by this heroic self-
dramatisation. For his agony is not done and Shakespeare again drives the
rest of the scene through fancy into nightmare. In his torrent of passion
before the silent Lavinia he had made a rhetorical offer to sever his own
hands:

> Give me a sword, I'll chop off my hands too;
> For they have fought for Rome, and all in vain;
> And they have nursed this woe, in feeding life;
> In bootless prayer have they been held up,
> And they have served me to effectless use. (III.i.72–6)

By employing a species of irony that we might claim to encounter in life but
which few authors would dare use in fiction, Aaron comes in with an offer
that Titus cannot refuse: his sons will be spared by the Emperor in return

for a hand severed from one of the Andronici. The announcement confirms our suspicion that the impassivity of the Tribunes was a symptom of the complete corruption of the new regime and begins an absurd comedy in which the men vie with one another for the privilege of losing a hand until Aaron intervenes with lines that might have come out of *Alice in Wonderland*:

> Nay, come, agree whose hand shall go along,
> For fear they die before their pardon come. (III.i.174–5)

After the fearsome clarity of this and the abrupt shock of seeing Aaron quickly cut off Titus' hand on stage, Titus' lament is magnificently emblematic and histrionic:

> If there were reasons for these miseries,
> Then into limits could I bind my woes:
> When heaven doth weep, doth not the earth o'erflow?
> If the winds rage, doth not the sea wax mad,
> Threatening the welkin with his big-swol'n face?
> And wilt thou have a reason for this coil?
> I am the sea. Hark how her sighs doth blow;
> She is the weeping welkin, I the earth:
> Then must my sea be movèd with her sighs;
> Then must my earth with her continual tears
> Become a deluge, overflowed and drowned;
> For why my bowels cannot hide her woes,
> But like a drunkard must I vomit them. (III.i.219–31)

In a way that neither Kyd nor Marlowe was able to do, Shakespeare is making Titus' consciousness the centre of the stage as his state of mind creates the place. Later in *Lear* he would use the technique in a more modulated form. The speech serves, however, only as a prelude to a further shock, the appearance of the Messenger bearing two heads and Titus' hand. Marcus and Lucius compete in insensitive exclamations, Lavinia in silent reproach to them kisses her father, but Titus' silence, a contrast with the fury of his tirade, is broken only by his line (cried or whispered?), 'When will this fearful slumber have an end?' (III.i.252), until, without warning, he laughs. This, rather than the speeches that came before, is Titus' recognition, a moment when, to quote Timon of Athens, language has ended, a recognition that what is horrible is defined not theologically by the absence of good but by a vision of a cosmos geared only to the survival of the fittest. The moment must have impressed contemporaries: Marston may have been parodying it when he has Pandulpho laugh at the catastrophes of I.ii. of *Antonio's Revenge*. Shakespeare uses the device to mark the moment when Titus realises that his compulsive energies must be harnessed to revenge. Now the thrustful energies he revealed as a warrior will be harnessed to the half-crazed half-witty contrivances of the revenger.

It is possible, moreover, that Aaron's confession in Act V describes a piece of stage action in this scene:

I played the cheater for thy father's hand,
And, when I had it, drew myself apart,
And almost broke my heart with extreme laughter.
I pryed me through the crevice of a wall
When, for his hand, he had his two sons' heads;
Beheld his tears, and laughed so heartily
That both mine eyes were rainy like to his. (V.i.111–17)

Aaron might have concealed himself in the discovery space and there would be a grim and ironic counterpoint if Titus were to thus unwittingly join him in a gale of laughter.

Shakespeare confirms this impression of Titus' monomania in the 'situational' scene (that appears only in the Folio) that follows. It demands a banquet, thus prefiguring the final Thyestean banquet and, as Nicholas Brooke suggests, it resembles the Painter scene in *The Spanish Tragedy*,[18] being an emblem of Titus' derangement. In it Titus' persistive laments give way to a sentimental plea for the kindred of the fly that Marcus stabs as the family sits at table. When Marcus remonstrates that the fly was as black as Aaron, Titus takes his knife to it himself in unremitting savagery. The scene works, concentrating the audience on the effects rather than the sensational spectacles of violence, so that Harold Hobson could write of the 1972 production: 'Mr. Nunn has decided not to do [the horror scenes] whole-heartedly. The most excessive horror to which he lends himself is Titus' savage stabbing of a fly' (*The Sunday Times*, 15 October 1972).

In Act IV the succession of violent spectacles abates in intensity for a while in preparation no doubt for the enormities of the play's conclusion. The Act opens with a scene where Lucius' son runs on stage fleeing from Lavinia. Her purpose is to obtain his copy of the *Metamorphoses* and to indicate that she like Philomel had been rudely forced. In an agonising sequence she writes out the names of her attackers in the sand with a stick held in her mouth and then quotes in Latin an anguished plea to the gods from Seneca's *Phaedra*. The moment is symmetrical with that when Demetrius, one of her violators, quoted from the same play (II.i.135), and like the use of divers languages in *The Spanish Tragedy*, gives the scene an archetypal significance. Although the scene is too obviously emblematic, there is also a more immediate awareness for the audience: that horror does not cease when the physical violence has abated, that to a child the innocent Lavinia is as terrible as the villainous Aaron. After his instinctive terror at this moment, the boy is converted to revenge by his grandfather and great uncle:

I say, my lord, that if I were a man
Their mother's bedchamber should not be safe

For these base bondmen to the yoke of Rome. (IV.i.108–10)
We might remember the pathetic moment when Lady Macduff's son boasts that he could be a warrior, but this is a horrible moment as the child puts on the antic and monstrous disposition of the revenger.

In the next scene another encounter with innocence is played out. We meet the steely Aaron who realizes that Chiron and Demetrius have not the wit to see that the weapons wound with mottoes sent them by Titus are a signal that they have been found out. He does not disclose the danger that they are in, thinking that he might leap to even higher power, but his mood is changed when the nurse brings him his bastard blackamoor child by Tamora. He is not moved to tenderness: on the contrary he coldly and cruelly dispatches the nurse:

'Wheak, wheak!'
So cries a pig preparèd to the spit. (IV.ii.146–7)

The sight of his child inspires him to a vitality and confidence of character that is shared by no one else in the play:

I tell you, younglings, not Enceladus,
With all his threat'ning band of Typhon's brood,
Nor great Alcides, nor the god of war,
Shall seize this prey out of his father's hands.
What, what, ye sanguine, shallow-hearted boys!
Ye white-limed walls! ye alehouse painted signs!
Coal-black is better than another hue,
In that it scorns to bear another hue;
For all the water in the ocean
Can never turn the swan's black legs to white,
Although she lave them hourly in the flood,
Tell the Empress from me, I am of age
To keep mine own – excuse it how she can. (IV.ii.93–105)

This borders on rant, but its lurching movement displays a nascent self-sufficiency and a celebration of natural values that is in its way attractive. As a politician too Aaron stands in contrast to the blundering of the Saturnines and the impotence of the Andronici who under the direction of the distracted Titus now shoot arrows to the gods and send a petition to the court to be carried by the unwitting Clown, with his pigeons on his way to the Tribunes over a threepenny brawl. There are elements of allegory here too: Titus proclaims that Astrea has left the earth and Lucius is said to have reached the constellation Virgo with his arrow. Frances Yates argues that this has to do with the Astrea cult that was built up around Elizabeth the Virgin Queen, and that the final enthronement of Lucius heralds the return to the golden age and is therefore an oblique compliment to the monarch.[19] But like the preceding Lavinia scene which also tended towards allegory or archtype it has a more immediate dramatic effect. In its mixture of grotesquerie created by the sight of arrows being fired into the playhouse gallery while the archers announce they are being sent to the heavens, pathos as we hear the rantings of Titus, cheerful obscenity when he remarks that Lucius has hit the virgin in the lap, and bathos when the Clown emerges to be the messenger, it serves as an emblem of the confusion in Titus' mind. It is a play within a play, like the trial scene in *Lear*, and the deliberate violation of decorum that occurs when a grand anagogic concept – communicating with the gods – is literally enacted on the stage is parallel to the indecorum of having Gloucester make an ungainly leap at his moment of spiritual enlightenment. In both cases Shakespeare seems to be deliberately disowning the significance of these climaxes in the dramatic action. It also serves to illustrate a point that Shakespeare was to raise repeatedly in his history plays, that the search for a final cause or providential pattern is fruitless. As Machiavelli had demonstrated and a popular audience would suspect, history is made by the actions of men, and we know that the fate of Rome will depend more on Aaron's conspiracy with the Goths than on any divine intervention. The casual execution of the clown, ordered by Tamora with as little concern as Aaron had shown over the death of the nurse, is scarcely noticed as we hear that at last the Andronici are on the march, having made a firmer alliance with the Goths than that Aaron boasted of.

With the Thyestean banquet, the final horror of the sons baked in a pie and served to their mother and the swift successions of stabbings, Act V offers a culmination to the nightmare of violence in the play. But it also contains a rising movement that is as strong as any in Shakespearean tragedy. It is not a question of good supplanting evil – the Thyestean banquet will strip Titus of any sympathy – but of a victory by main force of those who respect the state over those whose respect is only for themselves. There is an uncomfortable pause when it looks as though Lucius will hang Aaron's baby on the stage, but mercy prevails and the scene is resolved with a long confession of dastardly deeds from the captured Aaron. Among others, the speech describes one incident like that actually performed by Marlowe's Barabas when he set two dead men 'upright at their dear friend's door' (V.i.136). Here Shakespeare, however, cauterizes any humour. But the speech is at the centre of the first of two scenes in which Shakespeare, perhaps rather desperately, crystallizes themes out of the play's action, having, if my interpretation is correct, tried to eschew significance in some of the preceding sequences. As Muriel Bradbrook describes Aaron he is 'half-symbol, half stage formula'[20] and we may go further and say that he becomes the evil which Lucius must purge from the body politic. Or we may regard the speech as the equivalent to that at the end of *Richard III* in which Richard realises that he has become the part he had created to play before others ('I am I'). Aaron has become what the Goths needed in order to legitimise their invasion, a black devil, a stage villain.

In the second scene Shakespeare resorts to actual allegory as Tamora invests herself in the costume of Revenge. We are reminded of Death the Mower in *Edward II*, the Old Man in *Faustus*. The dividing line between realism and allegory was obviously less perceptible to the Elizabethans than to us. Tarquin moves towards the sleeping Lucrece through a landscape of the mind, Macbeth sees himself as 'withered Murder' (II.i.52), and we think of the way characters in Spenser easily become what they represent. In the visual arts, we might think of the allegorical portraits of the time such as the famous Eworth painting of Sir John Luttrell (1550) in the Courtauld Institute in which we see what is presumably a good likeness of the subject wading heroically as a bringer of peace through seas of wreck and turmoil. So Tamora enters as Revenge with her two sons. She may have been as Ripa describes her in the *Iconologia*, clad in red, bearing a naked dagger and biting a finger to express anguish,[21] or bearing a whip and sounding a drum as she appeared in Act II of an Admiral's play, Peele's *The Battle of Alcazar*, or dressed in imitation of the well-known figure from *The Spanish Tragedy*. Titus, in his madness, recognizes her immediately and begins the grim stage game that will end only with the deaths of them both. He names her sons Rape and Murder and invites her to 'Stab them, or tear them on thy chariot-wheels' (V.ii.47). This and the related lines describing a chariot may simply be a figment of Titus' festering imagination: they may, however, indicate that Tamora entered in a chariot, like Tamburlaine's drawn by her princely sons, a familiar figure of the Triumph of Revenge. If that is the case the entrance may have been into the playhouse yard to summon Titus out on to the stage for his final conflict. Alternatively the Goths might come out on to the stage (a chariot enters '*through the curtains*' in Act II of *The Battle of Alcazar*) and knock at one of the doors, for Titus to appear aloft in response to their knock. Strangely the Arden editor and Richard Hosley assert but without argument or evidence that the gallery was not in fact used.[22] Tamora's repeated bids to Titus to come down (ll. 33–43) and her covering aside while he descends, presumably down the stair within the tiring-house, seem sufficient evidence to me. Shakespeare may in fact have used the gallery as an ironic reminder of the action in Act I. There Tamora appeared aloft while her power was in the ascendant, here Titus has seen through to her true nature and is in a position to have her seized and brought to summary justice. The cruel Lavinia whom we have heard taunting Tamora reappears with a basin between her wrists to catch the blood of the sons, her violators, as her father slits their throats.

It must have been difficult to avoid excess. Shakespeare avoids it by invoking yet again a mythic archetype for the climax of the play, the Thyestean banquet, a suitable final image of the action. Familiar from *The Battle of Alcazar* (1588–9), *A Warning for Fair Women* (after 1585), and later to be used in *Antonio's Revenge* (1599), *The Golden Age* (1610), and *The*

Bloody Banquet (1639), it was presumably less sensational for Renaissance audiences than it is now. Shakespeare also lightens the sequence by bringing on Titus as a cook to serve up the cannibal's pie. The tone of nineteenth-century pantomime is heard here:

> Let me go grind their bones to powder small,
> And with this hateful liquor temper it;
> And in that paste let their vile heads be baked. (V.ii.198–200)

And yet this is not farce for children, but the kitchen humour of a distracted man. Its naïveté, however, serves a serious and humane purpose as the audience is delighted by the spectacle of politicians punished for their corruption. Once the spectacle is established the action moves very quickly as the pie is brought in, Lavinia is slain in imitation of the legend of Virginius' slaughter of his daughter, and Tamora, Titus himself, and Saturninus are despatched. The death of Lavinia may have quoted visually the scene in which she first appeared: there she knelt as Titus raised his hand to bless her, here she kneels as Titus raises his hand to kill her. A modern director might want to attempt the sequence in a kind of nightmarish slow motion, although a swift fury of slaughter might be equally effective, to contrast with the formalized pathos as the Andronici lament their dead and the ceremony of acclamation as Lucius is made Emperor. Peter Brook cut ruthlessly to avoid laughs and played the whole scene formally: 'in the glare of the torches the victims topple forward in succession across the dinner table like a row of ninepins skittled from behind. It was as if the actors were engaged in a ritual at once fluent from habitual performance and yet still practiced with concentrated attention.'[23] Rather, the scene has the combination of grotesquerie, savagery, and fundamentalist detachment from what is inhuman and inhumane that we find in *Alice in Wonderland*. Shakespeare, in other words, has taken what is naïve in folk culture and turned it into a sophisticated and serious kind of theatre. He marks this by turning from surrealist and fanciful nightmare to customary theatrical ceremony: the play must have ended with a double funeral procession, probably, as I noted, without music: the noble borne out shoulder high with due honour, the base drawn out ignominiously by their feet.

Abbreviations

Collections	Malone Society, *Collections* (1907—)
Diary	R. A. Foakes and R. T. Rickert (eds), *Henslowe's Diary*
ELH	*ELH: a Journal of English Literary History*
E.L.R.	*English Literary Renaissance*
E.S.	E. K. Chambers, *The Elizabethan Stage*
E.Sts	*English Studies*
Ind.	Induction
J.W.C.I.	*Journal of the Warburg and Courtauld Institute*
MLR	*Modern Language Review*
N.& Q.	*Notes and Queries*
R.E.S.	*Review of English Studies*
Ren.D.	*Renaissance Drama*
R.O.R.D.	*Research Opportunities in Renaissance Drama*
S.E.L.	*Studies in English Literature, 1500–1900*
S.P.	*Studies in Philology*
S.Q.	*Shakespeare Quarterly*
S.S.	*Shakespeare Survey*
Shak.S.	*Shakespeare Studies*
T.D.R.	*The Drama Review* (formerly *Tulane Drama Review*)
T.L.S.	*Times Literary Supplement*

Notes

Introduction

1 *The Boke Named the Governor* (ed. S. E. Lehmberg), London, 1962, p. 2.
2 For this concept and a fine general survey see Peter Burke, *Popular Culture in Early Modern Europe*, London, 1978.
3 For an argument for comparatively high literacy rates due to the Tudor revolution in education see Lawrence Stone, 'The Educational Revolution in England, 1560–1640', *Past and Present*, 28, 1964; cf. David Cressy, *Literacy and the Social Order: Reading and Writing in Tudor and Stuart England*, Cambridge, 1980.
4 Introduction to S. L. Bethell, *Shakespeare and the Popular Dramatic Tradition*, p. ix.
5 See John Willett (ed.), *Brecht on Theatre*, London, 1964, *passim*.
6 Quoted in Burke, p. 114.

Chapter 1   Playhouses and stages

1 Malone Society, *Collections*, I.3, 1909, p. 266; the University of Cambridge complained to the Privy Council in 1592 that the Queen's Men were diverting students to Chesterton just outside the town to see shows 'set up in open places' (*Collections*, I, pp. 193–5).
2 See K. M. Dodd, 'Another Elizabethan Theater in the Round', *S.Q.*, XXI, 1970, pp. 125–56.
3 W. W. Greg, *Dramatic Documents from the Elizabethan Playhouses*, I, p. 13.
4 E. K. Chambers, *The Elizabethan Stage* (hereafter this work will be abbreviated to *E.S.*), IV, p. 300.
5 *E.S.*, II, pp. 396ff; see Herbert Berry (ed.), *The First Public Playhouse: the Theatre in Shoreditch, 1576–1598*.
6 *E.S.*, II, p. 364.
7 *E.S.*, II, p. 405.
8 *E.S.*, III, p. 501.

9 *E.S.*, II, p. 534n.
10 *E.S.*, II, p. 437.
11 R. Cotgrave (ed.), *A Dictionary of the French and English Tongues*, London, 1611.
12 See A. Harbage, *Annals of English Drama*.
13 See A. Feuillerat (ed.), *Documents Relating to the . . . Revels at Court . . .*, *passim*; R. A. Foakes and R. T. Rickert (eds), *Henslowe's Diary* (hereafter *Diary*), pp. 319–21.
14 R. Southern, *The Staging of Plays before Shakespeare, passim*.
15 Ibid.
16 G. Wickham, *Early English Stages*, II.2, Plates X and XI.
17 Wickham, II.1, p. xii.
18 Ann Jennalie Cook, ' "Bargaines of Incontinencie": Bawdy Behaviour in the Playhouses', *Shak. S.*, X, 1977, pp. 271–90.
19 *E.S.*, II, p. 437.
20 Richard Hosley, 'A Reconstruction of the Fortune Playhouse', *The Elizabethan Theatre*, VI, 1978, pp. 1–20; see also J. W. Saunders, 'Vaulting the Rails', *S.S.*, VII, 1954, pp. 69–81.
21 *E.S.*, IV, p. 366; see W. J. Lawrence, *Those Nut-Cracking Elizabethans*, Ch. viii, 'The Evolution of the Tragic Carpet'.
22 See *E.S.*, III, pp. 79–80n.
23 R. Hosley, 'The Discovery-Space in Shakespeare's Globe', *S.S.*, XII, 1959, pp. 35–46.
24 E. L. Rhodes, *Henslowe's Rose: the Stage and Staging*, p. 31.
25 Vitruvius, *De Architectura*, V.ci.8; there is an interesting conjecture, that Barabas' body was thrown from the stage into the yard, in J. L. Simmons, 'Elizabethan Stage Practice and Marlowe's *The Jew of Malta*', *Ren.D.*, IV, 1971, pp. 93–104.
26 C. Walter Hodges, *The Globe Restored*, p. 43.
27 See G. E. Bentley, *The Jacobean and Caroline Stage*, Oxford, 1941–68, VI, p. 186n.; Herbert Berry, 'Dr. Fludd's Engravings and their Beholders', *Shak. S.*, III, 1967, pp. 11–21.
28 Rhodes, Ch. vi.
29 The Latin text is given in *E.S.*, II, pp. 361–2.
30 This case is well argued in D. F. Rowan, 'The English Playhouse: 1595–1630', *Ren.D.*, IV, 1971, pp. 37–52.
31 *E.S.*, II, p. 437.
32 In a Blackfriars play, *The Knight of the Burning Pestle*, the Wife draws attention to a painted cloth depicting the Conversion of St Paul (Interlude II, 11–12) which has nothing to do with the play's action.
33 Southern, pp. 266ff.
34 See Hosley, 'The Discovery-Space . . .'.
35 Their arguments are reviewed by T. J. King, 'The Stage in the Time of Shakespeare: a Survey of Major Scholarship', *Ren.D.*, IV, 1971, pp. 199–235.
36 Hosley, 'The Discovery-Space . . .'.
37 Some historians have inferred that the Fludd engravings represent the Blackfriars theatre, and the arrangement shown would accommodate the

opening stage direction of a Blackfriars play, *Eastward Ho* (1605): '*Enter Master Touchstone and Quicksilver at several [separate] doors . . . At the middle door, enter Golding, discovering a goldsmith's shop, and walking short turns before it.*'

38 See Rowan, op. cit.; John Orrell, 'Inigo Jones at the Cockpit', *S.S.*, XXX, 1977, pp. 157–68.

39 In other playhouses stage directions indicate that doors and not curtains were used. An example from Jonson's *Epicoene*, acted by the Children of the Revels in 1609 probably at the Whitefriars, suggests that this private playhouse, like the Rose (Rhodes, pp. 24ff.) had a recessed tiring-house façade fitted with doors in the side walls: 'Do you observe this gallery, or rather lobby indeed? Here are a couple of studies, at each end one: here will I act such a tragi-comedy . . . which of them comes out first, will I seize on; – you two shall be the chorus behind the arras, and whip out between the acts and speak' (IV.v.28–33). The arras hung between these two 'studies' and a reference later to locking the study doors (83) indicates that these were not, in this play at least, concealed by hangings.

40 Hosley, 'The Discovery-Space . . .'.

41 It could be used in the manner implied by some dialogue in *Much Ado About Nothing*: 'Stand thee close then under this penthouse, for it drizzles rain' (III.iii.96–7).

42 They are so designated in a stage direction in *The Devil is an Ass* (1616), where Jonson indicates that a scene (II.vi.) was '*acted at two windows, as out of two contiguous buildings.*' Admittedly this is a Blackfriars play, but there is no reason to doubt that the same fiction was used in the public playhouses (Hodges, pp. 61–2).

43 Ben Jonson, *Works* (ed. Herford and Simpson), Oxford, 1925–52, XI, p. 453.

44 The second Paul's playhouse, an indoor private theatre, evidently had a similar gallery divided into boxes. A stage direction from *Antonio's Revenge*, '*Andrugio's ghost is placed between the music-houses*' (V.iii.), indicates that two were used by musicians.

45 The height of the gallery is suggested by stage directions that call for players to leap from it to the stage below. An example is found in *I Henry VI*, probably a Rose play, where we find at II.i.38, '*The French leap over the walls in their shirts.*' These directions and the Swan drawing indicate a height of between 7 and 10 feet, although Hosley deduces that the Fortune gallery was 12 feet high (Hosley, 'A Reconstruction . . .'). The occurence of the word 'top' in stage directions has led some historians to conjecture the use of a second gallery above the first which may have doubled as a music room. There may even have been one at the Swan concealed in the drawing by the canopy. So we find in *I Henry VI* the stage direction '*Enter Pucelle on the top; thrusting out a torch, burning*' (III.ii.25) and in *The Tempest*, '*Solemn and strange music: and Prosper on the top, invisible*' (III.iii.17). In Fletcher and Massinger's *The Double Marriage* (1619–23), however, we find in a scene depicting a ship engaged in battle a prompter's warning '*Boy atop*' followed two lines later by a speech from '*Boy above*'. This suggests that 'top' was synonymous with 'above' – Hosley argues ('The Discovery-Space . . .') moreover that there was no such second gallery at the Globe. It is almost certain that players generally reached the gallery by

stairs within the tiring-house (Rhodes, p. 77) although when necessary stairs were sometimes set against the façade of the stage. *The Knight of Malta*, a King's Men play of about 1618, contains a notation apparently printed from a prompt copy: '*The scaffold set out and the stairs*' (II.v.). There is also mention in Henslowe's inventory of properties for the Lord Admiral's Men dated 10 March 1598, at which time the company was playing at the Rose, of 'i payer of Stayers for Fayeton' (*Diary*, p. 319).

46 *Diary*, p. 13.

47 Rhodes, pp. 84–5.

48 Andrew Gurr, *The Shakespearean Stage 1574–1642*, p. 96.

49 See G. Wickham, '"Heavens", Machinery, and Pillars in the Theatre and other Early Playhouses', in Berry op. cit., where it is argued that there was no canopy at the Theatre originally and that such a structure was added to the Rose only in 1592.

50 *E.S.*, II, pp. 466–7.

51 C. Walter Hodges, *Shakespeare's Second Globe*, Oxford, 1973, *passim*.

52 T. Heywood, *An Apology for Actors*, London, 1841 ed., pp. 34–5.

53 See Lawrence, Ch. vii, 'Bells in the Elizabethan Drama'.

54 *Diary*, p. 319.

55 B. Beckerman, *Shakespeare at the Globe*, p. 93.

56 *E.S.*, III, p. 77n.

57 *Diary*, p. 320; *E.S.*, III, pp. 76–7.

58 Heywood, *The Dramatic Works* (ed. R. H. Shepherd), London, 1874, III, pp. 135–7.

59 Rhodes, p. 18.

60 *The Silver Age* has a stage direction (Heywood, *Dramatic Works*, III, p. 159) that indicates that there might have been up to five traps: '*Hercules sinks himself; flashes of fire; the Devils appear at every corner of the stage with several fireworks. The Judges of Hell and the Three Sisters run over the stage, Hercules after them; fireworks all over the house. Enter Hercules.*' It is equally possible, however, that the devils simply came out into the yard and climbed onto the stage.

61 It seems that players may have brought out themselves the functional properties they required, a convention that violates naturalist concepts of dramatic illusion. So we find a stage direction in Wilson's *The Cobbler's Prophecy* (1590) where Ralph enters '*with his stool, his implements and shoes, and sitting on his stool, falls to sing*' (52–3). Shakespeare probably expected I.iii. of *Coriolanus* to begin in a similar manner:

> *Enter Volumnia and Virgilia, mother and wife to Martius. They set them down on two low stools and sew.*

Generally, however, such furniture would have been moved on and off by stage keepers. See Lawrence, Ch. ix, 'Bygone Stage Furniture and its Removers'.

62 Compare *Edward III*, III.iv; for spectacle in modern productions of *Tamburlaine*, see N. T. Leslie, 'Tamburlaine in the Theater: Tartar, Grand Guignol, or Janus?', *Ren.D.*, IV, 1971, pp. 105–20.

63 *Diary*, p. 321; see also W. J. Lawrence, 'Stage Dummies', Ch. ix of his *Speeding Up Shakespeare*.

64 See G. K. Hunter, 'The Theology of Marlowe's *The Jew of Malta*', *J.W.C.I.*,

XXVII, 1964, pp. 211–40; and cf. Kyd, *The Spanish Tragedy*, III.xi.26ff.

65 Lily B. Campbell, *Scenes and Machines on the English Stage*, pp. 63–4, 136–40, 212.

66 Heywood, *Dramatic Works*, III, pp. 67–70.

67 *Diary*, pp. 319–20.

68 *E.S.*, II, pp. 364–5. I have corrected the translation.

69 *Diary*, p. 319.

70 Similar scenes include a fragment from 'The Second Part of the Seven Deadly Sins', in W. W. Greg, op. cit., plate inserted between pp. 104–5; *2 The Iron Age*, II.i. (Heywood, III, pp. 371–2); see also *E.S.*, III, p. 53n.

71 *E.S.*, I, p. 229n.

72 G. F. Reynolds, *The Staging of Elizabethan Plays at the Red Bull Theater*, p. 153.

73 C. Walter Hodges, *The Globe Restored, passim*; Wickham, II.i., Ch. viii, 'Stage Furniture'; W. A. Armstrong, 'Actors and Theatres', *S.S.*, XVII, 1964, pp. 191–204.

74 *Diary*, p. 319.

75 This was how it was done at Court – see *E.S.*, I, p. 232.

76 *Diary*, p. 320.

77 A. Harbage, *Annals*, p. 58.

78 Sidney, *The Defence of Poesie*, London, 1595, Sig.G1ʳ.

79 *E.S.*, I, p. 234.

80 *E.S.*, II, p. 437.

81 *E.S.*, II, p. 362.

82 *E.S.*, II, p. 437.

Chapter 2   Performances

1   See Wickham, II.i., pp. 78ff.

2   Malone Society, *Collections*, I, 1907, p. 46.

3   See also the passages from Henry Crosse (1603) and 'I. H.' (1615) in *E.S.*, IV, pp. 247 and 254, and H. C. Gardiner, *Mysteries' End*, New Haven, 1946, *passim*, esp. p. 78; for a general survey see Margot Heinemann, *Puritanism and the Theatre: Thomas Middleton and Opposition Drama under the Stuarts*, Cambridge, 1980.

4   *E.S.*, IV, p. 322.

5   *E.S.*, IV, p. 291; the dating of this document is discussed by Wickham, II.i., p. 85.

6   *E.S.*, IV, p. 323.

7   *E.S.*, IV, p. 286.

8   *E.S.*, IV, p. 307.

9   *The Roaring Girl* (1608), I.i.

10 *E.S.*, II, p. 535.

11 *E.S.*, II, p. 549; see W. J. Lawrence, *Those Nut-Cracking Elizabethans*, Ch. i.

12 'Elizabethan Stage Gleanings', *R.E.S.*, I, 1925, pp. 182–6.

13 See p. 45 above.

14 See especially Alfred Harbage, *Shakespeare's Audience*; Harbage's conclusions have been questioned by Ann J. Cook, *The Privileged Playgoers of Shakespeare's London*.

15 See R. Schofield, 'Illiteracy in Pre-Industrial England', in E. Johansson (ed.), *Literacy and Society in a Historical Perspective*, Umea, 1973.

16 *E.S.*, II, p. 369n.

17 *E.S.*, II, p. 365; see Ernest Schanzer, 'Thomas Platter's Observations on the Elizabethan Stage', *N. & Q.*, CCI, 1956, pp. 465–7.

18 Gurr, p. 7.

19 Harbage, *Shakespeare's Audience*, p. 30.

20 *E.S.*, IV, p. 216; cf. Malone Society *Collections*, I, where in 1583 the Lord Mayor reports that at the Theatre and the Curtain 'do resort great multitudes of the basest sort of people; and many infected with sores running on them'.

21 Harbage, p. 59.

22 Quoted in *E.S.*, I, p. 265n. The subject of ritual misrule may be pursued in Keith Thomas's Stenton Lecture, *Rule and Misrule in the Schools of Early Modern England*, Reading, 1976.

23 Harbage, p. 82.

24 See n. 14 above.

25 Nashe, *Works* (ed. R. B. McKerrow), Oxford, 1958 ed., I, p. 149.

26 Harbage, p. 91.

27 Harbage, p. 76.

28 Malone Society, *Collections*, I, p. 74.

29 Ibid., p. 46.

30 Harbage, pp. 77–8.

31 *Diary*, p. 47.

32 Harbage has, however, calculated that *takings* (not necessarily attendances) were twice as large on holidays – see *Shakespeare's Audience*, pp. 174–8. Yet takings at the Theatre on Sundays were no higher than on other days – see H. Berry (ed.), *The First Public Playhouse*, p. 42.

33 B. Beckerman, *Shakespeare at the Globe, 1599–1609*, p. 12; *E.S.*, II, p. 143.

34 Peter Ure (ed.), *King Richard II*, London, 1956, p. lviii.

35 Beckerman, p. 10.

36 See E. Honigmann, *The Stability of Shakespeare's Text*, London, 1965, Ch. ii, 'The Transmission of Dramatic Manuscripts'.

37 *E.S.*, II, pp. 540–1; for Edward Knight, book-holder to the King's Men, see W. W. Greg, *The Shakespeare First Folio*, Oxford, 1955, p. 100.

38 Gurr, p. 137, and L. Hotson, 'False Faces on Shakespeare's Stage', *T.L.S.*, 16 May 1952.

39 Cit. *E.S.*, II, p. 540n.

40 *E.S.*, II, p. 219.

41 Gurr, p. 139.

42 Quoted by David Klein, 'Did Shakespeare Produce his own Plays?', *M.L.R.*, LVII, 1962, pp. 556–60; cf. W. A. Armstrong, 'Actors and Theatres', *S.S.*, XVII, 1964, pp. 191–204.

43 This has been argued chiefly by T. W. Baldwin, *The Organization and*

Personnel of the Shakespearean Company, Princeton, N.J., 1927; Baldwin's findings have been disputed by D. M. Bevington, *From 'Mankind' to Marlowe*, pp. 109ff.

44 A similar 'part' from a late miracle play is reproduced in *Collections*, II, pp. 239ff.

45 C. J. Sisson, 'Shakespeare Quartos as Prompt-Copies', *R.E.S.*, XVIII, 1942, pp. 129–43.

46 See Honigmann, op. cit.

47 Cit. H. A. Rennert, *The Spanish Stage in the Time of Lope de Vega*, New York, 1909, p. 159.

48 *E.S.*, II, p. 256.

49 *Collections*, I, pp. 53–4; see also pp. 70–1, 74, 92, 171, 174; II, p. 310. I was led to these references by Professor Peter Davison.

50 *E.S.*, II, p. 543n.

51 *E.S.*, I, p. 225.

52 *E.S.*, I, p. 220n.

53 Rhodes, pp. 143, 112.

54 Cf. Heywood, *Dramatic Works*, III, p. 269; Greene, *A Looking Glass*, V.ii.33, s.d. ('*with dispersed locks*').

55 Marston, *The Insatiate Countess*, in *The Plays of John Marsden* (ed. Harvey Wood), Edinburgh, 1939, p. 22.

56 Heywood, III, p. 161.

57 See J. Willett (ed.), *Brecht on Theatre*, London, 1964, *passim*.

58 Quotations from Marlowe are taken from *The Plays of Christopher Marlowe* (ed. Roma Gill), Oxford, 1971.

59 Rhodes, pp. 28ff.

60 *Diary*, p. 317.

61 D. H. Zucker, *Stage and Image in the Plays of Christopher Marlowe*, Salzburg, 1972, conjectures that Henslowe's 'clothe of the Sone & Mone' adorned the tiring-house for this play and that Tamburlaine may have gestured towards it at this point (p. 23).

62 *E.S.*, IV, p. 217.

63 *E.S.*, II, p. 455.

64 *1 Return from Parnassus*, l. 1601.

65 See J. S. Manifold, *Music in English Drama*, *passim*.

66 Gurr, p. 116; G. K. Hunter, 'Were there Act-Pauses on Shakespeare's Stage?', in S. Henning, R. Kimbrough and R. Knowles (eds), *English Renaissance Drama*, Carbondale, 1976.

67 *Diary*, p. 318.

68 *E.S.*, II, p. 343; see R. E. Morsberger, *Swordplay and the Elizabethan and Jacobean Stage*, Salzburg, 1974.

69 Quoted from the text in T. W. Craik (ed.), *Minor Elizabethan Tragedies*, London, 1974.

70 G. Puttenham, *The Arte of English Poesie*, London, 1589, I.xi., p. 21.

71 See Dieter Mehl, *The Elizabethan Dumb Show*, pp. 29ff.

72 Cf. Bacon's essay, 'Of Masques and Triumphs'.

73 Wickham, II.i., pp. 316–7.

74 T. W. Craik, *The Tudor Interlude*, p. 96.
75 Reprinted in Bevington, pp. 13–14.
76 See C. R. Baskerville, *The Elizabethan Jig*, and J. M. Nosworthy, 'An Elizabethan Jig', *Collections*, IX, pp. 24–9.
77 Modernised from J. B. Leishmann (ed.), *Three Parnassus Plays*, London, 1949, pp. 129–30.
78 *E.S.*, II, p. 365; I have emended Chambers's translation – see Schanzer, n. 17 above.
79 *E.S.*, II, p. 318.
80 *E.S.*, IV, p. 254.
81 Cit. Baskerville, p. 120.
82 *E.S.*, II, p. 551n.
83 *E.S.*, II, p. 553.
84 *E.S.*, II, p. 547.
85 *E.S.*, I, p. 311, II, p. 550.

Chapter 3 Players and playing

1 *E.S.*, I, p. 356.
2 *E.S.*, II, p. 153.
3 *E.S.*, I, p. 310; M. C. Bradbrook, *The Rise of the Common Player*, pp. 74–5; E. K. Chambers, *William Shakespeare*, Oxford, 1930, II, pp. 82ff.
4 J. B. Leishman (ed.), *The Three Parnassus Plays*, London, 1949, p. 350 (*2 Return*, ll. 1918ff.).
5 *E.S.*, II, p. 365; see W. A. Ringler Jr., 'The Number of Actors in Shakespeare's Early Plays', in G. E. Bentley (ed.), *The Seventeenth-Century Stage*, pp. 110–34.
6 D. M. Bevington, *From 'Mankind' to Marlowe*, p. 105.
7 Ibid., p. 107; there is useful material in Stanley Wells and Gary Taylor, *Modernizing Shakespeare's Spelling with Three Studies in the Text of Henry V*, Oxford, 1979, pp. 72ff.
8 See W. J. Lawrence, 'Shakespeare's Supers', in *Those Nut-Cracking Elizabethans*, pp. 44–58.
9 Eduard Eckhardt, *Die Dialekt- und Ausländertypen des älteren Englischen Dramas*, Louvain, 1910, pp. 4–79.
10 Nashe, *Works*, III, p. 311; cf. W. A. Armstrong, 'Actors and Theatres', *S.S.*, XVII, 1971, pp. 191–204.
11 Cf. Shakespeare, *Troilus*, I.iii.153ff., Marston, *Histriomastix*, V.
12 Nashe, *Works*, III, p. 236.
13 See, among others, Bertram Joseph, *Elizabethan Acting*; on acting and rhetoric, see Lise-Love Marker, 'Nature and Decorum in the Theory of Elizabethan Acting', *The Elizabethan Theatre*, II, 1970, pp. 87–107.
14 Bulwer, *Chironomia*, London, 1644, p. 24.
15 *Poetics* (tr. Butcher), ix.4.

16 Cotgrave, 'Faire la nique'. For lip-gnawing see Shakespeare, *Shrew*, II.i.241, *R3*, IV.ii.27, *Othello*, V.ii.42, *Coriolanus*, IV.i.48.

17 S. Rowlands, *The Letting of Humours Blood in the Head-Vaine*, London, 1600, Sig. A2ʳ (cit. Gurr, p. 81).

18 *E.S.*, IV, p. 251.

19 *The Arte of English Poesie*, London, 1589, III.iii., p. 119.

20 Malone Society, *Collections*, I, 1907, p. 128.

21 Ibid., p. 127.

22 Shakespeare, *Shrew*, Ind.ii.137.

23 We might compare another sequence in couplets between a father and his son, that between Talbot and John in Act IV of *1 Henry VI*, a figure of the relationship between Henry V and Henry VI.

24 Gurr, p. 116.

25 See J. B. Streett, 'The Durability of Boy Actors', *N. & Q.*, CCVIII, 1973, pp. 461–5; for a general discussion, see Michael Jamieson, 'Shakespeare's Celibate Stage', reprinted in G. E. Bentley (ed.), *The Seventeenth-Century Stage*, pp. 70–93.

26 *From 'Mankind' to Marlowe*, p. 95.

27 Heywood, III, p. 38.

28 See Marston, *Antonio's Revenge*, II.i.21ff.

29 *Diary*, p. 291; with this compare the catalogue of similar costumes prepared for James's visit to Oxford in 1605 (*Collections*, I, p. 251).

30 *E.S.*, II, p. 365.

31 *Diary*, p. 292.

32 See A. Harbage, *Annals*, p. 206.

33 *E.S.*, III, p. 452.

34 *Diary*, pp. 321–2.

35 See J. D. Wilson, '*Titus Andronicus* on the Stage in 1595', *S.S.*, I, 1948, pp. 17–22, and W. M. Merchant, 'Classical Costume in Shakespearian Productions', *S.S.*, X, 1957, pp. 71–6.

36 A. Latham (ed.), *As You Like It*, London, 1975, p. lv.

37 *A Warning for Fair Women*, Ind., 55.

38 *Diary*, p. 325.

39 C. R. Baskervill, *The Elizabethan Jig*, p. 93.

40 See Reynolds, *The Staging of . . . Plays at the Red Bull*, p. 43.

41 See W. J. Lawrence, 'Shakespeare's Use of Animals', in *Those Nut-Cracking Elizabethans*, pp. 9–27; *E.S.*, I, p. 232.

42 See R. Tarlton, *Tarlton's Jests* (ed. J. O. Halliwell), London, 1884, pp. 13–14.

43 *E.S.*, II, p. 344; see W. J. Lawrence, 'On the Underrated Genius of Dick Tarleton', in his *Speeding Up Shakespeare*, pp. 17–38.

44 *Tarlton's Jests*, pp. 24–5.

45 W. A. Armstrong, 'Shakespeare and the Acting of Edward Alleyn', *S.S.*, VII, 1954, pp. 82–9.

46 *E.S.*, II, p. 297.

47 Gurr notes that 'his "stalking Tamburlaine" drew similes from several pamphleteers at the end of the century. His own mocking name for himself in a family letter was "the fustian king"' (pp. 66–7).

48 *E.S.*, II, p. 309.
49 *Essays and Lectures on Shakespeare*, London, Everyman, n.d., p. 149.
50 See Hereward T. Price, *Construction in Shakespeare*, Ann Arbor, 1951.
51 W. Benjamin, *Illuminations*, London, 1973, pp. 152–3.
52 See my 'Marlowe and Brecht', in B. Morris (ed.), *Christopher Marlowe*, London, 1968, pp. 95–112.
53 D. Klein, *The Elizabethan Dramatists as Critics*, London, 1963, p. 222.
54 *E.S.*, IV, p. 370.

Chapter 4   *The Spanish Tragedy*: architectonic design

1 See Philip Edwards (ed.), *The Spanish Tragedy*, London, 1959, p. xxvii. Quotations, slightly modified, are taken from this edition of the play.
2 See Jean Fuzier, ' "La Tragédie espagnole" en Angleterre' in J. Jacquot (ed.), *Dramaturgie et société*, Paris, 1968, II, pp. 589–606.
3 See Edwards, p. lxvi.
4 Printed in F. S. Boas (ed.), *The Works of Thomas Kyd*, Oxford, 1901, pp. 348ff.
5 A review from *The Financial Times* is reprinted in *R.O.R.D.*, XXI, 1978, pp. 64–6.
6 *Diary*, pp. 182, 203.
7 See E. Auerbach, '*Figura*', in his *Themes from the Drama of European Literature*, New York, 1959, pp. 11–76.
8 For a contrary view see S. W. Dawson, *Drama and the Dramatic*, London, 1970, pp. 22–3 and Jonas A. Barish, '*The Spanish Tragedy* or The Pleasures and Perils of Rhetoric', in J. R. Brown and Bernard Harris (eds), *Elizabethan Theatre*, London, 1966.
9 Boas, p. xcvii.
10 Boas, p. 406.
11 See S. F. Johnson, '*The Spanish Tragedy*, or Babylon Revisited', in R. Hosley (ed.), *Essays on Shakespeare and Elizabethan Drama*, Columbia, Mo., 1962, pp. 23–36.
12 E. M. Tweedie, ' "Action is Eloquence": The Staging of Thomas Kyd's *Spanish Tragedy*', *S.E.L.*, XVI, 1976, pp. 223–39.
13 *Diary*, p. 321.
14 Printed in Boas, pp. 343–7.
15 See the introduction by Andrew Cairncross to his edition of *The First Part of Hieronimo* and *The Spanish Tragedy*, Lincoln, Nebr., 1967.
16 A. B. Grosart (ed.), *The Non-Dramatic Works of Thomas Dekker*, n.p., 1884–6, II, p. 253.
17 See S. Viswanathan, 'The Seating of Andrea's Ghost and Revenge in *The Spanish Tragedy*', *Theatre Survey*, XV, 1974, pp. 171–6.
18 *E.S.*, III, p. 92.
19 Quoted by Viswanathan, op. cit.
20 *Diary*, p. 319.

21 Quoted by Viswanathan, op. cit.
22 Cf. Emrys Jones, *The Origins of Shakespeare*, Oxford, 1977, p. 198.
23 See R. Southern, *The Staging of Plays before Shakespeare*, pp. 584–91.
24 Cf. the equivalent stage direction from the German version: '*Jetzt kompt Ernestus, der Hauptman, geht vor, als denn Lorentz, dess Königs Son, dann Balthazar, der gefangen Fürst von Portugall, als dann Horatius, Nicholaus, Famulus, Petrian vnd so vil man jhr haben kan; die gehen zu einer Thür ein, all für den König, neigen sich vnd zu der andern Thür wider hinauss*' (I.95).
25 *Coleridge's Essays and Lectures on Shakespeare*, London, Everyman, n.d., p. 149.
26 See Joel B. Altman, *The Tudor Play of Mind*, Berkeley, 1978, pp. 271–2.
27 See n. 5 above.
28 Cited in *E.S.*, I, p. 189n.
29 *E.S.*, I, p. 143n., see also Frances Yates, 'Elizabethan Chivalry: The Romance of the Accession Day Tilts', in *Astraea*, London, 1975, pp. 88–111.
30 See Edwards, pp. 34–5n.
31 Rhodes, p. 88.
32 M. C. Bradbrook, 'Marlowe's *Doctor Faustus* and the Eldritch Tradition', in Hosley, *Essays on Shakespeare* . . . ; Enid Welsford, *The Fool*, New York, 1935, pp. 301–2.
33 See n. 11 above.
34 Nashe, *Works*, III, p. 316.
35 Cf. D. F. Rowan, 'The Staging of *The Spanish Tragedy*', *The Elizabethan Theatre*, V, 1975, pp. 112–23.
36 Cf. ibid.; Rhodes, p. 88; Edwards, p. 110n.
37 See Arthur Freeman, *Thomas Kyd*, Oxford, 1967, p. 114.
38 Edwards, p. xxxvi.
39 William Empson, '*The Spanish Tragedy*', *Nimbus*, III, 1956, pp. 16–29.
40 G. Puttenham, *The Arte of English Poesie*, London, 1589, p. 119.

Chapter 5 *Mucedorus*: the exploitation of convention

1 C. F. Tucker Brooke (ed.), *The Shakespeare Apocrypha*, Oxford, 1908, p. xxvi.
2 See George F. Reynolds, '*Mucedorus*, Most Popular Elizabethan Play', in J. W. Bennett *et al.* (eds), *Studies in the English Renaissance Drama*, London, 1959, pp. 248–68.
3 *E.S.*, IV, p. 36.
4 C. R. Baskerville *et al.*, *Elizabethan and Stuart Plays*, New York, 1934, p. 525.
5 See Reynolds, op. cit.
6 A. Feuillerat (ed.), *Documents Relating to the . . . Revels at Court . . .* , pp. xvi–xvii.
7 Burke, *Popular Culture in Early Modern Europe*, London, 1978, p. 121.
8 *Diary*, p. 103.
9 Quotations are modernised from Brooke's text in *The Shakespeare Apocrypha*; cf. the portrait of Envy in Golding's Ovid, II.966–70.

10 Feuillerat, p. 159; cf. the figure of Tragedy in Heywood's *Apology for Actors*, reprinted in Allan H. Gilbert, *Literary Criticism: Plato to Dryden*, Detroit, 1962, p. 553.

11 C. R. Baskerville, *The Elizabethan Jig*, p. 180.

12 John Rowe, *Tragi-Comoedia*, Oxford, 1653, Sig. *2ʳ.

13 See L. Salingar, *Shakespeare and the Traditions of Comedy*, Cambridge, 1974, p. 76.

14 *An Apology for Poetry*, in Gilbert, pp. 451–2.

15 See Werner Habicht, 'Tree Properties and Tree Scenes in Elizabethan Theater', *Ren.D.*, IV, 1971, pp. 69–92.

16 *Diary*, p. 320.

17 Feuillerat, p. 365.

18 Feuillerat, p. 200.

19 Feuillerat, pp. 227, 458.

20 *Diary*, p. 318.

21 See Eduard Eckhardt, *Die Dialekt- und Ausländerntypen des älteren Englischen Dramas*, Louvain, 1910, I, 4–79.

22 See John Rowe, op. cit.

23 Baskerville, p. 137.

24 Patricia Russell, 'Romantic Narrative Plays: 1570–1590', in J. R. Brown and B. Harris (eds), *Elizabethan Theatre*, London, 1966, p. 118.

25 See Reynolds, op. cit.

26 *Diary*, p. 319.

27 Rowe, Sig. *2ᵛ.

28 See Robert Withington, *English Pageantry*, Cambridge, Mass., 1918, I, pp. 72ff.

29 Withington, I, pp. 208, 217.

30 Baskerville, pp. 284–5.

31 Feuillerat, pp. 227, 199–200.

32 Rowe, Sig. *2ᵛ.

Chapter 6   *Edward II*: dramatic documentary

1 Quotations are taken from *The Plays of Christopher Marlowe* (ed. Roma Gill), Oxford, 1971.

2 But see pp. 146 and 149.

3 Directed by Toby Robertson with Ian McKellen as the King (ZPR 113–15).

4 B. Brecht, *Collected Plays* (ed. R. Manheim and John Willett), London, 1970; New York, 1971, I, p. 228.

5 *E.S.*, II, pp. 128ff.

6 Cited in W. D. Briggs (ed.), *Marlowe's Edward II*, London, 1914, p. 152; cf. W. A. Ringler, 'The Number of Actors in Shakespeare's Early Plays', in G. E. Bentley (ed.), *The Seventeenth-Century Stage*, pp. 110–34.

7 Holinshed, *The Chronicles of England*, London, 1587, p. 319.

8 Cited by Caroline Bingham, 'Seventeenth-Century Attitudes towards Deviant Sex', *Journal of Interdisciplinary History*, I, 1970, pp. 447–72.
9 See Michel Foucault, *Histoire de la sexualité*, Paris, 1976, I, p. 59.
10 *E.S.*, I, pp. 122ff; Jean Wilson, *Entertainments for Elizabeth I*, Woodbridge; D. S. Brewer, 1980.
11 See Shakespeare, *Twelfth Night*, I.i.21–2; Chapman, 'Hymnus in Cynthiam', etc.
12 Holinshed, p. 318.
13 Judith Weil, *Christopher Marlowe, Merlin's Prophet*, Cambridge, 1977, p. 151.
14 *The Spanish Tragedy*, II.ii.6.
15 *Titus Andronicus*, II.i.72.
16 See E. H. Kantorowicz, *The King's Two Bodies*, Princeton, N.J., 1957.
17 They are described in *E.S.*, I, p. 143, and see Ch. 4, n. 29 above.
18 See E. Panofsky, *Studies in Iconology*, New York, 1962, p. 77.
19 Briggs, p. 182.
20 D. H. Zucker, *Stage and Image in the Plays of Christopher Marlowe*, Salzburg, 1972, p. 136.
21 Holinshed, p. 341.
22 This is suggested by T. W. Craik, 'The Reconstruction of Stage Action from Early Dramatic Texts', *The Elizabethan Theatre*, V, 1975, pp. 76–91.

Chapter 7 *Doctor Faustus*: **ritual shows**

1 *Marlowe's 'Doctor Faustus' 1604–1616*, (parallel texts edited by W. W. Greg), Oxford, 1950, p. vii.
2 *Diary*, p. 206.
3 *Marlowe's 'Doctor Faustus'*, p. vii–viii.
4 Ibid, p. 33.
5 *Diary*, p. 24.
6 *Marlowe's 'Doctor Faustus'*, pp. 61–2.
7 *E.S.*, III, p. 71.
8 W. J. Thoms (ed.), *A Collection of Early Prose Romances*, London, 1828, III, pp. 45–54.
9 Thomas Beard, *The Theatre of Gods Ivdgments*, London, 1631 ed., p. 553.
10 See P. M. Palmer and R. P. More, *The Sources of the Faust Tradition*, New York, 1936, pp. 239ff.
11 R. H. Perkinson, 'A Restoration "Improvement" of *Doctor Faustus*', *ELH*, I, 1934, pp. 305–324.
12 See Edward Ward, *The Dancing Devils: or, the Roaring Dragon*, London, 1724, and M. P. Wells, 'Some Notes on the Early Eighteenth-Century Pantomime', *S.P.*, XXXII, 1935, pp. 598–607.
13 Hazlitt, *Complete Works* (ed. P. P. Howe), London, 1930–4, VI, p. 202.
14 *E.S.*, III, p. 423.
15 John Melton, *Astrologaster*, London, 1620, p. 31.

16 *E.S.*, III, p. 423.
17 Ibid.
18 J. Grotowski, *Towards a Poor Theatre*, London, 1969, pp. 22–3; the ritual background to Marlowe's theme can be explored in E. M. Butler, *Ritual Magic*, Cambridge, 1949.
19 Compare G. K. Hunter, 'Five-Act Structure in *Doctor Faustus*', *T.D.R.*, VIII, 1964, pp. 77–91; and M. C. Bradbrook, 'The Tragic Pageant of *Timon of Athens*' in her *Shakespeare the Craftsman*, London, 1969.
20 H. Levin, *The Overreacher*, London, 1954.
21 See S. Hawkins, 'The Education of Faustus', *S.E.L.*, VI, 1966, pp. 193–209.
22 D. H. Zucker, *Stage and Image in the Plays of Christopher Marlowe*, Salzburg, 1972, p. 144.
23 Quoted in Gurr, p. 123.
24 Palmer and More, p. 136.
25 See Michael Hattaway, 'The Theology of Marlowe's *Doctor Faustus*', *Ren.D.*, III, 1970, pp. 51–78.
26 Samuel Rowlands, *The Knave of Clubs*, 1609.
27 Butler, p. 177.
28 W. W. Greg, 'The Damnation of Faustus', *M.L.R.*, XLI, 1946, pp. 97–100.
29 Cf. W. W. Greg, *Marlowe's 'Doctor Faustus'*, pp. 101–2.
30 Palmer and More, p. 164.
31 *Diary*, pp. 319ff.
32 Palmer and More, p. 138.
33 *Diary*, p. 320.
34 A. Feuillerat (ed.), *Documents Relating to the . . . Revels at Court . . .* , p. 345.
35 Ibid., p. 42, and cf. *Diary*, p. 318.
36 This is the opinion of T. W. Craik, 'The Reconstruction of Stage Action from Early Dramatic Texts', *The Elizabethan Theatre*, V, 1975, pp. 76–91.
37 *Marlowe's 'Doctor Faustus'*, p. 317, n.A378–81.
38 Zucker, p. 157.
39 It is reported in Guazzo's *Compendium Maleficarum*, Milan, 1610; see A. C. Kors and E. Peters (eds), *Witchcraft in Europe 1100–1700*, London, 1973, p. 150.
40 Dances were long associated with the play: see E. L. Avery, 'Dancing and Pantomime on the English Stage, 1700–1737', *S.P.*, XXXI, 1934, pp. 417–52.
41 See *Marlowe's 'Doctor Faustus'*, pp. 101–2.
42 See Hattaway, op. cit.
43 *Marlowe's 'Doctor Faustus'*, p. 108.
44 Ibid., p. 340, n. 669–70.
45 *Diary*, p. 319.
46 *Marlowe's 'Doctor Faustus'*, p. 351, n. 891ff.; the preliminary engraving in Volume II of the 1583 edition shows Henry VIII standing on the neck of the Pope.
47 *Diary*, p. 325.
48 Foxe, *Actes and Monuments*, London, 1563, pp. 23bff.
49 See Bent Suneson, 'Marlowe and the Dumb Show', *E.Sts*, XXXV, 1954, pp. 241–53.

50 See Jocelyn Powell, 'Marlowe's Spectacle', *T.D.R.*, VIII, 1964, pp. 195–210.
51 See Craik, op. cit.
52 M. C. Bradbrook, 'Marlowe's *Doctor Faustus* and the Eldritch Tradition', in R. H. Hosley (ed.), *Essays . . . in Honour of Hardin Craig*, London, 1963.
53 *Diary, Reminiscences, and Correspondence of Henry Crabb Robinson* (ed. T. Sadler), London, 1869, II, p. 434.
54 See Frank Kermode, 'The Banquet of Sense' in his *Renaissance Essays*, London, 1971.
55 Zucker, p. 167, and see Erwin Panofsky, *Studies in Iconology*, New York, 1962, pp. 86ff.
56 *Marlowe's 'Doctor Faustus'*, pp. 101–2.
57 B. Castiglione, *The Book of the Courtier* (tr. T. Hoby), Everyman ed., pp. 315–16; for the Neo-Platonists on the 'kiss of death' see E. Wind, *Pagan Mysteries in the Renaissance*, Harmondsworth, 1967, pp. 154ff.
58 W. Bridges-Adams, *The Irresistible Theatre*, New York, 1961, p. 128.
59 B. A. Young, in *Financial Times*, 28 June 1968.
60 William Empson, *Seven Types of Ambiguity*, London, 1930, pp. 261–2.

Chapter 8   *Titus Andronicus*: **strange images of death**

1   See the Arden edition (ed. J. C. Maxwell), London, 1961, p. xxiv.
2   See Ch. 4, n. 1.
3   See Nicholas Brooke, 'Marlowe as Provocative Agent in Shakespeare's Early Plays', *S.S.*, XIV, 1961, pp. 34–44.
4   *Diary*, pp. 21–2; for later productions see G. Harold Metz, 'The Stage History of *Titus Andronicus*', *S.Q.*, XXVIII, 1977, pp. 154–69.
5   See Gustav Ungerer, 'An Unrecorded Elizabethan Performance of *Titus Andronicus*', *S.S.*, XIV, 1961, pp. 102–9.
6   Roy Strong, *The English Icon*, London, 1969, p. 3.
7   See Ann Haaker, '*Non Sine Causa*: the Use of Emblematic Method and Iconology in the Thematic Structure of *Titus Andronicus*', *R.O.R.D.*, XIII–XIV, 1970–1, pp. 143–68.
8   See Eugene M. Waith, 'The Metamorphosis of Violence in *Titus Andronicus*', *S.S.*, X, 1957, pp. 39–49.
9   Richard David, 'Drams of Eale', *S.S.*, X, 1956, pp. 126–34.
10 Gareth Lloyd Evans, *Shakespeare*, I, Edinburgh, 1969, p. 73.
11 See David, op. cit.
12 See Haaker, op. cit.
13 See W. M. Merchant, 'Classical Costume in Shakespearian Production', *S.S.*, X, 1957, pp. 71–6; the fullest discussion of the drawing is to be found in R. A. Foakes, *London Theatres Illustrated* (forthcoming).
14 Kenneth Muir, *Shakespeare's Tragic Sequence*, London, 1972, p. 24.
15 Nicholas Brooke, *Shakespeare's Early Tragedies*, London, 1968, pp. 33–4.
16 J. Dover Wilson (ed.), *Titus Andronicus*, Cambridge, 1948, pp. li–lii.

17 See Waith, op. cit.; one might argue that like many men he is suppressing the hatred of women that has its end in rape.

18 Brooke, *Shakespeare's Early Tragedies*, p. 40.

19 Frances Yates, *Astraea*, London, 1975, p. 75. Cf. Haaker, op. cit.

20 Muriel Bradbrook, *Shakespeare and Elizabethan Poetry*, London, 1961, p. 107.

21 C. Ripa, *Iconologia*, Padua, 1611.

22 See V.ii.69n., and Hosley, 'Shakespeare's Use of a Gallery over the Stage', *S.S.*, X, 1957, p. 86, n. 4.

23 David, op. cit.

Select bibliography

This list contains the most useful books and articles on the staging of plays during the reign of Elizabeth. It can be augmented by reference to the appropriate sections of Stanley Wells (ed.), *Shakespeare*, Oxford, 1973 and *English Drama*, Oxford, 1975 – both in the Select Bibliographical Guides series – and of I. Ribner and C. C. Huffman (eds), *Tudor and Stuart Drama*, Arlington Heights, Ill., 1978.

Armstrong, W. A., 'Actors and Theatres', *S.S.*, XVII (1964), pp. 191–204.

Barroll, J. L. *et al.* (eds), *Revels History of Drama in English III: 1576–1613*, London, 1974.

Baskerville, C. R., *The Elizabethan Jig*, Chicago, 1929.

Beckerman, B., *Shakespeare at the Globe, 1599–1609*, London, 1962.

Bentley, G. E. (ed.), *The Seventeenth-Century Stage*, Chicago, 1968.

Berry, H. (ed.), *The First Public Playhouse: the Theatre in Shoreditch, 1576–1598*, Montreal, 1979.

Bethell, S. L., *Shakespeare and the Popular Dramatic Tradition*, London, 1944.

Bevington, D. M., *From 'Mankind' to Marlowe*, Cambridge, Mass., 1962.

Bradbrook, M. C., *The Rise of the Common Player*, London, 1962.

Campbell, L. B., *Scenes and Machines on the English Stage During the Renaissance*, Cambridge, 1923.

Chambers, E. K., *The Elizabethan Stage*, 4 vols, Oxford, 1923.

Cook, Ann J., *The Privileged Playgoers of Shakespeare's London, 1576–1642*, Princeton, N.J., 1981.

Craik, T. W., *The Tudor Interlude*, Leicester, 1958.

Edwards, C. (ed.), *The London Theatre Guide, 1576–1642*, Foxton, Herts., 1979.

Feuillerat, A. (ed.), *Documents Relating to the Office of the Revels at Court in the Time of Queen Elizabeth*, Louvain, 1908.

Foakes, R. A., *London Theatres Illustrated*, forthcoming.

Foakes, R. A. and R. T. Rickert (eds), *Henslowe's Diary*, Cambridge, 1961.

Galloway, David, 'Records of Early English Drama in the Provinces and What They May Tell Us About the Elizabethan Theatre', *The Elizabethan Theatre*, VII, 1980, pp. 82–110.

Greg, W. W., *Dramatic Documents from the Elizabethan Playhouses*, 2 vols, Oxford, 1931.

Gurr, A., *The Shakespearean Stage, 1574–1642*, Cambridge, 1970.

Harbage, A. (rev. S. Schoenbaum), *Annals of English Drama*, London, 1964.

Harbage, A., *Shakespeare's Audience*, New York, 1941.

Henslowe, *see* Foakes and Rickert.

Hodges, C. W., *The Globe Restored*, 2nd ed., London, 1968.

Hosley, R., 'A Reconstruction of the Fortune Playhouse', *The Elizabethan Theatre*, VI, 1978, pp. 1–20; Part II, VII, 1980, pp. 1–20.

Joseph, B., *Elizabethan Acting*, Oxford, 1951.

King, T. J., *Shakesepearean Staging 1599–1642*, Cambridge, Mass., 1971.

King, T. J., 'The Stage in the Time of Shakespeare: a Survey of Major Scholarship', *Ren.D.*, IV, 1971, pp. 199–235.

Klein, David, 'Did Shakespeare Produce his own Plays?', *MLR*, LVII, 1962, pp. 556–60.

Lawrence, W. J., *Speeding Up Shakespeare*, London, 1937.

Lawrence, W. J., *Those Nut-Cracking Elizabethans*, London, 1935.

Linnell, R., *The Curtain Playhouse*, London, 1977.

Linthicum, M. C., *Costume in the Drama of Shakespeare and his Contemporaries*, Oxford, 1936.

Manifold, J. S., *Music in English Drama*, London, 1956.

Marker, L. L., 'Nature and Decorum in the Theory of Elizabethan Acting', *The Elizabethan Theatre*, II, 1970, pp. 87–107.

Mehl, D., *The Elizabethan Dumb Show*, London, 1965.

Reynolds, G. F., *The Staging of Elizabethan Plays at the Red Bull Theater, 1605–25*, New York, 1940.

Rhodes, E. L., *Henslowe's Rose: the Stage and Staging*, Lexington, Ky, 1976.

Rowan, D. F., 'The English Playhouse: 1595–1630', *Ren.D.*, IV, 1971, pp. 37–51.

Southern, R., *The Staging of Plays before Shakespeare*, London, 1973.

Weimann, R., *Shakespeare and the Popular Tradition in the Theatre*, London, 1978.

Wickham, G., *Early English Stages, 1300–1660*, 3 vols in 4, London, 1959–80.

Index

1 Plays

Alchemist, The, 26, 113
Alphonsus, King of Aragon, 27, 31, 115, 131
Antonio and Mellida, 76, 77–8, 85, 114
Antonio's Revenge, 76, 114, 202, 206, 219
Antony and Cleopatra, 28, 84
Arraignment of Paris, The, 17
As You Like It, 134, 140

Bartholomew Fair, 21, 39, 43, 46, 89–90, 120, 186
Battle of Alcazar, The, 63, 115, 206
Believe as You List, 33
Black Joan, 36
Bloody Banquet, The, 207

Cambises, 24, 71
Captain Thomas Stukeley, 32
Captives, The, 52
Case is Altered, The, 58
Catiline his Conspiracy, 28, 114
Changes, 68
Chaste Maid in Cheapside, A, 12, 24, 29, 37
Clyomon and Clamydes, 135, 136
Cobbler's Prophecy, The, 214
Comedy of Errors, The, 85
Coriolanus, 62, 190, 214, 219
Cornelia, 112, 123–4
Cradle of Security, The, 65–6
Cymbeline, 122
Cynthia's Revels, 52

Damon and Pithias, 74
Daniel in the Lion's Den, 86
Dead Man's Fortune, The, 62
Devil is an Ass, The, 72, 213
Devil's Charter, The, 168
Dido, Queen of Carthage, 92
Doctor Faustus, 11, 18, 21, 29, 32, 51, 87, 93, 116, 123, 160–85, 206
Double Marriage, The, 213

Eastwood Ho, 213
Edward I, 38, 51, 56, 61
Edward II, 18, 31, 33, 77, 80, 95, 101, 141–59, 160, 161, 174, 190, 206
Edward III, 31, 32, 61, 117, 214
England's Joy, 13, 18
English Traveller, The, 59
Epicoene, 213
Every Man in His Humour, 18, 31, 73
Every Woman in Her Humour, 52

Famous Victories of Henry V, The, 18, 25, 89, 135, 139
Felix and Philiomena, 16
First Part of Hieronimo, The, 114
Five Plays in One, 134
Friar Bacon and Friar Bungay, 29, 46, 171
Fulgens and Lucrece, 19, 74–5

Gallathea, 134, 135
George-a-Greene, 37
Golden Age, The, 34, 37, 62, 85, 206

Gorboduc, 17, 63, 137

Hamlet, 10, 33, 50, 53, 62, 64, 76, 77, 84, 90, 92–3, 97, 106, 114, 118, 123, 143, 186
Harlequin Doctor Faustus, 165
Heir, The, 107
1 Henry IV, 83
2 Henry IV, 68, 86
Henry V, 46, 51, 218
1 Henry VI, 25, 34, 61, 62, 63, 64, 85, 101, 213, 219
2 Henry VI, 28, 32
3 Henry VI, 32, 35, 37, 56, 65, 88
Henry VIII, 32
Hey for Honesty, 112
History of Loyalty and Beauty, The, 130
History of the Solitary Knight, The, 130
Histriomastix, 16, 218

If it be not Good, the Devil is in it, 33
Insatiate Countess, The, 57
Iron Age, The, 215
Isle of Dogs, The, 12

Jack Drum's Entertainment, 48
James IV, 3, 36, 62, 80, 115, 130
Jew of Malta, The, 30, 36, 49, 51, 72, 81, 91, 103, 142, 143–4, 167, 193, 198, 205, 212, 214
Jocasta, 62, 65
Jugurtha, 49

Julius Caesar, 71

King John (Bale), 43
King John (Shakespeare), 54
King Lear, 69, 91, 122, 202, 205
Knight in the Burning Rock, The, 16, 130
Knight of the Burning Pestle, The, 1, 46, 129, 131, 212

Lingua, 53, 76
Locrine, 113, 115, 135
Look about You, 35, 36
Looking Glass for London and England, A, 32, 34, 27, 84–5, 116, 121, 135, 164, 175, 184, 217
Love's Labour's Lost, 46, 60, 63, 78, 117, 185

Macbeth, 65, 120, 175, 179, 206
Malcontent, The, 103
Mankind, 20–1
Marriage of Wit and Wisdom, The, 85
Masque of Blackness, The, 23
Massacre at Paris, The, 62
Medea, 167
Meleager, 115
Merchant of Venice, The, 135
Merry Milkmaids, The, 49
Messalina, 27
Midas, 69
Midsummer Night's Dream, A, 17, 19, 22, 46, 52, 68, 72, 192, 198
Misfortunes of Arthur, The, 112
Mucedorus, 1, 3, 17, 129–40, 142, 144, 193
Much Ado about Nothing, 63, 65, 68, 88, 90

Necromancer, The, 165
New Inn, The, 107

Old Fortunatus, 25, 31, 34, 137, 168
Old Wives Tale, The, 80, 130, 132
Orlando Furioso, 53, 81–2, 91
Othello, 91, 120, 219

Paris and Vienne, 88

Parnassus Plays, The, 67, 71, 90
Patient and Meek Grissell, 136
Pericles, 25, 80
Phaedra, 198, 203
Phaeton, 115, 214
Philaster, 111
Play of Robin Hood, The, 80
Poetaster, The, 115
Promos and Cassandra, 137
Puritan, The, 72
Pythagoras, 51

Ram Alley, 79
Rebellion, The, 112
Revenger's Tragedy, The, 80
Richard II, 44, 51, 61, 62, 72, 82–3, 88, 142, 144, 154, 155, 189, 201
Richard III, 36, 38, 57, 62, 78, 88, 91, 97, 101, 106, 145, 155, 159, 205, 219
Ritorno d'Ulisse in Patria, Il, 121
Romeo and Juliet, 63, 65, 90
Roxana, 27
Royal King, The, 86

Satiromastix, 103, 113
Scholars, The, 116
Search for Money, A, 81
Sejanus, 62
Seven Deadly Sins, The, 176, 215
Silver Age, The, 33, 57, 214
Sir Thomas More, 29, 63
Soliman and Perseda, 111, 115, 116, 120, 125, 126
Spanish Tragedy, The, 28, 65, 80, 91, 97, 101–28, 129, 131, 134, 142, 149, 160, 161, 170, 186, 193, 198, 203, 207, 215
Staple of News, The, 107
Summer's Last Will and Testament, 74, 86

Tale of a Tub, The, 169
Tamburlaine, 21, 30, 35, 39, 49, 51, 57–9, 61–2, 64, 65, 68, 73, 86, 87, 91, 93, 96, 141, 147, 149, 155, 174, 214
Taming of the Shrew, The, 80, 85, 115, 120, 139, 219

Tempest, The, 87, 120, 138, 213
Three Ladies of London, 85
Thyestes, 154, 205–7
Timon of Athens, 105, 201
Titus Andronicus, 1, 12, 60, 62, 87, 115, 186–207
Travels of the Three English Brothers, The, 12
Troilus and Cressida, 181, 218
Twelfth Night, 19, 28, 62, 68, 192
Two Gentlemen of Verona, The, 82, 135
Two Noble Ladies, The, 33, 87

Volpone, 27, 168

Warning for Fair Women, A, 24, 32, 37, 111–12, 114, 121, 206
White Devil, The, 31, 112
Whore of Babylon, The, 91
Widow's Tears, The, 97
Winter's Tale, The, 87, 90, 135, 149
Wise Man of West Chester, The, 103
Woman Killed with Kindness, A, 63
Woodstock, 25, 35, 87, 88

2 Names and topics

academic drama, 106, 113, 187, 189
acting styles, 41, 72–9, 83, 85, 91–2, 96, 105, 107–8, 114, 124, 127–8, 148, 156
actors, *see* players
Acts and Monuments (Foxe's *Book of Martyrs*), 177
Actor's Remonstance, The, 97
Admiral's Men, 10, 12, 32, 37, 50, 70, 103, 144, 162, 171, 206, 214
admission prices, 22, 47–8, 51
'alienation', 95–6, 108–9, 146, 188–9, 207
allegory, 87, 112–13, 115, 120, 130–1, 144, 146,

155, 180–1, 188, 204–5, 206
Alleyn, E., 13, 53, 58, 81, 86, 90–1, 96
animals, 82, 88, 135, 136, 171
Apology for Actors, An, 33, 222
apprentices, 45, 48–9
Aristotle, 11, 60, 77, 168, 184
Armin, R., 12
asides, 74, 81, 92, 124
audiences, 11, 13, 15, 22, 23, 30–1, 40–1, 43, 44–50, 161
auditoria, 13, 16, 20–1, 30, 40–1, 46, 48, 51, 70, 212

Bacon, A., 186
Bale, J., 43
banquets, 36, 110, 120, 179–80, 205–7
Barry, L., 79
battle scenes, 29, 31–2, 61, 131, 153–4, 163–4, 182
bear-baiting, 13, 43, 60–1, 80
beards, 72, 85
bears, 136
Beaumont, F., 1, 46, 78
beds, 36–7
bells, 32, 140, 183–4
Belsavage Inn, 166
Betterton, T., 52
Black Book, 166
Blackfriars Playhouse, 10, 44, 53, 103, 212
boats, 25
Book of the Courtier, The, 181
book-holders, 45, 70
boy players, 83–5, 97, 118–19, 148
boys' companies, 10, 70
Brecht, B., 3, 57, 92–6, 108, 109, 146, 149
'breeches parts', 85
Britannia's Pastorals, 24
Brome, R., 64
Browne, W., 24
Brueghel, P. (the elder), 138
Buchell, A. van, 15
Bull Inn, 89
Bulwer, J., 76
Burbage, J., 9, 11, 22
Burbage, R., 11, 78, 91–2, 97–8, 103

Calvin, J., 125
canopy, 15, 30–1, 38, 164, 214
Castiglione, B., 181
catch phrases, 78, 90, 107
cellarage, 32, 103
Caveat for Common Cursitors, A, 188
censorship, 44
Chamberlain's Men, 12, 13, 51, 88, 111, 186
Chapman, G., 12, 64, 97, 122, 191
chariots, 33, 65, 206
Chaucer, G., 197
Chirologia and *Chiromania*, 76
choruses, 29, 31, 77, 86, 111–12, 116, 168–9, 184
City petitions against the players, 42–4, 50
classical drama, 1, 37, 43, 187–8
clowns, 11, 12, 37, 61, 67, 69, 87, 88–90, 96, 101, 123, 135–6, 160, 173, 204–5
Cockpit at Court, 26
Cockpit in Drury Lane, 28
columns, 30–1, 122
commedia dell'arte, 54, 123
Commentaries on Genesis, 125
companies, 9–10, 42, 71, 98
Compendium Maleficarum, 224
continental performances, 5, 68, 104, 130, 165
costumes, 21, 53, 58, 65, 72, 86–8, 111–13, 118, 124, 130, 135, 141, 148, 160, 172, 189, 193–4, 206
Cotgrave, R., 56
court performances, 4, 9, 10–11, 16–17, 38–9, 44, 56, 69, 84, 88, 101, 112, 129–30, 134, 161, 162–4, 168, 172
Cross Keys Inn, 9, 103
Curtain Playhouse, 11–12, 38, 103, 216
curtains, 16, 27, 28, 38, 126, 176, 184, 206, 212, 213

dances, 59, 60, 63, 68, 165, 174

Davenant, W., 53
Dawes, R., 55
dead marches, 61–2, 122, 126, 159
débats, 130
decorum, 2, 17, 73–6, 205
Dee, J., 160
Defence of Poesie, The, 132
Dekker, T., 12, 24, 33, 34, 45, 68, 91, 103, 113, 115, 137
delight, 2, 132
'delivery', 91, 97–8, 101, 107, 110
devils, 20, 33, 87, 116, 157, 163, 166–7, 170–1
'directors', 45
discoveries, 27–9, 30, 36, 87, 101, 126, 159, 164, 168–9, 172, 176, 180, 183–4, 194, 202
disguisings, 20
Dish of Lenten Stuff, A, 47
'documentary characters', 150, 154
Donne, J., 145, 169
doors, 15, 20, 21, 24, 25, 27–8, 57, 124, 170, 173, 176, 212
doubling, 20, 71–2, 85, 144, 152
Downes, J., 52
dragons, 171
Drayton, M., 12
Dryden, J., 34
dumb shows, 59, 62, 63–5, 110–11, 120, 125, 149, 178
duration of performances, 144

eccyclema (*exostra*), 37
Edwards, R., 74
Eisenstein, S., 150
'eldritch' humour, 20, 123, 169–70, 178, 198, 207
Eliot, T. S., 3
elocution, *see* 'delivery'
Elyot, T., 1
emblems, 64, 93, 109, 154, 175, 189, 191–2, 197–8, 203
Euripides, 1
Eworth, H., 206

Faerie Queene, The, 35, 77, 175, 212

fairground theatres, 14, 21–2
fencing, 63
Festivous Notes upon Don Quixote, 49
Field, N., 13
'figures', 3, 63, 83, 93–5, 104–6, 124, 159, 170, 173, 175, 178–9, 189, 203, 219
fireworks, 13, 31, 60–1, 174–5, 177, 214
Flecknoe, R., 97–8
Fletcher, J., 78, 213
flying, 31–2, 115–16, 164, 177, 182
Florio, J., 2, 38
Fludd, R., 25, 27–8, 30, 116
folk-plays, 14, 17, 79–80, 82, 109, 130, 138
fools, 87; *see also* clowns
Fortune Playhouse, 12, 13, 15, 22, 23, 25, 26, 40, 45, 68, 91, 103, 166
Foxe, J., 177

'gag', 90, 147, 173, 177
gallery ('aloft'), 15, 29–30, 40, 101–2, 115, 120, 126, 161, 170–2, 176, 179, 182, 188, 193, 205, 206, 213
games (plays as), 79–83, 132
Garlick, 68
gatherers, 22, 24, 70
Gawdy, P., 50
Gayton, E., 49
'gests', 3, 57–9, 91, 105–6, 119, 124, 148–9, 177, 193–4
gestures, 76, 78, 96
ghosts, 33, 85, 87, 112, 115
Globe Playhouse, 11–13, 23, 25, 28, 30, 32, 37, 47, 51, 68, 103, 168; second Globe, 30
Goethe, W., 166
Gosson, S., 48, 60
Greene, R., 12, 27, 31, 34, 47, 80, 81, 84, 85, 116, 129, 175
Greene, T., 78
Greenwich, 112, 134
groundlings, 11, 17, 44–5, 48, 64
Gull's Hornbook, The, 24

hangings (executions), 122–3, 126, 205
Harman, T., 188
Harrington, J., 186
Henslowe, P., 10, 11, 13, 16–17, 30, 31, 32, 36, 38, 39, 50, 55, 65, 70–1, 86, 87, 103, 104, 111, 134, 135, 162, 171, 214, 217
Hero and Leander, 93–4, 200
Heywood, T., 13, 31, 32, 33, 34, 45, 57, 59, 64, 71, 78, 86, 222
hirelings, 70
history plays, 77, 102, 143–4
homosexuality, 145
Hope Playhouse, 13, 22, 30, 39, 40, 46, 186
horses, 25, 88
'houses', *see* mansions
Howard's Men, 130
huts, 15, 31–2, 40

Iconologia, 206
'identification', 78–9, 97–8
idolatry, 43
illusion, 3, 9, 14, 18, 23, 29, 34, 36, 41, 59–61, 97–8, 109, 135, 142, 199, 214
impersonation, 58, 77–8, 80, 91, 97–8, 108–9
improvisation, 21, 54, 69, 89–90
Inductions, 80, 89–90, 111, 130–1
inns, 14, 22, 43–4
'inner stage', 27, 37
Inner Temple, 17
Inns of Court, 9, 49, 50
interior scenes, 26–7, 29
interludes, 19–20
intermezzi, 19
interruption, 2, 55–6, 123, 130, 155, 172, 177
intervals, 47, 62, 83
investiture scenes, 21, 58, 135, 136, 147, 155, 159, 174, 196, 206
invisibility, 87, 177

jigs, 67–9, 135, 165
Johnson, S., 34
Jones, I., 23, 26, 28, 30
Jonson, B., 18, 21, 23, 29, 31, 39, 46, 52, 58, 62, 64,

73, 91, 103, 104, 107, 113, 169, 186, 213

Kempe, W., 67, 90
King's Men, 10, 13, 28, 69, 129, 214
Knight, E., 216
Kyd, T., 1, 10, 12, 101–28 *passim*, 142, 187, 191, 202

Langland, W., 35
Langley, F., 12
Lanman, H., 11
lazzi, 130, 136, 139
Leicester's Men, 71
licensing of plays, 9, 44, 52
Life and Death of Doctor Faustus, The, 165
lighting, 17, 35, 56, 65, 106, 157
literacy, 11, 47, 211
'liveliness', 80, 108
localization, *see* place
Lodge, T., 12, 34, 116, 129, 175
Lopez, R., 51
Lovelace, R., 116
Lowen, J., 53
Luttrell, J., 206
Lyly, J., 69, 134

Machiavelli, N., 81, 101, 118, 143–4, 168, 205
Machin, L., 52
machinery, 31, 32, 115–16, 120, 164, 171, 182–3
make-up, 85, 112
mansions, 10, 37–9, 60, 101–2, 134, 162–4, 176
maps of London, 40
Marlowe, C., 1, 2, 10, 21, 57–9, 72, 80, 83, 84, 92–6, 101, 118, 141–85 *passim*, 186, 196, 198, 200, 202, 205
Marston, J., 16, 57, 76, 114
masques, 120, 137, 149
Massinger, P., 33, 213
Master of the Revels, 44, 52
May, T., 107
Mayne, J., 29
Meade, J., 55
Medwall, H., 74
Middle Temple, 28
Middleton, T., 12, 13, 24, 45, 166
Midsummer Shows, 19

mirror scenes, *see* 'figures'
montage, 123, 124–5, 146, 153, 168, 176
Monteverdi, C., 121
Mountfort, W., 165
mummers' plays, 20, 136, 137
music, 61–3, 64, 120, 125, 127, 130, 139, 153, 183, 190–3, 198
music-room, 29–30, 213
musical instruments, 62

narrative speeches, 108–9, 117–19, 152
Nashe, T., 2, 49, 72, 74, 79, 86, 125, 187
naturalism, 73–4, 83, 88, 95, 157–8, 190
Newington Butts Playhouse, 12, 103, 186

opposition to the players, 42–4
Ovid, 1, 189, 192, 197, 199–200
Ovid's Banquet of Sense, 122
ownership of the playhouses, 70

Palladio, A., 25
Palsgrave's Men, 13
parody, 76, 103, 111, 114, 173, 202
'parts', 52–4
'passing over the stage', 25, 117–18, 180
'passions', 54, 123
patronage, 42–3, 70
Paul's Boys, 10, 48, 72
Paul's Playhouse, 48, 213
Peacham, H., 87, 193–4
Peele, G., 17, 38, 51, 63, 80, 118, 129, 132
Pembroke's Men, 12, 144, 161, 186
performance times, 55–6
perspective, 14
Petit, J., 186
Phillips, A., 51
place (localization), 17, 18, 26, 29, 34, 37–41, 102, 134, 197, 202
plague, 12, 44, 161, 186
platea, 10
Platter, T., 12, 37, 47–8, 68, 71, 86

players, 19, 80
players' organizations 42–3, 70–1
playhouse furnishing, 4, 24, 26–7, 31, 33–40, 43
playhouses, 11–14
Plays Confuted in Five Actions, 48, 60
playwrights, 52–3
plot, 59
'plots', 52, 54
popular drama, 1–5, 10, 80, 109, 111
Preston, T., 71
Prince Henry's Men, 13
printed texts, 44, 54–5, 66–7, 129, 130, 131–2, 154, 160, 175
private playhouses, 1, 10, 24, 25, 40–1, 62, 140
Privy Council, 12, 39, 43–4, 50, 53, 55, 211
processions, 25, 35, 61, 64, 121, 177, 193, 207
prologues, 28, 61, 86, 87, 143, 163
prompt-books, 52, 161
properties, 17, 32, 34–7, 57–9, 62, 65, 93, 101, 115, 123–4, 131, 138, 160–1
proscaenium, 15
proscenium arches, 14, 23, 27
prostitutes, 46, 49, 50
provincial performances, 5, 9, 10, 14, 65–6, 103, 129, 146, 160, 166–7, 175, 186, 211
Prynne, W., 166
psychomachia, 144
public playhouses, 1, 10, 22, 24–5, 69
'puritan' attacks on the stage, 26, 42–3, 68, 71
Puttenham, G., 64, 79

Queen Anne's Players, 9, 144
Queen's Men, 12, 16, 63, 88, 90, 115, 129, 134, 135, 211
'quotable gestures', 96, 111, 149, 150; *see also* figures

ragmen, 87
Randolph, T., 112

Red Bull Playhouse, 5, 13, 29, 32, 33, 38, 40, 47, 87, 144
rehearsals, 51–5
repertory system, 50–1
revelry, 18–19, 44, 80, 130, 178, 186
Revels Office, 17, 38–9, 44, 62, 130, 134, 137
revenge, 101, 112–3, 116–17, 188, 202
revivals, 5, 103, 104, 110, 160
Rhenanus, J., 53
Rich, J., 165
Ricius, A., 176
riots, 49
Ripa, C., 206
Rojas, A. de, 55
romances, 16–17, 130–3
Rose Playhouse, 9, 10, 12, 16, 25, 27, 29, 30, 31, 32, 37, 38, 56, 63, 71, 103, 115, 116, 121, 131, 162, 168, 170, 186, 213, 214
Rowlands, S., 219
Rowley, W., 13, 81
rustics, 72, 75, 87, 89, 135

'scenery', 14, 34, 35
Second Report of Doctor John Faustus, The, 162–4, 166, 167
Seneca, 1, 28, 154, 167, 187, 189–90, 198, 203
Seven Deadly Sins of London, The, 115
Shadow of Night, The, 191
Shakespeare, W., 1, 2, 10, 11, 13, 40, 52, 57, 64, 71, 72, 77, 84, 101, 103, 129, 159, 186–207 *passim*
'sharers', 24, 70, 71
Shirley, J., 78, 79
Sidney, P., 3, 39, 74, 132, 135
Sincklo, J., 113
Sir Gawayn and the Green Knight, 20, 80, 178
soliloquies, 88, 97, 145, 154, 198
songs, 62, 131, 138
sound effects, 31–2, 114–15, 131, 134, 183; *see also* bells
spectacle, 11, 58–61, 66–7, 131, 134, 141–2, 165,

(spectacle – *Contd.*)
170, 175–6, 178–9, 187,
199, 203, 214
Spenser, E., 35, 77, 80
stage directions, 53, 56, 60,
66–7, 71, 144, 184, 193
stage-keepers, 52, 54, 71,
89, 126
stages, 14, 15–16, 22, 23–4,
101–2, 111
stairs, 36, 115, 127, 214
Stationers' Company, 52,
106
stichomythia, 119, 172
Strange Horse Race, A,
68–9
Strange's Men, 9, 12, 103,
144, 162, 186
Street, P., 13
'studies', 27, 29, 169, 175,
213
supernumerary actors, 52,
71
Sussex's Men, 12, 186
Swan Playhouse, 4–5,
12–13, 15–16, 23, 26–7,
28, 30, 40, 47

'tableau scenes', 28–9,
56–9, 64, 95–6, 101,
110–11, 126, 146, 151,
178
Tarlton, R., 11, 17, 63, 69,

88–90, 129, 130, 135–6,
139, 176
tents, 12, 15, 21, 28, 38, 134
Terence, 25
Theatre, The, 9, 11, 13, 22,
25, 50, 68, 103, 161, 166,
216
theatre history, 14, 27, 104
This World's Folly, 68
thrones, 37, 116, 133–4,
144, 183
tire-men, 54, 70
tiring-house, 15, 21, 24–7,
33, 40, 103, 121
token properties, 34–5, 58,
66, 93, 117, 123, 151
Tomkis, T., 53, 76
tournaments, 3, 20
tragedy, 2, 81, 102–3, 144,
155–6, 160, 167–8, 187,
189–90, 222
traps, 16, 28, 33, 115, 120,
131, 157, 170, 182, 184,
188, 194, 199, 214
trees, 31, 37, 121–2, 134,
171, 178
Thurmond, J., 165
Turner, W., 47
type characters, 73, 77,
93–5, 103, 133, 188–9,
198

Unton, H., 39

Vennar, R., 13
verisimilitude, 2–3, 21, 73,
80, 86–7, 97–8, 106–8,
125, 132, 158, 190, 200
verse-speaking, *see*
'delivery'
'Viage entretenido', 55
Vitruvius, 25

'waits', 63
Warwick's Men, 16, 38, 130
Webster, J., 31, 123
Wedel, L. von, 60
wells, 134
Whetstone, G., 137
Whitefriars Playhouse, 213
Whitehall, 10, 17, 129
wigs, 81, 84–5, 124, 131,
138
wild men, 63, 80, 134,
137–8
Willis, R., 65
Wilson, R., 12, 69
windows, 29, 116, 170–1,
213
Witt, J. de, 12, 15–16, 26,
30, 40
women in audience, 24, 31,
50
Worcester's Men, 70, 144

yards, 15, 16, 22, 25, 31,
44–5, 65, 119, 180, 206